YALE SERIES IN THE
PHILOSOPHY AND THEORY OF ART

Handel's monument in Westminster Abbey. Engraving from Charles Burney's *An Account of the Musical Performances in Westminster-Abbey, and the Pantheon.*

The Possessor and the Possessed

HANDEL, MOZART, BEETHOVEN, AND THE IDEA OF MUSICAL GENIUS

PETER KIVY

YALE UNIVERSITY PRESS/NEW HAVEN & LONDON

Copyright © 2001 by Yale University.
All rights reserved.
This book may not be reproduced, in whole or in part, including illustrations, in any form (beyond that copying permitted by Sections 107 and 108 of the U.S. Copyright Law and except by reviewers for the public press), without written permission from the publishers.

Designed by Mary Valencia
Set in Galliard Old Style and Cezanne type by Tseng Information Systems, Inc.
Printed in the United States of America by Sheridan Books.

Library of Congress Cataloging-in-Publication Data
Kivy, Peter.
The possessor and the possessed : Handel, Mozart, Beethoven, and the idea of musical genius / Peter Kivy.
p. cm. (Yale series in the philosophy and theory of art)
Includes bibliographical references.
ISBN 0-300-08758-6 (cloth : alk. paper)
1. Handel, George Frideric, 1685–1759. 2. Mozart, Wolfgang Amadeus, 1756–1791. 3. Beethoven, Ludwig van, 1770–1827.
4. Genius—History. 5. Creation (Literary, artistic, etc.)—History.
6. Composers. I. Title. II. Series.
ML390 .K595 2001
781'.1—dc21
2001017785

A catalogue record for this book is available from the British Library.

The paper in this book meets the guidelines for permanence and durability of the Committee on Production Guidelines for Book Longevity of the Council on Library Resources.

10 9 8 7 6 5 4 3 2 1

For Noel Carroll

I am sensible, that, according
to the past experience of mankind,
friendship is the chief joy of human life. . . .

David Hume

> "What! you teach me Music?
> It is your words is bad. Hear the passage again.
> There! Go you, make words to that music."
>
> GEORGE FRIDERIC HANDEL

> "Stu! Knaller Praller
> Schnip-Schnap-Schnur Schenepeperl—Snai!—"
>
> WOLFGANG AMADEUS MOZART

> "I may do it, but not you."
>
> LUDWIG VAN BEETHOVEN

Contents

PREFACE xi

I Time out of Mind 1

II Greatness of Mind 13

III Breaking the Rule 22

IV The Saxon or the Devil 37

V The Genius and the Child 57

VI The Little Man from Salzburg 78

VII Giving the Rule 97

VIII An Unlicked Bear 119

IX Mozart's Second Childhood 149

X Odd Men Out 164

XI Beethoven Again 175

XII Gendering Genius 218

XIII Reconstructing Genius 238

NOTES 255

BIBLIOGRAPHY 271

INDEX 277

Preface

This book is about the concept of artistic genius and the way it came to be symbolized by three great composers of the modern era: Handel, Mozart, and Beethoven. The choice of these three is not an expression of personal preference, but dictated by historical fact: in their own times their contemporaries so singled them out, and the latter two were so singled out in our own times as well, not as symbols of musical genius alone but of genius *tout court*.

I shall begin by delineating two basic concepts of genius that were already well formed in the ancient world. It is the historical and philosophical argument of my book that in the period from Handel's hegemony in England to the present, these two concepts have been in a kind of pendulum swing, first one, then the other holding sway. Why these swings should have taken place is part of my subject.

Both of these concepts were given philosophical reformulations in modern times, and it is, in part, these reformulations that came to be seen as peculiarly instantiated by the three composers I have named. The journey has been from Handel to Mozart to Beethoven to Mozart again. And although I am no believer in cyclical theories of historical process, I seem to detect some few signs, at least in musicological circles, of a move to Beethoven again.

The origins of my thesis, in my own thinking, go back to two of the very first essays I wrote (as a graduate student, in fact) on what is now more and more being referred to as a separate branch of philosophical aesthetics: the "philosophy of music." The first of these, "Mainwaring's *Handel:* Its Relation to English Aesthetics" (1964), had as its main topic the significance of what is sometimes described as the first full-blown biography of a composer, for Enlightenment philosophy of art.[1] But it treats, as a result, the view of Handel as musical genius that his contemporaries in England held. The second article, "Child Mozart as an Aesthetic Symbol" (1967), examined how Mozart's genius was represented by his contemporaries and his immediate posterity.[2] I saw, at the time, no particular connection between these two juvenilia, and they have lain dormant lo these many years. But the material in both of them, now considerably reworked and rethought, is part of my argument here.

The occasion on which the argument of this book began to emerge, and the content of the essays on Handel and Mozart to matter to me once again, was the opportunity afforded me by Cambridge University Press to publish a collection of my essays, both historical and analytic, on the philosophy of music. I decided to include the essay on Mozart, but not the one on Handel, because the volume was growing too large, and something had to go. But in rereading the Mozart piece, the following question posed itself to me. I quote from my preface to that volume:

> [T]he "idea of Mozart," . . . it seems to me, has replaced the "idea of Beethoven" as the dominating *musical* image of genius and creative intellect. I think this replacement of the "Beethoven idea" by the "Mozart idea," if I am right about it, must tell us something important about the difference between the way music, as a human enterprise, was viewed in the nineteenth century and the way it is viewed now. Indeed, I think it must tell us something about changing attitudes toward all the arts. I wish someone would take up this theme. It seems to me rich in possibilities for the history of ideas.[3]

No one, so far as I know, has taken the theme up. So I thought I had better take it up myself.

As can be seen, I originally viewed the theme as one swing of the pendulum from the nineteenth century's enshrinement of Beethoven as the symbol of creative genius, to what I perceived to be the recent enshrinement of Mozart as the symbol, even in the popular culture —

but a symbol of a very *different* kind of genius altogether. However, I quickly saw that what my 1967 essay, together with my perceptions of the new Mozart "craze," suggested was two swings of the pendulum: from Mozart to Beethoven to Mozart again. Furthermore, it seemed clear that not only was the swing from Mozart to Beethoven a swing from one notion of genius to another, different notion; the swing away from Beethoven and *back* to Mozart was a *return both* to the same composer, *and* to the same concept of genius.

Once, however, one sees that the oscillation from Mozart to Beethoven to Mozart is an oscillation between *two* concepts of genius, not a progression from one, to a second, to a third, one then sees, as I soon did, that the picture of Handel's genius, as formed in his own day, is at least the preliminary sketch for the picture that another age executed, more elaborately, and in more detail, of the genius of Beethoven. The story now has three characters. But the pendulum analogy is still in place, for there remain but two concepts of genius between which it oscillates, and three swings to make, from the Enlightenment to today. That is the historical story I wish now to tell, beginning with the ancient origin of the two concepts of genius, ending with what might be called the "new Mozart."

But, though the historical story ends with the "new Mozart," my book does not, for the philosopher in me has not allowed this book to be a purely "disinterested" account. So the final three chapters undertake an examination of the recent "critique" of the traditional concept of genius, and a defense of the traditional concept against this "critique"—or, at least, against two well-known examples.

Of the historical part of this book, let me conclude with a warning. Even though I begin with ancient texts, and go on to discuss various eighteenth-, nineteenth-, and twentieth-century ones, this should not by any means be seen as a historical tract. It is not, and scarcely could be a history of the concept of genius, musical or otherwise. I present, rather, some philosophical and musical reflections on some "moments" in the history of an idea, in which the concept of musical genius, and the three musical figures that were then (and still are) seen to instantiate it, play a prominent role.

PREFACE

I thank Nicholas Wolterstorff for undertaking to read the entire manuscript of this book. That there are historical and philosophical errors still remaining I know full well. I wish I knew where they were. But wherever they are, for *them* I have only myself to thank.

THE POSSESSOR AND THE POSSESSED

I
Time out of Mind

Vienna celebrated Haydn's seventy-sixth birthday with a performance of *The Creation* in his honor. The aging master was carried into the Great Hall in a chair, to the accompaniment of fanfares and cheers—fitting tribute to his genius—and seated beside the Princess Esterhazy. "When the passage [in *The Creation*], 'And there was Light,' was reached, Haydn (as Carpani, who was an eye-witness, relates) 'raised his trembling arms to Heaven, as if in prayer to the Father of Harmony.'"[1] Another version of the incident has it that he spoke words to the effect that "Not from me, from thence comes everything."[2]

More than twenty centuries before, Homer, though he prayed to other divinities, said much the same thing when he began the *Iliad* "Sing, goddess, the anger of Peleus' son Achilleus. . . ," and the *Odyssey*, "Sing in me, Muse, and through me tell the story. . . ."[3]

I suppose one might be tempted to call this a "theory" of "creativity," and where the "creativity" is at a high enough level, a "theory" of "genius." But what it *really* is, I think, is a way of suggesting that such a "theory" is impossible. It is a way of suggesting that there is *no* explanation for how someone "gets a bright idea." For convenience, though, I will call this the "inspiration theory" of "creation," and later, when it becomes appropriate, the "inspiration theory" of "genius." I say when it becomes appropriate, because although Haydn certainly had available to him something like the modern notion of "genius" and "*a* genius," certainly the Homeric poets did not.

Now the inspiration theory of creativity is, as the openings of the *Iliad* and *Odyssey* demonstrate, a very old idea in Western thought. But it can hardly be taken seriously as a "theory," or even called that until given a philosophical analysis. And that too came early on in the history of Western thought. It was given definite conceptual outline in Plato's wonderful little Socratic dialogue, the *Ion*. It is there that the story I wish to tell in my book really begins in earnest.

Ion, with whom Socrates has his brief colloquy, follows the profession of "rhapsode." He recites poetry, or "sings" it, to the accompaniment, one supposes (or knows?), of a stringed instrument. But he also—and this seems, I think, strange to us—interlards his performance with interpretive comments on the poetry he is reciting or singing. In other words, he is a performer and "critic" all wrapped into one. I suppose his performance might have been something like an "illustrated lecture."

Furthermore, if Plato's description, in the *Republic,* is to be credited, the recitation was accompanied not only by music, and by critical comment, but by "sound effects" as well. As Plato describes the affair, clearly with contempt, the rhapsode "will be inclined to omit nothing in his narration, and to think nothing too low for him, so that he will attempt, seriously, and in the presence of many hearers, to imitate everything without exception, . . . claps of thunder and the noise of the wind and hail, and of wheels and pulleys, and the sounds of trumpets and flutes and pipes and all manner of instruments; nay even the barking of dogs, the bleating of sheep, and the notes of birds. . . ."[4] The rhapsode, then, as we might put it, is a veritable one-man band.

Now what particularly engages Plato's attention, in the *Ion,* is that the rhapsode is, so to say, a kind of "specialist." Ion seems good only at commenting on Homer. At that he is top dog. But he is at a loss commenting on anyone else. As he puts it to Socrates, in the form of a question: "Then what can be the reason, Socrates, why I pay no attention when somebody discusses any other poet, and am unable to offer any remark at all of any value, but simply drop into a doze, whereas if anyone mentions something connected with Homer I wake up at once and attend and have plenty to say?"[5] Socrates wonders the same thing; it is the object of his inquiry.

To understand Socrates' problem, we must backtrack a bit in the dialogue to see how the problem was reached in the first place.

Early on, Socrates asks Ion, "[A]re you skilled in Homer only, or in Hesiod and Archilochus as well?," to which Ion's prompt reply is: "No, no, only in Homer; for that seems to me quite enough."[6] Socrates' next question, obviously a rhetorical one, is: "Does Homer speak of any other than the very things that all the other poets speak of?"; Ion gives the sought-for answer: "What you say is true, Socrates."[7]

The problem then is this. When a group of people talk, *professionally*, about the same things, the same subject matter, they constitute a craft, a "techne," an "art" (as our translator, and most others, render it). And if I am able to talk intelligently and well about what *one* member of the group says, it follows that I must be able to talk intelligently and well about what *all* of them say. That is because in order to talk intelligently and well about even what one of such a group says, you must have learned his craft or techne or art. There is no other way to accomplish that. And if one *has* learned his craft or techne or art, then there is no reason one cannot talk intelligently and well about what every member of that craft may say.

Now we can see Socrates' problem emerging. For if the poets all talk about the same things, as Socrates and Ion agree they do, why then *they* must constitute a craft or techne or art. And since Ion can talk intelligently and well about what Homer says, it follows that he *must* be able to talk about what Hesiod says, and Archilochus, and the rest. For he must be talking intelligently and well about Homer by applying the poetic techne or art; and that techne or art can be applied to *any* poet with equally satisfactory results. Yet Ion cannot talk intelligently and well about the rest of the poets—only about Homer.

And when brought to this point in the inquiry, Ion is driven to ask the question with which we began: "Then what can be the reason, Socrates, why I pay no attention when somebody discusses any other poet, and am unable to offer any remark at all of any value, but simply drop into a doze, whereas if anyone mentions something concerned with Homer I wake up at once and attend and have plenty to say?"

Socrates' answer to this question is more or less straightforward, at least for our purposes. But it does leave a relevant loose end in the dialogue that is difficult, if not impossible, to tie up. Let me first present the straightforward part, and then go on to the more doubtful.

If Ion were using techne or art to speak intelligently and well about Homer, then it would follow that he could speak intelligently and well about *any* poet. But he can speak intelligently and well *only* about Homer. It would seem to follow that Ion is not speaking intelligently and well about Homer by the application of techne or art. And that is exactly the conclusion Socrates reaches: "this is not an art in you, whereby you speak well on Homer, but a divine power which moves you like that in the stone which Euripides named a magnet. . . ."[8] In other words, Ion is "possessed."

Were Socrates' conclusion applicable merely to the rhapsode it would be of limited interest. But the image of the magnet extends the conclusion in two opposite directions: from the rhapsode to his audience, and, more important still, for present purposes, from the rhapsode to the poet. For magnetism is "transitive": what the magnet attracts will itself attract because it has been "infected" by magnetism itself. "In the same manner also the Muse inspires men herself, and then by means of these inspired persons the inspiration spreads to others, and holds them in a connected chain." Most important, the magnet first "infects" the poets themselves. "For all the good epic poets utter all these fine poems not from art, but as inspired and possessed, and the good lyric poets likewise. . . ."[9]

Put another way, it is not the poet who speaks but the Muse or the God *through* the poet; and this we conclude for the same reason we were forced to conclude the very same thing about the rhapsodes. For like the rhapsodes, the poets are "specialists," each speaking about the same things, as we have seen, *but* not in the same way. Poets, that is to say, have different "styles." And so the inspiration theory turns out to be not merely a theory of "content" (for the rhapsode) but a theory of "style" (for the poet) as well.

Seeing then that it is not by art that they compose and utter such fine things about the deeds of men—as you do about Homer—but by a divine dispensation, each is able only to compose that to which the Muse has stirred him, this man dithyrambs, another laudatory odes, another dance-songs, another epic or else iambic verse; but each is at fault at any other kind. For not by art do they utter these things, but by divine influence; since, if they had fully learnt by art to speak on one kind of theme, they would know how to speak on all. And for this reason God takes away the mind of these men and uses them as his ministers.[10]

Here then, in brief (to summarize), is the straightforward part of Socrates' argument. Rhapsodes and poets are alike in that they seem to be "specialists": each rhapsode seems to be able to speak intelligently and well about only one poet, and each poet intelligently and well in only one manner (or "style"). If they all had a rational method, if they had "art," however, each rhapsode would be able to speak intelligently and well about *every* poet; and each poet would be able to speak intelligently and well in *any* manner or style. But if they have *no* rational method or art, how do they speak intelligently and well at all? The answer must be that someone *else* speaks through them intelligently and well. It is the God or the Muse. *They* are simply the "possessed."

Later on I will examine Socrates' "theory" of "possession" more closely, to see what significance it can have for those of us who do not believe in gods and muses. But before I do that I must, as promised, try to pick up the loose end. What might it be?

Shoemakers have an art, a techne, and make shoes by applying it. The same is true of charioteers and doctors and mathematicians, who all possess rational methods appropriate to their disciplines, and fabricate the "products" of these disciplines by employing them.

Similarly, those who are capable of passing judgment on the products of an art or techne must themselves possess that art or techne, else how could *they* make such judgments? On Socrates' view, it *does* take a jockey to know a horse—or it takes someone at least somewhat versed in the "art" of horsemanship.

But what of *poetry*? If poems are neither produced by poets nor judged by rhapsodes through art or techne, but are produced and judged through possession by the God, doesn't it follow that poetry is not an art or techne? Yet that does not appear to be Socrates' view. For he says to Ion: "anyone can see that you are unable to speak on Homer with art or knowledge. For if you could do it with art, you could speak on all the other poets as well; since there is an art of poetry, as a whole, is there not?"[11] And so we are stuck with the somewhat cumbersome, inelegant position that poetry, in contrast to all other arts, is created, interpreted, and evaluated not by means of its "art," but by divine afflatus. Why so? We are owed an explanation, but none is in evidence.

In this connection it is interesting to examine the examples Socrates gives of "arts" where at least "interpretation" and "evaluation" are the result of rational method, of techne. They are all arts of "representation," *mimesis*—what *we* would call the "fine arts." (Plato of course had no such concept.)

Socrates begins: "And when one has acquired any other art whatever [besides poetry, that is] as a whole, the same principle of inquiry holds through all the arts?"[12] Again, a rhetorical question which elicits from Ion the called-for affirmative response.

There then follows a series of rhetorical questions of the same kind, all requiring Ion to respond in the negative, which he obligingly does. "Now have you ever found anybody who is skilled in pointing out the successes and failures among the works of Polygnotus son of Aglaophon, but unable to do so with the works of the other painters . . . ?" "Or again, in sculpture, have you ever found anyone who is skilled in expounding the successes of Daedalus son of Metion, or Epeius son of Panopeus, or Theodorus son of Samos, or any other single sculptor, but in face of the works of the other sculptors is at a loss and dozes, having nothing to say?" "But further, I expect you have also failed to find one in fluting or harping or minstrelsy or rhapsodizing . . . ," and so on.[13]

One crucial thing Socrates does not tell us explicitly is whether the *making* of pictures, statues, and the rest is the result of art or of divine possession. It would be hard, though, not to surmise the former. If painting and sculpture and musical performance are art, and if it is art that produces interpretations and evaluations of them—which it *must* be, since the interpreter and evaluator can pass judgment not on the work of just one practitioner but all in the discipline—then it would be odd in the extreme to deny that it is also art that produces the works in the first place. It seems an anomaly that poetry should *both* be an art *and* produce both poems as well as their interpretations not through art but through divine possession. It would be an anomaly on top of an anomaly to maintain that painting, sculpture and musical performance, all arts, as poetry apparently is, should, *like* poetry, produce works through divine inspiration but, *unlike* poetry, interpretations and evaluations through art. And Socrates, although giving us no positive statement to rule this double anomaly out, gives us no reason either for us to subscribe to it. One anomaly is enough!

We are then apparently stuck with the anomalous position that poetry, alone of all the arts, representational and non-representational, generates both its products and its interpretations (and evaluations) of them through the God. But *are* we really stuck with even this single anomaly? A look at the Greek text and an alternative translation suggest otherwise: suggest a plausible way out, a more rational interpretation of Plato's position on poetry in the *Ion*.

Generations of readers have been made acquainted with Plato's dialogues through Benjamin Jowett's famous translation. His rendering of our problematic passage is revealing: it does *not* contain mention of poetry as art or techne at all. As Jowett has it: "No one can fail to see that you speak of Homer without any art or knowledge. If you were able to speak of him by rules of art, you would be able to speak of all other poets; for *poetry is a whole*."[14]

Throughout the *Ion* Plato makes the claim that something is "a whole" in conjunction with the claim that it is an "art" or "techne." Our modern translator, W. R. M. Lamb, has obviously interpreted Plato to the effect that if something *is* "a whole," it is an "art"; and since the word "art" does not appear in the Greek text of our troublesome passage (which it does not) he *adds* it, as does the most recent translator of the dialogue, Paul Woodruff.[15] But Jowett does *not* add it. And the question now arises whether, nevertheless, it *must* be understood as *implied*. I think not. It makes far better sense of the argument of the *Ion* to have Plato saying that poetry is distinct from all the other "wholes," in that it is "a whole" but not an "art." In other words, the doctrine of the *Ion* is that if something is an art, it is a whole, but if a whole, not necessarily an art—poetry being an instance, and prophecy, perhaps, another.

If this is what Plato is saying in the *Ion*—that unlike other wholes, which *are* arts, poetry is a whole without being an art—then the rest of what he is saying makes perfect sense, namely, that poetry is made and talked about not by art but by divine possession. For it cannot be made or talked about by art, since it *isn't* one.

Perhaps, furthermore, we may add to the evidence that Plato did not think poetry an art the passage from the *Gorgias* where Plato is contrasting the "arts" with such non-arts as rhetoric and cookery—the non-arts in question not, by the way, inspired activities like poetry and prophecy, but empirical ones: "experiences," as Plato calls them (in Jowett's translation). They too, like poetry, are not practiced by art, that is, by rational method (although not by divine possession either). "And," Plato says, apropos of this, "I do not call any irrational thing art. . . ."[16] But poetry is, according to the *Ion,* quintessentially an "irrational thing," even when practiced by Homer, the greatest practitioner of them all. For the poet is possessed, literally "out of his mind," when in the throes of creation. No productive activity could be a more irrational thing than that, and irrational things, Plato says straight out, in the *Gorgias,* are *not art*. I think this strongly supports the interpretation of the *Ion* I am urging—if not directly, then at least by pretty direct implication.

The only question that now remains is whether we can make sense of the notion of something's being "a whole," but not an art, as I am saying Plato thought poetry to be. If being a whole is equivalent to being an art, then we know pretty well what it means to be a whole: it means to be something practiced by a rational method: by a "techne." But what might Plato mean by something's being a whole, if being a whole and being an art are not the same thing? What does it mean to call poetry a whole but not an art, as I think Plato is doing? I think he has left us a pretty broad hint.

Recall the question that Socrates asks Ion very early on: "Does

Homer speak of any other than the very things that all the other poets speak of?" Ion answers in the negative; and that is the conclusion Plato wants us to draw. But *that* is exactly, I suggest, what makes poetry, or anything else, "a whole," in Plato's sense. What makes poetry a whole is that it is a single universe of discourse: all the poets (and rhapsodes) talk about the same sorts of things; and that is also what makes medicine a whole, or generalship, or any of the others. The difference is that poetry, though a whole, a single universe of discourse, is *not,* like the other wholes Plato mentions, the other universes of discourse, an *art.* And so it is a whole, a universe of discourse governed not by art but by inspiration. That, I believe, is what Plato is saying in the *Ion.*

R. G. Collingwood, in his *Principles of Art,* is well known for claiming that the ancients thought poetry, and all the other of what we would call fine arts, were what he called "crafts"; or, in other words, "techne," "arts." But he adds the caveat: "There are suggestions in some of them, especially in Plato, of a quite different view. . . ."[17] Was Collingwood thinking here of the *Ion;* and is the "quite different view" the view that poetry, unlike other wholes, is not a "craft"? If that was what Collingwood had in mind, he was, I think, right; and so was Jowett in translating our recalcitrant passage in the way that he did.

I have spoken at some length, now, about a sticky point in the interpretation of Plato's doctrine in the *Ion,* claiming that Plato thought poetry a whole but not an art, and that that is why he thought poetry a practice governed by inspiration rather than by art. But whether I am right or not about this particular point of interpretation is of no particular importance for the present enterprise, although it certainly is for the history of aesthetics. What *is* important is the theory of poetic inspiration itself, whether or not poetry is, for Plato, an "art." It is time now, therefore, that we went on to a consideration of what significance Socrates' "theory" of poetic inspiration has for the future, and for the argument of this book.

Let us remember, to begin with, a few things about Plato's theory of poetic inspiration. First, it is not a theory about "genius" *in the fine arts.* Plato had no concept of the fine arts, at least as we understand that concept. It had to await formulation in the eighteenth century.

Second, it is not really a theory of *genius.* Nowhere in the *Ion* does

Plato use any word that a translator has so rendered. Whatever Plato's theory was a theory of, it was not a theory of *that*.

Third, it must be remembered that our concept of genius and, to remain in the Platonic world, our concept of poetic creation are both highly charged evaluative concepts of a *positive* kind. To call someone a genius or to refer to her poetic "inspiration" is to give her powerful praise: the ultimate accolade. Such is not the case with Plato; indeed, just the very opposite. As we know primarily from the *Republic*, but from other dialogues as well, Plato cast a baleful eye on both the epistemic pretensions and moral effect of what we now call the fine arts. He is, therefore, offering no praise of the states of mind of Ion, Homer, or their audience, but harsh disapproval when he says of them all, in a revival of the magnet metaphor: "And are you aware that your spectator is the last of the rings which I spoke of as receiving from each other the power transmitted from the Heraclean lodestone? You, the rhapsode and actor, are the middle ring; the poet himself is the first but it is the god who through the whole series draws the souls of men whithersoever he pleases, making the power of one depend on the others." [18]

In other words, Homer and Ion and their audience, when in the throes of poetic creation, interpretation, or appreciation are quite mad, irrational, out of control—a state, for Plato, *not* devoutly to be wished. Ion himself, thick though he is, understands quite well the reproof in Socrates' words: "Well spoken, I grant you," he acknowledges, "but still I shall be surprised if you can speak well enough to convince me that I am possessed and mad when I praise Homer." [19]

So we must remember how far Plato is from any modern notion of artistic genius. And yet how close! So in spite of what I have just said, I will, more than somewhat anachronistically, call what Plato is talking about in the *Ion* "genius." At least that is what later ages made of it. What, then, was Plato doing? I can begin to answer this question by mentioning two more or less well-known stories.

According to folk tradition, Isaac Newton thought of the law of gravity after an apple fell on his head. And, according to a well-known story, Henri Poincaré got the basic idea for one of his mathematical theories while stepping off a London omnibus. Both stories are supposed to tell us something about how the genius gets his or her "inspirations." Only one of them is telling the truth.

Newton's story is, of course, telling us that "strokes of genius" can be provoked by accidental, trivial events; and that indeed is so. The omnibus story tells us the very same thing. But there is a very big difference. For Newton's story suggests there is a relevant *connection* between the accidental occurrence and the insight. It is a *falling* apple that gives the genius the insight into the law that governs *all* falling bodies. *Eating* an apple would not have done the trick. In the omnibus story, however, there is absolutely *no relevant connection* between the event, stepping off the omnibus, and the brilliant idea: that is the whole point of the story. And it is *that* aspect of the omnibus story that contains the truth that Plato already revealed in the *Ion*.

Bright ideas are not generated by acts of will through the application of some "method." Bright ideas just "happen" to people. People who get them are patients, not agents. That was Plato's (or Socrates') discovery. Insight is a kind of "infectious disease" that one succumbs to. One might well call it the "passive" notion of genius.

Is Plato's a "theory" of genius? The answer depends upon how literally one wants to take Plato's "theology."

Ion and the poets have ideas happen to them stepping off the omnibus. If we take Plato's "theology" literally, it is an "explanation" of this fact. *Where* do these bright ideas come from? *How* do they happen? The explanation is "supernatural." The gods funnel their ideas through the poets and rhapsodes. (Of course it is a nice question where and how the gods get the ideas they impart to the poets and rhapsodes. But perhaps to consider thus is to consider too curiously.)

But how literally Plato took the various myths and appeals to the divine that he used to depict our epistemic situation is not at all clear. And in the present case I am inclined to see Plato's story of divine possession not so much as an "explanation" for how poets and rhapsodes do their work, get their "bright ideas," but as merely an elaborate metaphorical description of the phenomenon, which itself has no explanation at all and no rule-governed "method" for its generation.

Of course bright ideas occur only to people who prepare to "receive" them, just as the oracle needs *his* preparation, whether it be ritual or mushroom. You cannot step off the omnibus and think of how to prove a theorem unless you are a trained mathematician. You cannot be "inspired" to write *The Creation* unless you study harmony and counterpoint. But once having made the preparations, nothing you have learned will equip you to generate, by rational decision and acts of will, great ideas. As the logicians say, there is no "decision procedure" for that. Plato discovered this for poetry—*great* poetry, that is.

This, then, is Plato's non-theory of poetic creation: poetry *happens* to you; *you* don't *do* it. The Elizabethan critics called it the "Platonic furor."

Plato, then, had neither a "theory" of "genius" nor even a *concept* of it. He *did* have a metaphor for poetic creation that can easily be made into a description of human invention at its highest level, wherever it may manifest itself. And *that* latter *is* an account (or perhaps a "theory") of genius.

The "Platonic furor" served future ages as a source for various concepts of genius, reformulated, of course, in terms more congenial to a world no longer inhabited by muses and divinities (in the plural), even to serve as metaphorical props. But its general outline will be met again, in different philosophical trappings from those of Plato's *Ion*. We shall meet the theory again, recognizable though transformed. Now, however, we must confront a very different picture of genius that also had its source in the ancient world.[20]

II
Greatness of Mind

The "inspiration" or "possession" picture of genius is a perennial favorite. But it is ill-suited to certain of what we take to be paradigmatic cases. If, for example, you think of genius as epitomized by Beethoven's vow to "seize Fate by the throat . . . ,"[1] the "Platonic furor" will hardly serve; for according to *it, Fate,* rather, is seizing *Beethoven* by the throat. Beethoven is its passive victim. Hardly our image of "Beethoven the Creator."

But the Beethovenian concept of genius too had its precedent in an ancient text, one that made a very big noise in the eighteenth century. I have reference to the incomplete treatise, *On the Sublime,* once attributed to the third century A.D. critic, Longinus of Palmyra, but now thought to be a work of the first century A.D. by a yet-to-be identified author. It is customary to refer to the author in quotation marks as "Longinus." He is also sometimes called the pseudo-Longinus. The former becomes a nuisance, and the latter is cumbersome. So I will simply call him Longinus and let it go at that.

Peri Hupsos, On the Sublime, is concerned with literary style in prose as well as poetry, as *Ion* was not. But like Plato, Longinus had no word for genius, and where both his early and modern translators use that term, which they consistently do, the literal translation is more like "greatness of mind." Although, however, Longinus did not have the word, he does seem to have had something close to *one* modern concept of the thing. And I shall, therefore, follow his translators in using the term for what Longinus was talking about.

What the translators render as "genius," indeed, rears its head at the very beginning of the treatise, where Longinus is in the process of defining his terms. The subject is the sublime in writing. And Longinus, in addressing one Postumius Terentianus, for whom the work is ostensibly composed, says that

> writing for a man of such learning and culture as yourself, dear friend, I almost feel freed from the need of a lengthy preface showing how the Sublime consists in a consumate excellence and distinction of language, and that this alone gave to the greatest poets and historians their pre-eminence and clothed them with immortal fame. For the effect of genius is not to persuade an audience but rather to transport them out of themselves.[2]

Very soon thereafter, we get at least a hint of what the nature of genius might be. "Again inventive skill and the due disposal and marshalling of facts do not show themselves in one or two touches: they gradually emerge from the whole tissue of the composition, while, on the other hand, a well-timed flash of sublimity scatters everything before it like a bolt of lightening and reveals the full power of the speaker at a single stroke."[3]

Genius, *roughly,* is the ability to achieve sublimity in writing. And it is *power,* not skill, although the full meaning of this is yet to be seen.

Longinus subscribes to a concept of genius, "natural genius," that must have been a commonplace by his time—which, I assume, with those who seem to know, is the first century A.D. This concept first enters Longinus' argument very close to the beginning, directly after the passages just quoted above. He introduces it with some hesitation, as a concept held by others, but not wholeheartedly by him. For Longinus, it requires qualifications, at least in the extreme form in which he first states it. "Genius, it is said, is born and does not come of teaching. Works of natural genius, so people think, are spoiled and utterly demeaned by being reduced to the dry bones of rule and precept."[4]

It is not that Longinus does not believe in the adage that genius is born, not made. Rather, it is the rider, that strokes of genius are spoiled by the application of "rule and precept," which he rejects. "For," he says, "genius needs the curb as often as the spur." Or, put less epigrammatically: "In all production Nature is the prime cause, the great exemplar; but as to all questions of degree, of the happy moment in each case, and again of the safest rules of practice and use, such prescriptions are the proper contribution of art or system."[5]

As the argument of Longinus proceeds, the concept of genius, and its relation to "rule and precept," are re-introduced on a number of occasions, and Longinus' belief in the concept of natural genius is expressed in stronger terms, perhaps, than at the outset. By examining the major passages on natural genius, one by one, we will be able to flesh out, insofar as is possible, what exactly he had in mind, although in the end we get, I think, a collection of ideas, not necessarily consistent, rather than a "theory." "Theories" were to come only upon the reemergence of *On the Sublime* in the eighteenth century.

The next passage in which the concept of genius is discussed presents a number of new elements. Longinus states that of the main sources of the sublime (five in number), "The first and most powerful is the command of full-blooded ideas. . . ."[6] Shortly thereafter he tells us that another name for "the command of full-blooded ideas" just is "natural genius," of which he then goes on to say, "although it is rather a gift than an acquired ability, we should still do our utmost to train our minds into sympathy with what is noble and, as it were, impregnate them again and again with lofty inspiration."[7]

Again, "Sublimity is the true ring of a noble mind," and "a great style is the natural outcome of weighty thoughts, and sublime sayings naturally fall to men of spirit."[8]

What begins to emerge, then, is a picture of the genius as a figure of weight, spirit, nobility, loftiness of thought—in a word, a figure of *power*. Not, one is beginning to suspect, the passive conduit of another force, but a force unto itself—not the possessed but the possessor.

The Longinian genius is a "take-charge guy." And that impression is reinforced as the argument progresses.

Furthermore, there is just a hint here, but an intriguing one, of a very Romantic notion: the so-called expression theory of art. Notice, in this regard, Longinus' striking statement, just quoted above: "Sublimity is the true ring of a noble mind." (There are other such in the text.) If this statement stood alone, its significance might pass us by. But if we read it with hindsight we can see lurking here the notion that in sublime writing, we are, so to say, put in contact with a noble mind. The nobility of that mind is being "expressed" in sublime composition: that mind is *communicating* its nobility to us, and therein, at least in part, lies the value of the sublime. It imparts to us, at least for a moment, a nobility of mind we ourselves do not possess. (I shall say a bit more about this "expression theory" shortly.)

To return to the concept of genius as *power,* one vagrant point is worth noticing in this regard. Longinus, as was customary, believed the *Iliad* and *Odyssey* to be two works of the same single poet, the latter a product of old age, the former "the heyday of his genius."[9] And of the latter Longinus remarks: "throughout the *Odyssey* . . . Homer shows that as genius ebbs, it is the love of romance that characterizes old age."[10] Completing the thought, a few sentences later, "I have led into this digression to show you, as I said, that natural genius with the decline of vigour often falls very easily into garrulity. . . ."[11]

How natural for genius to decline with age, if, as Longinus characterizes it, it is an attribute of vigorous, powerful minds! For vigor and power of mind, as of body, we would expect to ebb with the ebbing of life. (Recall the argument of Lucretius to that effect!) And here, again, the Longinian notion of natural genius contrasts sharply with the Platonic afflatus.

For there is no reason to think that "inspiration," possession by the God, should be any less common in old age than in youth. And not only is there no evidence in the *Ion* that Socrates thought poetic inspiration declines with age, there is at least some evidence to show that he thought it flourishes. For one thing, Socrates' references to the *Odyssey,* unlike those of Longinus, are always of a positive kind. It serves as an exemplar of the inspired in poetry no less than does the

Iliad, even though it seems likely that Socrates shared Longinus' view of the former as a work of the poet's old age.

Second, Socrates thinks poetic inspiration of a piece with the inspiration of prophets and oracles: ". . . God takes away the mind of these men and uses them as his ministers, just as he does soothsayers and godly seers. . . ."[12] And our image of "soothsayers and godly seers" is far more likely to be one of aged, white-bearded sages than youths in the prime of life.

And, finally, Socrates, in support of the inspiration theory of poetic creation, gives us the intriguing example of the poet, Tynnichus the Chalcidian, "who never composed a single poem in his life that could deserve any mention, and then produced the paean which is in everyone's mouth, almost the finest song we have, simply—as he says himself—'an invention of the Muses.'"[13] Here, then, an example of poetic "genius" not declining in old age but, rather, appearing for the first (and only) time in a man whose creative life has been until then a history of mediocrity.

So Longinus gives us a theory of genius as strength and power and "expression," which grows, flourishes, and perforce must decline; Socrates, a theory of genius as a thing that comes when it will at the bidding of the God or the Muse. For Longinus genius must seize the day; for Socrates the day must seize the genius.

The richest, fullest of the passages on genius in *On the Sublime* occur toward the middle of the treatise, as we have it. (A substantial portion is lost.) I turn to these passages now.

We saw early on that Longinus is concerned about the relation between what is "natural" in literary composition, which is to say, inborn genius, and what is artificial and acquired, which is to say "rule and precept." The later passages concerning genius speak very much to this point. But there is something of a reversal of fortunes. For whereas in the earlier passages there was a rather vigorous defense of "rule and precept" against those who think brilliant strokes are spoiled by art and method, the later ones defend, rather, the prerogative of genius to—at least in some sense or senses we must ultimately determine—kick over the traces to gallop unhindered.

Longinus inaugurates his "defense" of "literary incorrectness" with a question: "... Which is the better in poetry and in prose, grandeur with a few flaws or correct composition of mediocre quality, yet entirely sound and impeccable?"[14]

The question that would immediately occur to us as a response to Longinus' one is: "Why can't we have grandeur without any flaws at all? Why the disjunction: either grandeur without perfection or perfection without grandeur?"

The answer to this second question is that Longinus thinks "flaws," flouted precepts and broken rules of correct literary composition, are a *necessary* part of great, sublime writing: a necessary concomitant of genius: "the greatest natures are least immaculate.... [I]n great writing as in great wealth there must needs be something overlooked."[15]

It is not altogether clear, in the part of Longinus' text that we possess, just *why* genius should be any more prone to mistakes than is mediocrity. (Why not the other way round?) A number of metaphors and "old sayings" are marshalled in that regard. The more interesting question, however, as we shall see, is: What is the nature of these "infractions" of the rules? Longinus' first stab at answering that question is to characterize them simply as mindless errors of an aesthetically disagreeable kind. He says of the "good many faults in Homer and the other authors, ... though these slips certainly offend my taste, yet I prefer to call them not wilful mistakes but careless oversights, let in casually almost at random by the heedlessness of genius."[16]

What should first be noted here is that the violations of rule are represented completely in the negative. They are offensive to taste, and they are "mistakes," "oversights." There is no virtue in *them*, only in the result of which they are the unwanted side effect. And, second, they are not the direct result of intentional choice but, rather, are "careless oversights," "random heedlessness." It is not as if the genius, knowing full well that these defects, these violations of rule and precept, would be the foreseen outcome of aiming at and achieving loftier, more important aesthetic goals, chose those loftier, more important goals nevertheless. On the contrary, they slip by in the rush of genius.

This view of the relation of genius to the breaking of the rules still suggests the notions of power and will mentioned previously. But certainly it pays genius no very great compliment in charging it with what might be called the aesthetic version of "reckless endangerment." With regard to the violation of rule and precept, the genius is as passive a "victim" as the Platonic "genius possessed."

Furthermore, I think this wholly negative characterization of the genius' prerogative to violate the rules and precepts of correct literary composition runs counter to one of our deep aesthetic intuitions about the view of natural genius Longinus is putting out. It is the intuition that the broken rules and precepts are a positive aesthetic virtue, not a fault. They are broken for the positive effect of breaking them, not out of mindless carelessness. Only thus can full justice be done to the power of natural genius. I do not think that Longinus ever comes to this. That is left for Kant and his posterity. But he does, later on in the treatise, make intimations.

It is not that Longinus ever does take a positive attitude toward rule-breaking. But the passages in which it is defended become more and more effusive in their praise of the genius who breaks them. Thus he speaks of "those demi-gods who aimed only at what is greatest in writing and scorned detailed accuracy."[17] Or he says of these geniuses of the sublime that "sublimity lifts them near the mighty mind of God," and so "each of these great men again and again redeems all his mistakes by a single touch of nobility and true excellence. . . ."[18] No recognition here, to be sure, that broken rules and flouted precepts of correct literary composition are anything but lapses in "accuracy" that must be "redeemed." There is still, in Longinus, something of a Beckmesser, toting up the credits against the debits. Yet the terms in which the sublime rule-breakers are praised have become inflated to fairly impressive proportions. And that leads to a further observation.

What *are* the terms of praise? The genius has now become "demigod" and "near the mighty mind of God." Whereas in Plato God speaks through the poet, in Longinus the poet has taken on the persona of God.

The God-poet is not, indeed, even within his own literary world, the God of Genesis and the Christian theologians. *That* God does not, like Longinus' poet-God, break the rules: he *makes* the rules. Indeed, Longinus' poet-God, pagan God that he is, forgets himself. (As Elijah says of Baal, "Perchance he sleeps.") He becomes carried away and forgets the rules. Or He does the best He can by seeing that, though He cannot *both* achieve sublimity *and* obey the rules, He can do better *by* breaking the rules rather than obeying them, in His sublime "strokes of genius." He is demiurge, not omnipotent and omniscient Divinity.

Longinus' last word on genius and the rules and precepts, at least in that part of the treatise *On the Sublime* we possess, presents an interesting volte-face, in a way disappointing. For it seems to be a step back from the notion of genius as *necessarily* a departure from the rules and precepts. Before, we were assured that genius and perfection are necessarily, *interestingly* incompatible. But in the end, Longinus seems to retreat from that appealingly "Romantic" notion. He writes that "since the merit of impeccable correctness is, generally speaking, due to art, and the height of excellence, though not sustained, to genius, it is proper that art should always assist Nature. Their co-operation may thus result in perfection."[19]

Recall that when the notion of natural genius was introduced, Longinus took issue with what might be called the "super-Romantic" notion that genius is always spoiled by the application of art. So Longinus at no time denied that natural genius requires rule and precept. But he goes on to present what might be called the "moderately Romantic" notion that even with the application of rule and precept, works of genius must perforce be *contrary* to rule and precept, hence "imperfect," but in a praiseworthy way. Now, however, he is saying something different again, namely, that the application of "art"—which is to say, rule and precept—*can* make the work of genius *both* sublime *and* perfect. The "pizzazz" now seems to have gone out of the doctrine, and it has become a rather pallid, not too convincing attempt to have and to eat.

But it was the interesting, "moderately Romantic" view that resurfaced, and persisted in the eighteenth century, when *On the Sublime* was rediscovered and translated into French and English. That is the Longinus that made the big noise.

Nor should we forget that Longinus' treatise contained (as we have seen) the seed of another distinctly "Romantic" notion, the expression theory of art, in the characterization of the sublime as putting one in contact with a noble mind. The "inspiration" theory could provide no such idea, in a secular context. It is true, of course, that the God, or Muse, through the poet and rhapsode, puts the audience in contact with a noble enough mind: a divine one, in fact. And for a Christian aesthetics, this is obviously a welcome conclusion.

But for a secular aesthetics, whereas on the Longinian view the audience is put in contact with a noble mind, that of the artist, on the Platonic view, in the absence of the God or the Muse, the audience is put in contact with *no mind at all*. After all, the poet and rhapsode are both "out of their minds," hence "mindless." There is no "source" in a mental act of will. There is just the passive recipient of brilliant invention from "we know not where": from "nowhere." This does not mean there can be no theory of value for secularized Platonism. There cannot, however, be the value of "expression"—communication with the great human spirit—so dear to the Romantic heart.

So antiquity gave us two notions of creative genius in the arts: the genius of the possessed and the genius of the possessor; the passive genius, possessed by the God, and the active genius, a God himself, possessor of the table of the laws which he gives to his work; a genius to which creation happens and a genius who makes creation happen. Both of these concepts of genius, we shall presently see, manifested themselves in modern times, expressed in modern terms. And as we shall also see, Handel, Mozart, and Beethoven, each in his turn, came to represent for the musical world and the world at large one or other of these notions. That story I now begin to tell. It begins with the rediscovery of Longinus in the eighteenth century. Where it ends, no one can say.

III

Breaking the Rule

By the purest of coincidences the year 1711 is doubly significant for the argument of my book. It is the year of Handel's first musical triumph in London, where he remained for fifty years the dominant figure on the English musical landscape. And it is the year that Joseph Addison published in the *Spectator* (Monday, September 3) a modest little paper on genius that, along with the paper on taste of the following year, and the eleven papers called "On the Pleasures of the Imagination," to which it was prefixed, arguably constitute the inauguration of the modern discipline of Aesthetics and the Philosophy of Art.

The beginnings of Aesthetics and the Philosophy of Art, as we understand them today, are but one of a number of crucial ideas and institutions that came into being in the eighteenth century, and that we take for granted in our thinking about the fine arts. They are important, some crucial in the eventual enshrinement of Handel as a symbol of musical—and *artistic*—genius. They shall be discussed in the following chapter. What we must do in this one is to become acquainted with the Longinian concept of natural genius as it was reexpressed and reformulated in the years between Handel's entrance onto the English musical scene in 1711 and his death in 1759. And it is with Addison that it is not only convenient to start but logical as well. For it is Addison's paper on genius that marks the real beginning of the British fascination with the concept in the eighteenth century—a fascination that ultimately had its full philosophical payoff in Kant's *Critique of Judgment*.

Addison begins by suggesting that "genius" is rather indiscriminantly bandied about in the literary world. He says: "There is no character more frequently given to a writer, than that of being a genius. ... There is not an heroic scribbler in the nation that has not his admirers who think him a great genius. . . ." It is Addison's intention to set matters aright by giving genius its true character and (thereby) determine which literary figures merit the appellation. "My design in this paper is to consider what is properly a great genius, and to throw some thoughts together on so uncommon a subject."[1]

Addison distinguishes between two kinds of genius, the first, and, apparently, the most to be admired, very much in the Longinian mold of natural genius. Of such, Addison writes:

> Among great geniuses those few draw the admiration of all the world upon them, and stand up as the prodigies of mankind, who by the mere strength of natural parts, and without any assistance of art or learning, have produced works that were the delight of their own times and the wonder of posterity. There appears something nobly wild and extravagant in these natural geniuses, that is infinitely more beautiful than all the turn and polishing of what the French call the *bel esprit,* by which they would express a genius refined by conversation, reflection, and the reading of the most polite authors.[2]

I say that this first, natural kind of genius is in the Longinian mold. That I think is obvious. Perhaps less obvious, but of great significance, are the new suggestions—distinctive of the discussion as it was evolving in the early years of the eighteenth century—in the country that was, for more than fifty years, to lead in the philosophical discussion of art and the aesthetic.

It might be remarked upon, first, that Addison far outdistances Longinus in his emphasis on the *naturalness* of "natural genius." For

Longinus, the issue was to what *extent* learning was to influence or control genius. For Addison, there is no such issue at all. The natural genius creates "by the mere strength of natural parts, and *without any assistance of art or learning* . . . ," the implication, made explicit a moment later, being not that natural genius ignores the rules and precepts of literary composition but that it operates quite in the absence of any knowledge at all. The natural genius, in others words, is a "primitive," it would seem.

This implication is drawn, unequivocally, and significantly, in the next paragraph, where Addison locates the majority of such natural geniuses in antiquity, with Homer and the Old Testament as his primary examples. "Many of these great natural geniuses that were never disciplined and broken by rules of art, are to be found among the ancients, and in particular among those of the more eastern part of the world. Homer has innumerable flights that Virgil was not able to reach; and in the Old Testament we find several passages more elevated and sublime than anything in Homer."[3]

Why the ancients should provide the major instances of natural genius we shall understand in a moment. But it is necessary now to point out that Addison has introduced, in the comparison of Homer to Virgil, a trope that characterizes the discussion of genius in England in the eighteenth century, and the discussion of the contrast between the sublime and beautiful around which it revolves.

A further point to be noticed, in which Addison departs from the Longinian mold, is in his introduction of the concept of imitation. And we comprehend that fully only with the introduction of Addison's second kind of genius. Of this genius, he writes: "There is another kind of great geniuses which I shall place in a second class, not as I think them inferior to the first, but only for distinction's sake, as they are of a different kind. This second class of great geniuses are those that have formed themselves by the rules, and submitted the greatness of their natural talents to the corrections and restraints of art."[4]

On Addison's view, then, the Longinian, natural genius is complemented by a "learned" genius who operates through rules and precepts. But exactly *what* constitutes the application of rules and precepts? Is it like following a recipe in a cookbook? Apparently not. This we can see from Addison's cautionary note *to* the learned genius: "The great danger in the latter kind of geniuses is, lest they cramp their own abilities too much by *imitation*, and form themselves altogether upon models, without giving full play to their own natural parts."[5] I conclude from this that following rules and precepts is not so much applying recipes as it is emulating models that might be thought to embody the accumulated rules and precepts in palpable form. And this certainly accords well with the way any artist learns her trade, who, not being a natural genius, has to learn it rather than possessing it as a gift of birth.

This introduces a second, distinctly "modern" concept to the discussion of artistic genius. Addison's age conceptualized, as Longinus' age did not, *two different worlds of literature* (as, of course, did the Renaissance): ancient and modern. They were involved, and would be for some time to come, in what has come to be known as the "quarrel between the ancients and moderns": a dispute about whether or not modern literature could surpass or even equal the ancient. For those who took the side of the ancients, "genius," if that was the right name for it, could but imitate ancient models. For those who took the side of the moderns, however, it was Longinian natural genius that suited their purpose. *It* was the concept of genius as scorning the rules, ignoring the rules (in Addison's case, indeed, not even knowing the rules); it was the concept of genius as an originating font of literary works, neither in need of nor prone to the imitation or emulation of classical models.

Which concept of genius does Addison incline toward? He *says* that he does not think the cultivated genius "inferior to" the natural one. Of course, any logic student can tell you that that is compatible with believing either that they are equal or that the cultivated genius is *superior* to the natural kind. But classroom logic is notoriously cavalier concerning idiomatic English, and Addison's sense here is clearly that he is indifferent between the two.

Furthermore, I am inclined to think that although Addison gives lip service to the equality of natural and imitative genius, the spirit of the piece points in the opposite direction: that is, to the superiority of the former. Recall how he introduces the concept of natural genius, in what superlatives he paints it. "Among great geniuses those few draw the admiration of all the world upon them, and stand up as the prodigies of mankind, who by the mere strength of natural parts, and without any assistance of art or learning, have produced works that were the delight of their own times and the wonder of posterity." And, again, having warned against the dangers one runs as a genius of the cultivated, imitative kind, he adds: "An imitation of the best authors is not to compare with a good original; and I believe we may observe that very few writers make an extraordinary figure in the world who have not something in their way of thinking or expressing themselves that is peculiar to them and entirely their own."[6] Originality was to become a hallmark of Longinian genius, as we shall see, a sine qua non of genius in general, and of greatness in art. Addison had sounded the clarion call at the very beginning of modern aesthetic theory.

Finally, let me again return to the previously quoted characterization of natural genius to remind the reader of the following passage, from which two rather important conclusions can be drawn. The passage is this: "There appears something nobly wild and extravagant in these natural geniuses, that is infinitely more beautiful than all the turn and polishing of what the French call the *bel esprit*. . . ."

The first conclusion to be drawn is that, right here, at the outset of his paper, Addison is already contrasting the wild, natural genius with the correct, cultivated one, much to the favor of the former, being "infinitely more beautiful." We may, then, sum up the case for Addison's favoring of natural over cultivated, imitative genius in three points, as follows. First, few but natural geniuses "draw the admiration of all the world upon them. . . ." Second, imitative genius, unlike the natural kind, seldom achieves originality. (How could it?) And, third, the successes of natural genius are "infinitely more beautiful" than those of the correct variety. And thus I am going to conclude that, in spite of Addison's rather polite assurance that he does not favor one form of genius over the other, it is clear that in spirit it is Longinian natural genius—the genius that operates above and beyond rules, precepts and models of correct composition—that most properly deserves the name of "genius," in Addison's account. This, more and more after him, is the judgment of his century.

But I said that there was a second conclusion to be drawn from the passage just quoted. It is this. In spite of the fact that neither the name of Longinus, nor the word "sublime" ever occurs in Addison's paper on genius, a fairly recognizable description of the sublime, as the eighteenth century was beginning to understand it, is apparent in the passage in question, in the phrase "nobly wild and extravagant." Nor can there be any doubt that Addison knew his Longinus, as his name crops up in a number of the *Spectator* papers around this time. Indeed, in a paper of 1714, not only does Addison refer to him as one of the "true" critics of antiquity whom he "esteem[s]," but he again presents the now all too familiar Longinian picture of genius versus the rules. This new statement of the position is instructive not only because it occurs soon after the mention of Longinus, but also because it makes no secret of Addison's inclination toward the Longinian natural genius over the cultivated emulator. Thus, in excoriating the critics of his time who "are so stupid, that they do not know how to put ten words together with elegance or common propriety," Addison writes: "They are often led into these numerous absurdities in which they daily instruct the people, by not considering that, first, there is sometimes a greater judgment shown in deviating from the rules of art than in adhering to them; and, secondly, that there is more beauty in the works of a great genius who is ignorant of all the rules than in the works of a little genius who not only knows but scrupulously observes them."[7]

Addision, then, revived for the British Enlightenment the Longinian theory of natural genius: if he was not the first, he was certainly the most impressive of the "firsts." He did this before the Longinian "craze" took over, and no doubt contributed materially to its development.[8] But already clearly discernible in Addison's account of genius are: first, the notion of genius as wild and powerful; second, as (therefore) the breaker of rules; third, as original rather than derivative; and, fourth, as peculiarly prone to the production of sublime rather than beautiful works.

This conception of genius, sketched by Addison, was given a more aggressive, though certainly not more elegant, form some fifty years later in Edward Young's intriguing *Conjectures on Original Composi-*

tion. Between Addison's writings on genius and Young's, perhaps the most germane literary and philosophical events were the appearance in 1739 of William Smith's translation of Longinus, the most influential in the century, and in 1757 the publication of Edmund Burke's *Philosophical Enquiry into the Origin of Our Ideas of the Sublime and Beautiful,* undoubtedly the most admired and widely read aesthetic treatise of the British Enlightenment, both at home and abroad.

There can be no thought of recounting, here, the adventures of the sublime from Addison to Burke.[9] A brief comment will suffice.

As Addison was the logical place to begin an account of genius as an aesthetic concept in eighteenth-century Britain, he is the logical place, because of his influence and ingenuity in these matters, to begin a brief characterization of the sublime. Indeed, William Smith, in the introduction to his translation of *On the Sublime,* makes the connection himself. "An *Essay on Criticism* appears but once in an Age; and what a tedious Interval is there between *Longinus* and *Addison!*"[10]

In his highly influential *Spectator* papers "On the Pleasures of the Imagination," Addison distinguishes among three kinds of what we would want to call "aesthetic qualities" and their concomitant pleasures. "I shall first consider those pleasures of the imagination which arise from the actual view and survey of outward objects: and these, I think, all proceed from the sight of what is great, uncommon, or beautiful."[11] Addison is beginning, then, with our aesthetic appreciation of nature—of natural objects—and the two categories there, of concern to us, are the beautiful and (principally) the "great," by which Addison clearly means what was subsequently to be called almost universally the "sublime" or "grand."

Addison's description of the great (or sublime) is two-pronged: a description of the objects and of our experience of them. This becomes characteristic of the speculation surrounding the sublime throughout the eighteenth century, which tended to be centered more on the "subjective" aspects of the aesthetic. Of the objects, Addison writes: "By greatness, I do not only mean the bulk of any single object, but the largeness of a whole view, considered as one entire piece." And of the experience: "Our imagination loves to be filled with an object, or to grasp at any thing that is too big for its capacity. We are flung into a pleasing astonishment at such unbounded views, and feel a delightful stillness and amazement in the soul at the apprehension of them."[12]

In Burke's far more detailed and elaborate picture of the sublime, the idea of greatness remains. But a very significant new element has entered the picture: that of terror. For Burke, and for Kant later, the experience of the sublime is not an unalloyed pleasure, as it appears to be for Addison. Terror, the perception of potential danger, and other such usually unpleasant as well as unwanted reactions to the great or terrifyingly powerful have worked their way into the occasion, producing a well-known aesthetic "paradox" of the "painful pleasure" or "pleasing pain."

A typical example of this terror-ridden sublime is the passage in Burke's *Enquiry* in which the concept of the sublime is introduced to the reader. I quote it in full.

> The passion caused by the great and sublime in *nature*, when these causes operate most powerfully, is Astonishment; and astonishment is that state of the soul, in which all its motions are suspended, with some degree of horror. In this case the mind is so entirely filled with its object, that it cannot entertain any other, nor by consequence reason on that object which employes it. Hence arises the great power of the sublime, that far from being produced by them, it anticipates our reasonings, and hurries us on by an irresistible force. Astonishment, as I have said, is the effect of the sublime in its highest degree; the inferior effects are admiration, reverence and respect.[13]

The influence of Burke's characterization of the sublime was widespread, both in his own country and abroad. It is echoed, for example, early on by Kant, in his charming pre-Critical work, *Observations on the Feeling of the Beautiful and Sublime* (1764). The pain-pleasure paradox is inherent there as well.

> The sight of a mountain whose snow-covered peak rises above the clouds, the description of a raging storm, or Milton's portrayal of the infernal kingdom, arouse enjoyment but with horror; on the other hand, the sight of flower-strewn meadows,

valleys with winding brooks and covered with grazing flocks, the description of Elysium, or Homer's portrayal of the girdle of Venus, also occasion a pleasant sensation but one that is joyous and smiling. In order that the former impression could occur to us in due strength, we must have a *feeling of the sublime,* and in order to enjoy the latter well, a *feeling of the beautiful.*[14]

Both Addison and Burke introduce the concept of the sublime by discussing the sublime in nature; and it is in nature that (as the casual reader tends to forget) the eighteenth century most frequently detected the quality.[15] But Addison, like Longinus, associated it too with literature, as did Kant, in his pre-Critical days, as we have just seen. Burke, indeed, extended the concept, apparently, to music as well—a point of considerable importance, obviously, to my project here. The connection is through the role of "obscurity" in the arousal of the feeling of sublimity.

The argument goes something like this. Sublimity involves not merely a perception of power or greatness but a perception of *danger* as well. And the sense of danger is enhanced by the obscurity of the threat, reduced or even removed by its clear perception. (Fear of the unknown is obviously being appealed to.) "To make any thing very terrible, obscurity seems in general to be necessary. When we know the full extent of any danger, when we can accustom our eyes to it, a great deal of the apprehension vanishes."[16]

So, in literary description, obscurity enhances sublimity, clarity reduces or destroys it. But what, after all, is more "obscure" in comparison with the descriptive powers of language than music? Thus: "so far is a clearness of imagery from being absolutely necessary to an influence on the passions, that they may be considerably operated upon without presenting any image at all, by certain sounds adapted to that purpose; of which we have a sufficient proof in the acknowledged and powerful effects of instrumental music."[17] And although Burke is appealing here to the familiar notion that music can arouse any of the passions or affections—as Dryden put it, "What Passion cannot MUSIC raise and quell!"—it is, manifestly, the "passion" of *sublimity* that is the subject here.

The importance of the question of whether music can be sublime will become obvious enough in the next chapter, when we discuss Handel's ascendency to the Pantheon of genius. So, having mentioned it in anticipation, I will let it alone for now and go on to one further matter concerning the sublime, before I return to the concept of Longinian genius in its late flowering in eighteenth-century Britain.

For Longinus, we saw in the previous chapter, genius and the sublime in literature were inextricably connected, as cause and effect. Natural genius was the necessary condition for sublimity, whatever the role of "rules" or the breaking thereof might be. In eighteenth-century Britain that connection was established for the other fine arts, as well as for literature, to the extent that they gained the necessary intellectual clout. And it is for that reason that we must know at least the general character of the sublime, as the British Enlightenment conceived it, as well as its connection to the concept of artistic genius, which is, of course, the center of our concern—musical genius in particular. For the presence of sublimity in art became, for the British Enlightenment, the litmus test for the artist's genius.

Having now at least a general idea of the concept of the sublime as an aesthetic category, in two of its most characteristic formulations—Addison's in the early stages, Burke's at its fullest flowering—it remains for us to make the connection with genius, before we go on in the closing pages of this chapter, to look at the concept again in its later form.

The connection between genius and the sublime in the period from Addison to Burke is easily stated. The basic division of artistic styles, in literature, and, gradually, in music and the visual arts, was that between beauty and sublimity, the former being couched in the classical mode of harmony and proportion, the latter in the more "Romantic" mode of the great, powerful, dark, obscure, even terrible (in the eighteenth-century sense of that term). In literature, the highest model for the former was Virgil, for the latter Homer. And as harmony and proportion were easily seen as falling under rules and precepts, the sublime qualities came, rather, to be seen as violations of them—beyond the control of artistic "method." Or, seen in another way, the growing taste for "aesthetic qualities" other than those of "harmony and proportion," the grandeur of mountains, the obscurity of dark, wooded glens, was, ipso facto, a taste for qualities beyond "the rules and precepts"; for "the rules and precepts" just *were* the rules and precepts directed toward achieving harmony and proportion, which is to say, "beauty," not "the other thing."

Addison, as we have seen, had already made a special connection between genius and the sublime, even though he still wished to call talent for the beautiful a kind of "genius" as well. But as the connection between a Longinian version of natural genius and the sublime became more and more firmly cemented, other terms such as "taste" or "judgment" became more and more reserved for those with a penchant for the beautiful. (Young called it "good understanding.") In short, the sublime became, in eighteenth-century Britain, the exclusive preserve of Longinian, natural genius, and the presence of the sublime in any work of art became evidence of its creator's genius, be it Homer, Shakespeare, Milton, or, as we shall soon see, Handel.

With this general background concerning genius and the sublime in tow, we can now go on to complete our picture of Longinian genius in eighteenth-century Britain. In the last half of the century, the British produced two notable works on the concept of genius: *Conjectures on Original Composition,* by the distinguished poet Edward Young, and Alexander Gerard's *Essay on Genius,* one of the major productions of the so-called Scottish Enlightenment. The second-named work will concern us at a later stage in our discussion. The former naturally falls into place here as perhaps the closing act of the pure Longinian tradition of genius.

Young's *Conjectures* appeared in 1759; and, again, we are presented with two significant events in our story occurring, by pure coincidence, in the same year. For 1759 was also the year of Handel's death.

Edward Young is well known in literary circles for his melancholy poem, *Night Thoughts,* a work often associated with the growing "Romantic," anti-Enlightenment tendencies in eighteenth-century English literature. It is full of just those dark, brooding, obscure, "terrible" qualities that epitomize Burke's version of the sublime (among others). And his elegant (if somewhat overwrought and overwritten) little treatise on genius and originality is fully in accord with the nature of his poetic production, advocating, as it does, originality over imitation, natural genius over "good understanding," the sublime over the beautiful, the "moderns" over the "ancients."

The "quarrel" between the "ancients" and the "moderns" is, indeed, the setting in which Young places his reflections on genius and "original composition."

In works of literature (literature being Young's major concern) there are, he maintains, "imitations" and "originals": in other words, works that are, and works that are not "*Imitations* . . . of authors . . ." by other authors. Of these, he maintains, ". . . *Originals* are the fairest flowers: *Imitations* are of quicker growth but fainter bloom."[18]

As is to be expected, Young presents a basically Longinian picture of originality, and its source, genius, as innate, not acquired: "An *Original* may be said to be of a *vegetable* nature; it rises spontaneously from the vital root of genius; it *grows*, it is not *made: Imitations* are often a sort of *manufacture* wrought up by those *mechanics, art,* and *labour*, out of pre-existent materials not their own."[19] Clearly, then, it is "natural genius" that Young is talking about.

What immediately catches one's eye, here, if one has become familiar with the distinction I drew early on between the *passivity* of Plato's "inspired" genius and the aggressive *agency* of Longinus' "natural" one is that Young appears to be ascribing to *Longinian* genius a passive character as well. Its product grows like a *vegetable:* hardly an image of human will and rational choice.

But we must not be misled. The product of genius may grow like a vegetable, for Young, while the imitative product of understanding requires "*manufacture*," which is to say, "*labour*," but genius does not *use itself;* it must first be *recognized* by its possessor, and then "*consciously applied.*" "Therefore," Young admonishes, "dive deep into thy bosom; learn the depth, extent, bias, and full fort [*sic*] of thy mind; contract full intimacy with the stranger within thee; excite and cherish every spark of intellectual light and heat, however smothered under former negligence, or scattered through the dull, dark mass of common thoughts; and collecting them into a body, let thy genius rise (if a genius thou hast) as the sun from chaos. . . ."[20]

BREAKING THE RULE

The original may, indeed, be a "vegetable," a wild, uncultivated one at that. But even a wild flower must first be *found,* and then be *picked.* These are the acts of men, not the deliverances of gods, although it is a god-like act to "let genius rise," as it was an act of God to create "the sun from chaos." So, Young continues,

> let not great examples, or authorities, browbeat thy reason into too great a diffidence of thyself: Thyself so reverence, as to prefer the native growth of thy own mind to the richest import from abroad; such borrowed riches make us poor. The man who thus reverences himself, will soon find the world's reverence to follow his own. His works will stand distinguished; his the sole property of them; which property alone can confer the noble title of an *author;* that is one who (to speak accurately) *thinks,* and *composes;* while other invaders of the press, how voluminous and learned soever, (with due respect be it spoken) only *read* and *write*.[21]

No, it is imitation that is *passive;* genius, in its originality, in its creativity, active. For it is *mental* acts that are here at issue, and *imitation* is a passive "act," origination an *act* properly so called. Genius is power, and power properly pays homage to itself.

What further characterizes genius for Young? The descriptions offered, although distinctively *his* in expression (as befits an author who praises original composition), all converge on two familiar Longinian themes, as we have met them in Addison, and in Longinus originally: freedom from the rules, freedom to break the rules.

Of freedom from the rules, Young writes: "Genius is a master-workman, learning is but an instrument; and an instrument, tho' most valuable, yet not always indispensible." And, in amplification of this thought: "Nor is it strange; for what, for the most part, mean we by genius, but the power of accomplishing great things without the means generally reputed necessary to that end? A *genius* differs from a *good understanding,* as a magician from a good architect; *that* raises his structure by means invisible; *this* by the skilful use of common tools."[22]

The analogy of genius and learning to magician and architect is a most revealing one. For what would a magician who worked "by means invisible" to fulfill the same function as "a good architect" call to mind but the Divine Architect in the work of Creation? The genius is being analogized, as Longinus already had done, to God. Small wonder, then, that Young admonishes the genius: *Reverence thyself!* For do we not owe reverence to "God"?

The prerogative, indeed, the necessity of genius to break the rules and precepts is stated by Young in this wise:

> *Learning* destitute of this superior aid [i.e. genius], is fond, and proud, of what has cost it much pains; is a great lover of rules, and boaster of famed examples: As beauties less perfect, who owe half their charms to cautious art, learning inveighs against unstudied graces, and small harmless inaccuracies, and sets rigid bounds to that liberty to which genius often owes its supreme glory. . . . For unprescribed beauties, and unexampled excellence, which are characteristics of *genius*, lie without the pale of *learning*'s authorities and laws. . . . For rules, like crutches, are a needful aid to the lame, tho' an impediment to the strong.[23]

We get the suggestion here, as I think we never do in Longinus or Addison, that breaking the rules is not merely a necessary evil in genius, to some greater good, but, at least at times, a positive virtue in its own right. That is the intuition that, I suggested early on, Longinus failed to do justice to. Young I think has begun to do it justice. But the note is not paid in full, as we shall see, until Kant gets his hands on the concept of artistic genius in 1790.[24]

Addison's paper on genius (1711) and Young's *Conjectures on Original Composition* (1759), of which I have given some brief account here, frame the entire period of Handel's almost permanent sojourn in London. Into the intellectual ferment of which the developing idea of Longinian genius was an integral part, Handel plunged in 1711; from it he was unwillingly removed by death in 1759. (He worked almost to the last.)

Handel, as no other composer of music before him in the history of the West, played his part on the great stage of great ideas, among some of the largest intellects of his times. Some praised him. Some ridiculed him and his trade. Many simply ignored him. But he was *there;* the times were propitious for the elevation of a *musician,* for the first time in European history, to the pantheon hitherto reserved for the likes of Homer, Shakespeare, and Milton.

That Handel *was* a genius of course was part of the price of admission—but, after all, neither necessary nor sufficient. What had to be in place was an intellectual environment in which such an elevation was possible. Handel was obviously neither the first nor the greatest musical genius yet to be seen. But he moved in an intellectual world—as, for example, neither Bach nor Josquin did—in which, for the first time, it was possible to be recognized as such. (In a world without cans, a can opener doesn't stand a chance of winning a prize.)

Part of what made Handel the first successful candidate was the Longinian concept of genius that prevailed, and part was the *nature* of his genius itself. But that is hardly the whole story. And to that full story of Handel's apotheosis, at least as I am able to understand it, I will turn in the next chapter, the materials necessary for such an understanding now in hand.

IV

The Saxon or The Devil

If you are interested at all in the history of musical scholarship, then you may know that what is generally considered the first "modern" history of music, Charles Burney's *General History,* began to appear, volume by volume—there were to be three—in 1776. It was a landmark in the historical study of Western music—arguably its inauguration.

Lesser known, but of no small significance nevertheless, is the Reverend John Mainwaring's *Memoirs of the Life of the Late George Frederic Handel,* published in 1760.[1] It is the first book devoted solely to the life and works of a musical composer. In this sixteen-year period, then, two of the most central projects of historical musicology, the history of music, and the musical biography were given their first fully recognizable examples. Mainwaring's work, I shall argue in this chapter, is the instrument by means of which Handel was initiated into the pantheon of artistic genius—the first composer to be so recognized. Mainwaring's model, I shall further argue, is the genius of the sublime, the Longinian genius, as sketched in the previous two chapters.

Mainwaring's *Memoirs* is by no means a contemptible beginning for the recorded history of musical biography. It is a serious attempt to understand both Handel's life and his works. Mainwaring chooses for his format the straightforward one in which first the life is told and then the works are analyzed, rather than the more integrated (and difficult) one of mingling life with works. But he is not to be scorned for that. Some of the masterpieces of nineteenth- and twentieth-century musical biography display the same sharp division between biography and musical analysis.

My theme is the concept of musical genius, and it is Mainwaring who presents the world with the first "philosophical" sketch of the animal, in the person of Handel, as he emerges from this epoch-making little volume. The nature of Handel's genius, as Mainwaring and his age saw it, emerges most fully (it should come as no surprise) in the *Observations* on his works. But it is of no small interest to us that the foundations are already being laid in the *Life*. It behooves us, therefore, to cull both the biography and the musical analysis for our picture of musical genius, as Mainwaring paints it. And we will begin, as Mainwaring does, with the biography.

It is no part of my business here, I should warn, and this goes as well for the discussion of Mozart and Beethoven to come, to separate the fact from the fiction, the musicology from the myth. For what is important to us is not what may be true about the nature of Handel's genius, or Mozart's or Beethoven's, but what was taken for truth by those who were in the process of constructing the concept of musical genius, and who found their exemplars in the three composers discussed in these pages. What is important here is not whether the anecdotes of Handel's life, or Mozart's or Beethoven's, are true, but what was taken for truth as an illustration of what the nature of musical genius must be, given the life that was led. With due warning given, then, we can turn to the life of Handel as Mainwaring thought he knew it.

It is of special interest for us that the early pages of Mainwaring's *Life* provide material for what could have become quite another philosophy of genius: a philosophy of genius along Platonic rather than Longinian lines, predicated upon the child prodigy and the childlike creator—just the picture, so we shall see, that the Mozart myth

THE SAXON OR THE DEVIL

evolved into at the hands of the early Romantics. For Mainwaring spends a good deal of time presenting Handel as a *Wunderkind,* very much in what became the familiar Mozartian vein. From Handel's precocity, however, he drew a very different lesson from the one the nineteenth century drew from Mozart's. The times were not yet propitious for genius as the eternal child.

The first event in Handel's musical odyssey, as recounted by Mainwaring, is well known to students of the composer:

> From his very childhood HANDEL had discovered such a strong propensity to Music, that his father, who always intended him for the study of the Civil Law, had reason to be alarmed. Perceiving that this inclination still increased, he took every method to oppose it. . . . All this caution and art, instead of restraining, did but augment his passion. He had found means to get a little clavichord privately convey'd to a room at the top of the house. To this room he constantly stole when the family was asleep.[2]

The story is not as implausible as it may first seem. For the clavichord produces a sound quite inaudible even a few yards away—it was known in its time as the "dumb spinet"—so our infant prodigy could well have practiced to his heart's content in the attic without in the least disturbing the sleeping household below. In any event, such musical accomplishments in one so young, Mainwaring concludes, "tho' not attended to at that time, were no slight prognostics of his future greatness." And he then goes on to draw an illuminating analogy between Handel's precocity and that of Pascal in mathematics.

> And here it may not be unpleasing to the reader, just to remind him of the minute and surprising resemblance between these passages in the early period of HANDEL's life, and some which are recorded in that of the celebrated monsieur Pascal, written by his sister. Nothing could equal the bias of the one to Mathematics, but the bias of the other to Music: both in their very childhood out-did the efforts of maturer age: they

pursued their respective studies not only without any assistance, but against the consent of their parents, and in spite of all the opposition they contrived to give them.³

As I suggested earlier, the lesson to be drawn from Handel's precocity, for Mainwaring, has nothing to do with the possible relation of genius to childishness. Rather, it must somehow fit the Longinian genius of the sublime, the concept of *natural* genius. And so, for Mainwaring, the early appearance of musical ability in Handel is taken as a sign that Nature has planted it there right from the start, and it must by natural compulsion force itself to the surface at the earliest possible moment, inevitably and irresistibly. So, according to Mainwaring's narrative, the opposition of Handel's father to the son's musical pursuits was served the admonition to not attempt the staying of nature's course. "It was observed with reason, that where Nature seemed to declare herself in so strong a manner, resistance was often not only fruitless, but pernicious."⁴

The theme of nature manifesting herself irresistibly endures throughout the *Life,* but nowhere more insistently than in the period of Handel's childhood and youth. Thus, in another well-known anecdote, Handel is taken on a visit to his father's half-brother, the Duke of Saxe-Weisenfels, after following his father's coach on foot, against paternal wishes. He is discovered playing the organ in the Duke's chapel, whereupon the Duke admonishes the father that "for his own part, he could not but consider it as a sort of crime against the public and posterity to rob the world of such a rising Genius!" And, furthermore, "he observed how much more likely he would be to succeed, if suffered to pursue the path that Nature and Providence seemed to have worked out for him. . . ."⁵

It is of some interest that almost one third of Mainwaring's *Life* concerns what might be called Handel's "prodigy years." And the early flowering of the composer's genius, the prodigality of its possessor, are frequently adverted to.

On his return to Halle from the court of Saxe-Weisenfels, Handel, Mainwaring tells us, was put under the tutelage of "one ZACKAW, who was organist to the cathedral church."⁶ This was Friedrich Wilhelm

THE SAXON OR THE DEVIL

Zachow (1663–1712), not a mean practitioner of the art. The *Wunderkind* soon became his "assistant," upon which occurrence Mainwaring remarks: "It may seem strange to talk of an assistant of seven years of age, for he could not be more, if indeed he could be quite so much, when first he was committed to the care of this person. But," Mainwaring continues, "it will appear much stranger, that by the time he was nine he began to compose the church service for voices and instruments, and from that time actually did compose a service every week for three years successively."[7] So in a brief period "the pupil surpassed the master, the master himself confessed his superiority."[8]

Thus far, if you substituted Leopold for Zachow, you might think yourself reading one of the early biographies of Mozart. And Mainwaring's *Life* continues in the same vein as Handel's *Wanderjahre* begin. For, like Salzburg, "Hall [i.e., Halle] was not a place for so aspiring a youth to be confined to."[9] And so: on to Berlin and the King of Prussia.

Once in Berlin, "the little stranger had not been long at court before his abilities became known to the King, who frequently made him large presents."[10] And Attilio Ariosto, then composing for the Berlin opera, "would often take him on his knee, and make him play on his harpsichord for an hour together, equally pleased and surprized with the extraordinary proficiency of so young a person; for at this time he could not exceed thirteen. . . ."[11] This is an anecdote of truly Mozartian flavor (although Handel must have been small for his age if it is to be credited).

The prodigy years continue in Hamburg, the way Mainwaring tells his story, where Handel, a young teenager, plied his trade as violinist, harpsichordist, and, ultimately, opera composer. Handel's first operatic venture, Mainwaring tells us, was *Almira;* which occasions another of Mainwaring's references to the child prodigy. "The success of it was so great, that it ran for thirty nights without an interruption. He was at this time not much above fourteen: before he was quite fifteen, he made a second, entitled FLORINDA; and soon after, a third called NERONE, which were heard with the same applause."[12]

As I suggested earlier, Mainwaring draws an entirely different conclusion from the *Wunderkind* phenomenon to that which a later age drew from the case of Mozart, even though all the materials for the other conclusion were in place. For those who experienced or knew through the tradition the extraordinary musical exploits of the child Mozart, the moral to be drawn was the relation of genius to the childlike, whereas for Mainwaring it was quite another, the early appearance of musical skills being, rather, evidence of genius as the pure gift of Nature. But that Longinian view, as we have seen, associates genius with the power of the sublime, the power of the rule-breaker and lawgiver, things one would hesitate to ascribe to the child or the childlike. It is not surprising, therefore, that not until the prodigy years were, in Mainwaring's account, almost over, did his picture of Handel's genius begin to emerge along clearly recognizable Longinian lines.

Thus, toward the end of the Hamburg years, Mainwaring observes, of the variety of musical styles with which Handel was confronted: "So little are they to be learnt by rule, that they are not infrequently direct violations of rule." And to leave no doubt that it is Handel's character as a composer to which he refers, he adds in a footnote: "The very first answer of the Fugue in the overture to MUCIUS SCAEVOLA, affords an instance of this kind." Furthermore, in the same footnote, he draws a direct connection between rule-breaking and genius, as well as a direct connection between music and the other fine arts in this regard. "It is needless to observe the exact analogy which Poetry and Painting bear to Music in respect to these licences, to which the slender company of great Genius's seem to claim an exclusive previlege."[13] We are now, clearly, in familiar Longinian territory, from which Mainwaring seldom departs through the rest of his book. From Hamburg Handel embarked on the composer's customary tour of Italy—*de rigueur* for any one of that profession aspiring to an operatic career. In Mainwaring's account he first spent a year in Florence, where, among other accomplishments, "At the age of eighteen he made the opera of RODRIGO, for which he was presented with 1000 sequins, and a service of plate." The aura of the *Wunderkind* lingers still, here, as it does in the final reference Mainwaring makes to Handel's youth, when he gushes over the overture to *Agrippina*, "this effort of his genius before he was well nineteen."[14]

From Florence Handel's Italian odyssey took him to Venice, where, anecdote tells us, he met the great Domenico Scarlatti. His reputation had preceded him. "He was first discovered there at a Masquerade, while he was playing on a harpsichord in his visor. Scarlatti happened to be there, and affirmed that it could be no one but the famous Saxon, or the devil."[15]

Anecdote also has Handel called "the divine Saxon," which comports well, as we have seen, with the Longinian description of the sublime genius, having been sanctioned by Longinus "himself" (whoever that might be). But how much more appropriate, in a way, to associate the Longinian genius with the other guy. For he is the breaker of rules, the "bad boy of music" (as Henry Cowell was called when he started playing the piano with his elbows and wrists). And God, after all, is the *maker* rather than the breaker of rules—which is what the sublime genius became, so I shall argue, later on, when Kant got his hands on the concept of genius in the third *Critique*.

In any event, Handel's demonization in Venice was followed directly by his deification in Rome (where else?) where "He was compared to ORPHEUS, and exalted above the rank of mortals" by the Cardinal Panfili.[16] It is further reported "that SCARLATTI, as oft as he was admired for his great execution, would mention HANDEL, and cross himself in token of veneration."[17]

By the time Mainwaring's *Life* brings its hero to England, in 1710, the evolution of the Longinian musical genius has already been completed, from its natural flowering in the *Wunderkind* to its deification in Handel's young maturity. Perhaps sensing this, Mainwaring tells the rest of his story with little further reference to genius or the sublime. But these subjects are taken up again, with a vengeance, in the *Observations* on the works. Here the enshrinement of Handel as the first musical genius is completed in all its detail. We turn to it now.

Mainwaring begins his *Observations* on Handel's works with something like a statement of theoretical principles, or, as he puts it, an attempt "to settle the meaning of some words, which, on other subjects have been used with no great care, but never perhaps with so little as when they have been applied to music."[18] Actually, the point of view expressed is familiar to anyone acquainted with the literature in aesthetics from Addison to Burke. In sum:

> Music is founded on established rules and principles.... The rules are derived from experience and observation, which informs us what particular system or disposition of sounds will produce the most pleasing effects. A clear comprehension of those rules, and the ability to apply them, are called *knowledge:* and this alone, without any great share either of *invention* or *taste,* may make a tolerable Composer. But either of these joined with it, forms a Master.[19]

The theoretical structure is familiar. That the "rules and principles" of musical composition are "derived from experience" is a reflection of well-entrenched British empiricist tenets. And it is difficult not to think that Mainwaring is directly echoing either Addison, here, or the sentiments of David Hume, expressed but three years earlier in the essay "Of the Standard of Taste," to wit:

> It is evident that none of the rules of [literary] composition are fixed by reasoning *à priori,* or can be esteemed abstract conclusions of the understanding, from comparing those habitudes and relations of ideas which are eternal and immutable. Their foundation is the same as with that of all the practical sciences, experience; nor are they any thing but general observations, concerning what has been universally found to please in all countries, and in all ages.[20]

As for the contrast between *invention* and *taste,* it is the familiar one between the Homeric and the Virgilian; between the breaker of rules and the follower. As Mainwaring spells it out: "Those who have an *inventive* genius will depart from the common rules, and please us the more by such deviations," while, "On the other hand, they who have *taste,* or a nice discernment of the minuter circumstances that please, will polish and improve the inventions of others," and "adhere strictly to rules...." Nor is the inventive genius merely the breaker of rules, but, thereby, the maker of rules as well—a distinctively Kantian spin on things, as we shall see later on. Where the inventive genius violates the received principles of musical composition, in Mainwaring's words, "Such passages are not founded on rules, but are themselves the foundations of new rules."[21]

It is this theme, the contrast between invention and taste, the sublime and the beautiful, the breaker (or maker) of rules and their follower, that is played out in the subsequent *Observations* on Handel's works, with Handel emerging as the quintessential genius of overwhelming power and disdain for established compositional principles —in short, the Longinian natural genius in the British Enlightenment pattern. I shall need to spend some time filling in this picture.

Immediately after his general statement of critical "philosophy," Mainwaring makes it clear where Handel stands within it.

> [The] merit of HANDEL'S Music will be least discerned by the lovers of elegance and correctness. They are shocked with every defect of this sort, while their very character hinders them from entering into these excellencies of higher nature, in which he so much surpasses all other Musicians: excellencies, which are hardly consistent with a constant regard to those minuter circumstances, on which beauty depends.[22]

As can be gathered from this passage, it is not as if Handel is being placed in one category of genius rather than another, invention rather than taste. (It will be recalled that this is much the way Addison seemed to see a very similar distinction in the *Spectator* paper on genius.) It is that in being preeminent in the former, he is preeminent *tout court:* he is characterized by "excellencies of a higher nature" than those of taste and beauty, in which he "surpasses all other Musicians." He is the breaker and maker of rules, they the followers and imitators. This is the Handelian (and Longinian) theme. Here follow some of the variations thereupon.

Handel is straightaway identified with the sublime: "by the greatness and sublimity of his genius, he has worked up effects that are astonishing."[23] And again: "For in his sublime strokes, of which he has many, he acts as powerfully upon the most Knowing, as upon the Ignorant."[24]

The character of sublimity is associated, most notably, with the oratorio choruses. "As his Oratorios are all, or most of them, on scripture-subjects, so the Chorusses in them are quite in the church-style; and it may be said without extravagance, that the sublime strokes they abound with, look more like the effects of illumination than of mere natural genius."[25] Or, in a similar vein: "it is very remarkable that some persons, on whom the finest modulations would have little or no effect, have been greatly struck with HANDEL's Chorusses. This is probably owing to that grandeur of conception, which predominates in them; and which, as coming purely from Nature, is the more strongly, and the more generally felt."[26]

In both of these passages, Mainwaring makes it clear that it is Longinian *natural* genius that he ascribes to Handel. The "grandeur" is "purely from Nature," he says in the latter one. And in the former, although he suggests divine inspiration, it is rather a metaphorical figure of praise than a serious suggestion: "the sublime strokes," although the result of "mere natural genius," are so marvelous as to "look more like the effects of [divine] illumination." We can be absolutely certain, in any case, that Mainwaring had Longinian natural genius in mind for Handel, for he refers to Longinus specifically, in what follows immediately after the discussion of the choruses, and in obvious allusion to them. Of the composer of those sublime musical objects, he writes, "there are no words capable of conveying an idea of his character, unless indeed I was to repeat those which LONGINUS has employed in his description of DEMOSTHENES, every part of which is so perfectly applicable to HANDEL, that one would almost be persuaded it was intended for him."[27] Mainwaring does not quote the passage he mentions, but it will be instructive for me to do so. I will use Smith's translation, since it is in these words, or words like them that Mainwaring would have understood Longinus.

> Whereas *Demosthenes* [in contrast to Hyperides] adding to a continued Vein of Grandeur and to Magnificene of Diction (the greatest Qualifications requisite in an Orator) such lively Strokes of Passion, such Copiousness of Words, such Address and such Rapidity of Speech; and what is his Masterpiece, such Force and Vehemence, as the greatest Writers besides durst never aspire to; being, I say, abundantly furnished with all these

divine (it would be Sin to call them human) Abilities, he excells all before him in the Beauties which are really his own, and to atone for Deficiencies in those he has not, overthrows all Opponents with the irresistible Force, and the glittering Blaze of his Lightning. For it is much easier to behold with stedfast and undazzled Eyes the flashing Lightning than those ardent Strokes of the Pathetic, which come so thick one upon another in his Orations.[28]

That the Longinian description of Demosthenes should be thought altogether appropriate, by Mainwaring, to Handel, at a single stroke enshrines the composer in the temple of the immortals, where Demosthenes resides, as *artist* and *genius*.

I have, so far in my discussion of Mainwaring's *Observations* on Handel's works, been dealing almost exclusively with the characterization of the music in terms of the largeness of the sublime as a sign of genius. But the close of the Longinian description of Demosthenes reminds us that there is another, accompanying theme to the largeness of the sublime genius and its products—the theme, namely, of the rule-breaker. Indeed, the quotation from Longinus that serves for Mainwaring's epigraph refers exclusively to that, suggesting how large it loomed in Mainwaring's thinking about Handel's genius. An epigraph, after all, is supposed to encapsulate an author's major thesis. Here it is in Smith's translation (Mainwaring gives it in Greek): "I readily allow, that Writers of a lofty and tow'ring Genius are by no means pure and correct, since whatever is neat and accurate throughout, must be exceedingly liable to Flatness."[29] I will turn to this thesis now.

Of the oratorio choruses, which, as we have seen, for Mainwaring represented the highest form of the musically sublime, he remarks, nonetheless, that "there are great inequalities, as in most of HANDEL'S [music]. . . ."[30] Of the chamber duets he writes: "It is not to be dissembled that the manly cast of HANDEL'S mind often led him into a kind of melody ill suited to the voice; that he was apt to depart from the style which the species of composition demanded, and run into passages purely instrumental."[31] And of the instrumental works: "In his music for instruments there are the same marks of great genius, and likewise some instances of great negligence."[32]

Nor was Mainwaring by any means the first to remark on Handel's defects in direct contrast with his sublimity and genius. In a similar vein, Charles Avison, Handel's contemporary and a well-known writer on music, averred that: "Mr. HANDEL is in Music, what his own DRYDEN was in Poetry; nervous, exalted, and harmonius; but voluminous, and, consequently, not always correct. Their Abilities equal to every Thing; their Execution frequently inferior. Born with Genius capable of *soaring the boldest Flights;* they have sometimes, to suit the vitiated Taste of the Age in which they lived in, *descended to the lowest.*"[33]

Both Mainwaring and Avison try to mitigate the presence of these faults, these violations of the rules of musical composition in Handel's works. What is noteworthy, though, is the way in which each goes about it. For Avison it is merely that the virtues outweigh the vices in Handel (and Dryden). "Yet, as both their Excellencies are infinitely more numerous than their Deficiencies, so both their Characters will devolve to latest Posterity, not as Models of perfection, yet glorious Examples of those amazing Powers that actuate the human Soul."[34] But in Mainwaring the defense is sometimes more subtle than that: not merely that the good overshadows the bad; rather that, somehow, the bad *is* at the same time a good—that it cannot simply be treated as a grammatical error to be corrected (the way the English of a later age "corrected" Purcell's false relations), for correction will lead to a lesser effect. This line of defense comes out most clearly in Mainwaring's discussion of Handel's writing for voices in the chamber duets, which, as we have just seen, is judged unvocal—too instrumental in style. Of this "defect" Mainwaring writes: "Yet so admirable is the contrivance, and so beautiful the modulation in some of these pieces, where this deviation is most conspicuous; that the best judge of Music, who examines them as a critic, will hardly have the heart to execute his office; and while the laws compel him to assign the fault, will almost be sorry to see it corrected."[35]

This kind of defense, which Mainwaring launches to mitigate Handel's "mistakes," is the transfiguration of the more primitive Longinian model of deviation from rule as a defect to be outweighed by virtues into the more subtle one of deviation from rule *as* an aesthetic virtue in its own right. We saw it developing in Young, prefigured vaguely in Longinus, and will see it again, solidified in Kant's account of genius to come. It is, preeminently, the picture of Beethoven as rule-disdaining genius, for which Mainwaring's Handel is, I suggest, the preliminary sketch.

If John Mainwaring, in his pioneering biography, was the "philosophical" instrument through which Handel became the first "official" genius among musical composers, two subsequent—what might be called "public"—events institutionalized that genius, making it, in fact, not merely a British phenomenon but an international one. The first of these events was the installation in 1762 of a statue of Handel, sculpted by Louis-François Roubiliac, in Westminster Abbey, where the composer had been interred. The occasion was reported in the *London Chronicle* of 15 July 1762.

> Last Saturday [the 10th] was opened in Westminster-Abbey near the Poet's Corner the monument in memory of the late George Frederick Handel, Esq. He is represented pointing to the back of the monument, where David is playing on the harp. In Mr. Handel's right hand is a pen, writing part of the Messiah, "I know that my Redeemer liveth, &c. . . ."[36]

Roubiliac had, in 1738, made a bust of Handel that was placed in Vauxhall Gardens, where his music was popular. But it is one thing to have one's statue in an entertainment park, and quite another to have it in the Abbey, "near the Poet's Corner." The Poet's Corner is where certified *artistic* geniuses are memorialized. Handel's placement there officially enshrined him among the poetic, therefore *artistic,* immortals.

How did Roubiliac view his subject? As shown in both the frontispiece to this book and figure 1, clearly Handel is in the throes of creation. And it is by no means a tranquil activity that is depicted. The figure is in a somewhat violent *contraposto*. There is power in that figure, at least within the capabilities of Roubiliac to capture it. (He was, after all, no Michelangelo.) Handel seems to be *doing,* not

Figure 1. Handel's monument in Westminster Abbey. Photograph by Helmut Gernsheim, Warburg Institute, London.

being done to: the Longinian rather than the Platonic representation of genius.

But Roubiliac was, it appears, not of one mind in the matter of artistic creation. For there is that figure of an angel, above Handel, to his left, playing a harp—a figure that the *London Chronicle* reporter takes to be David. And Handel appears to be gesturing toward him with upraised hand and extended index finger. Is he, like Haydn, indicating the divine source of his music, his "inspiration"?

It is amusing to note that the statue, at present, is missing that extended finger (see Figure 1). I rather think its absence improves the work. The gesture now appears less artificial to me, and the rendering more Longinian. But of course I have an ax to grind, and what Roubiliac originally intended, it would seem, is something of a mixed message: a Longinian figure of genius, yet a divine rather than a natural source. But that does not take away from the significance of placing the statue near the Poet's Corner. It was a public act of homage, a public stamp of approval on the "philosophical" concept of Handel as *musical* and *artistic* genius. He was the first to be so designated in Western musical culture.

Of further interest for us concerning the statue is the tablet that appears above. It memorializes the great Handel festival of 1784, commemorating the one hundredth anniversary of the composer's birth. (The perpetrators were off by one year, as was Roubiliac in his inscription—Mainwaring had it right.) Dr. Burney was its official "program annotator," and left us a full account of this unprecedented musical event in his *Account of the Musical Performances in Westminster-Abbey and the Pantheon*. . . . It surely puts the final public imprimatur upon Handel's genius, and the esteem in which it was held in Britain.

Of the great festival, Burney writes in his preface to the *Account:*

> Such a gigantic idea of commemoration as the present, for the completion of which it was necessary that so many minds should be concentrated, must have been long fostering ere it took a practicable form, and was matured into reality. But from the conception of this plan to its full growth, there was such a

concurrence of favorable circumstances as the records of no art or science can parallel: the Royal Patronage with which it was honoured; the high rank, unanimity, and active zeal of the directors; the leisure, as well as ardour and skill of the conductor; the disinterested docility of individuals; and liberal contributions of the public; all conspired to render this event memorable, and worthy of a place, not only in the annals of Music, but of mankind.[37]

And of the subject of this great public event he writes:

HANDEL whose genius and abilities have lately been so nobly commemorated, though not a native of England, spent the greatest part of his life in the service of its inhabitants: improving our taste, delighting us in the church, the theatre, and the chamber; and introducing among us so many species of musical excellence, that, during more than half a century, while sentiment, not fashion guided our applause, we neither wanted nor wished for any other standard.[38]

No doubt to the detriment of native British music, the commemoration of 1784 put the final touches on Handel as the country's "official," anointed musical genius, the first so honored in music history.

Why Britain? Why Handel? Why this time and place? There is a fairly convincing answer to all these questions.

Two philosophical developments of some importance in the history of ideas took place during Handel's hegemony in the United Kingdom, and had a direct impact on his future elevation to the status of musical genius. They were the formulation of what Paul Oskar Kristeller called, in a seminal article, "the modern system of the arts,"[39] and the concomitant emergence of the branch of philosophy commonly called in the Academy, today, Aesthetics, or the Philosophy of Art. Kristeller's main point was that before the first quarter of the eighteenth century, the notion of what *we* think of as the "fine arts"—in particular, literature, the visual arts, and music—did not exist at all. These endeavors were not regarded as of a piece. But in the early years of the eighteenth century, and most especially in Britain, this notion of the fine arts did indeed become common coin. In Kristeller's words: "During the first half of the eighteenth century the interest of amateurs, writers and philosophers in the visual arts and in music increased. The age produced not only critical writings on these arts composed for laymen, but also treatises in which the arts were compared with each other and with poetry, and thus finally arrived at the fixation of the modern system of the fine arts."[40]

The emergence of the modern system of the arts posed, for the Enlightenment, the philosophical task of detecting just what it was that made these seemingly disparate practices of literary composition, painting (and sculpting), and the composing of music three instances of the *same* practice: the practice of fine art. It was this task that, in turn, solidified a diffuse collection of art-theoretic and critical practices into the *philosophical* practice of *aesthetics*. And because *music* had now passed from being seen as a craft to being seen as a fine art, composers now became possible candidates for the rank of genius; for the fine arts, unlike the craft arts, could be seen the way poetry had been seen since antiquity, as the arts of genius. All the philosophical ingredients were now in place, especially in England, for the first elevation of a composer to the pantheon of artistic genius. Into this mix Handel plunged in 1710, to emerge fifty years later as a philosophically certified genius. But why Handel?

If England was, in the first half of the eighteenth century, particularly suited philosophically to anoint the first "genius composer," then Handel, Dr. Burney clearly saw, was the musical genius particularly suited to the English taste. As he remarked in the *Account* of the 1784 Handel Commemoration: "The English, a manly, military race, were instantly captivated by the grave, bold, and nervous style of Handel, which is congenial with their manners and sentiments."[41] What Burney gives here, in characterizing Handel's music, is a fairly recognizable description of the sublime, a word he uses specifically in regard to Handel elsewhere, on numerous occasions. And since the reigning concept of genius in England *was* the Longinian one, Handel was the predictable, and predictably successful, candidate for the honor.

The path that the writer of music took from the Medieval period to the Enlightenment might be described as from *maker* to *composer* to at least candidate for *genius*. I take the distinction between maker and composer from an intriguing and learned study by Rob C. Wegman. I base what I have to say about it on that study, which aims to show that during a seventy-five-year period in the Netherlands, ending in the 1540s, " 'the composer,' specifically of vocal polyphony, proffesionalized and acquired increasing cultural status—not only in the eyes of those who began to describe themselves as such, but also in the popular consciousness."[42]

Prior to the beginning of the sixteenth century, those who wrote vocal polyphony, as opposed to those who improvised it, were known as "makers," the word "composer" having not yet been coined for them, either in Latin or in the vernacular, "the crucial point . . . [being] that 'maker,' unlike 'composer,' never became invested with the overtones of a later aesthetic, and retained the basic connotation of craftsmanship (not necessarily musical) that made it once synonymous with composer."[43] Which is to say, before the sixteenth century there was no word to describe the special craft of composing music, and so those who pursued that craft were given merely the generic name for those who make rather than do. "Even the internationally famous composer Jacob Obrecht was simply identified, in 1488 and 1492, as master of arts and priest."[44]

Wegman tells us that "in Insbruck on 3 April 1497, Heinrich Isaac had signed a contract that almost certainly marks the beginning of professional composition in the proper sense."[45] At this point, "Isaac had become a professional composer, and was so described as such, not only in the court accounts of Maximilian . . . or the chapter acts of Constance cathedral . . . but even in the correspondence of a politician like Niccolò Machiavelli. . . ."[46]

The status of professional composer was more emphatically achieved shortly thereafter by Josquin Des Prez (c. 1440–1521), "the man," Wegman writes, "who was to become associated with a newly emerging aesthetic of the composer. . . ."[47] But even he, who "reserved the right to compose 'when he wants to,' " failed to become "a prototypical Renaissance genius, breaking free from the suffocating bonds of medieval craftsmanship in order to assert his artistic freedom."[48] Composing had now become a recognized profession, not merely the generic craft of "making"—but a *craft* it remained, and a craft may allow of excellence but never genius.

This is not, of course, to say that there were no composers until Josquin and Isaac came to be called that at the beginning of the sixteenth century. Or that there were no genius-composers before Handel came to be called *that* by Mainwaring and Burney in the eighteenth. Obrecht, as we have seen, had not gained the title of composer as late as 1492. But in 1504 he was appointed "compositore de canto" in Ferrara.[49] Surely it would be absurd to claim that he was not *composing* music in 1492, and was twelve years later. Nor, indeed, would it make sense to deny that Obrecht or Josquin were genius-composers, their compositions works of art merely because during their lives they and their works were not so conceived of. Kristeller was certainly not claiming that there were no musical art works before the formulation of the modern system of the arts, and the concept of the fine arts itself.

The transition from thinking of the musician as a generic maker to thinking of him as a specific kind of craftsman, the composer, which Wegman so carefully documents, nevertheless still leaves the idea of the composer some distance from the modern concept, as Wegman himself recognizes. What needs to be in place before that distance can be traversed is the concept of music as a fine art and the consequent concept of the composer as candidate for genius, which the modern system of the arts makes possible. A craftsman is not a possible genius; an artist is. Perhaps it is that, at least in large part, which separates the two. The newly made philosophical discipline of aesthetics put all these pieces in place in Britain in the first quarter of the eighteenth century, along with the Longinian concept of natural genius. Handel arrived in London with all the requisite qualities and there for almost fifty years displayed them forth. The result, as we have seen, was his philosophical enfranchisement as Longinian genius of musical composition—the first genius-composer recognized as such.

But even as Mainwaring, the first musical biographer, was fashioning Handel into the first genius-composer in the Longinian mold, the possessor of the law, another image of genius, and of *musical* genius, was beginning to take shape, one that would swing the pendulum from the Longinian concept to the Platonic one—at least so I shall argue. The man who was to embody this other, Platonic genius was already four years old—indeed, already a *composer,* if the well-known anecdotes of his childhood are true. It is from the possessor to the possessed, then, that we now turn: from the genius of Handel to the genius of Mozart. Before we do that, however, I must lay the philosophical foundations. That requires a turn from British philosophy to German.

V

The Genius and the Child

Immanuel Kant is responsible for two nineteenth-century concepts of genius. Directly, in his own treatment of genius in the *Critique of Judgment,* he is responsible for the Romantic version of the Longinian genius, which finds its prime exemplar in Beethoven. Indirectly, as I shall argue in this chapter, he is responsible, through the third *Critique,* for the Romantic version of the Platonic genius, which I identify, as will become apparent at the close of this discussion, with the child-genius, exemplified for the Romantics, needless to say, by Mozart.

The identification of genius with the childlike I lay at Schopenhauer's door. But as is well known in philosophical circles, the basis for Schopenhauer's aesthetics, of which his concept of genius is an important part, was put in place by Kant. So it is to this Kantian foundation that we first turn our attention.

The most familiar, and surely most influential notion in Kant's philosophy of beauty is the notion of "disinterestedness." This is the source and inspiration, so I shall argue, of Schopenhauer's concept of genius, and its identification with the childlike. So it is the logical place to begin my discussion.

Kant introduces the notion of disinterestedness at the very beginning of his analysis of beauty and taste, in Part I of the *Critique of Judgment,* which he calls the Critique of Aesthetic Judgment. The Critique of Aesthetic Judgment is divided into two sections, and the first section, "Analytic of Aesthetic Judgment," into three books. The first of these books, "The Analytic of the Beautiful," contains four "Moments," which are, essentially, four categories of logical judgment as traditionally conceived: quality, quantity, relation, and modality. The first and second of these Moments, the Moments of quality and quantity, comprise the portion of Kant's philosophy of beauty that I am primarily interested in.

The place where I think it convenient to begin is the conclusion of the First Moment. It reads: "*Taste* is the faculty of estimating an object or a mode of representation by means of a delight or aversion *apart from any interest.* The object of such a delight is called beautiful."[1]

It is important to note, before we go any further, that Kant employs the term "aesthetic" in a sense only distantly related to ours. He means by it neither something having to do especially with what we call aesthetic qualities—such as beauty, grace, sublimity, and the like—nor something having especially to do with art. An *aesthetic* judgment, as Kant uses that term, is, quite simply, a judgment based upon *feeling,* as opposed to a logical judgment in which some subject is placed under a concept. Thus a judgment that something is beautiful is, on Kant's view, an *aesthetic* judgment, because we make it in virtue of experiencing a certain kind of delight. But a judgment that some particular food tastes good to us is also an aesthetic judgment, for Kant, because it too is made in virtue of our experiencing a pleasurable sensation. The judgment that something is beautiful is an *aesthetic* judgment, then, the way Kant uses that term, not because it predicates of a subject what *we* would call an "aesthetic" quality. And Kant distinguishes judgments of beauty from other aesthetic judgments by calling them "pure judgments of taste." I shall be careful to preserve Kant's terminology in what follows.

In the First Moment, as we have just seen, Kant characterizes pure judgments of taste as judgments made on the basis of a felt delight *apart from any interest,* or "disinterested," as contemporary philosophers of art frequently say. Our task here is to understand what it means, for Kant, to make such a *disinterested* judgment: what it means to make a judgment based on delight *apart from any interest*.

Kant begins, as seems reasonable, by stating what it would mean to feel delight in an *interested* fashion, since *disinterested* delight is its opposite. He says: "The delight which we connect with the representation of the real existence of an object is called interest." In stark contrast to delight based on the real existence of its object, which Kant denominates "desire," is the delight we take in the beautiful and express in the pure judgment of taste. "Now where the question is whether something is beautiful, we do not want to know whether we, or any one else, are, or even could be, concerned in the real existence of the thing, but rather what estimate we form of it on mere contemplation (intuition or reflection)."[2]

Two preliminary points concerning this contrast between interest and disinterest must be made straightaway before we dig any deeper into it. To start with, the reader not familiar with Kantian terminology may be puzzled by the juxtaposition of "intuition" and "reflection" as both modes of "contemplation." This puzzlement can immediately be dissolved by it being pointed out that Kant means by intuition nothing like what we would ordinarily take it to mean (as in "intuitive knowledge") but simply presentation to the senses, or, not to put too fine a point on it, sense perception. He is, thus, juxtaposing sense perception with reflection and saying, simply, that these are the two ways we can "contemplate" the beautiful: in perception or in thought.

Kant's use of the word "contemplation" also invites comment, for it is directly connected with the notion of disinterested delight that we are trying to understand. The notion of disinterestedness as somehow characterizing our experience of the beautiful—what we would call more generally today "aesthetic experience"—already had a nearly one-hundred-year-old history, beginning with the third earl of Shaftesbury, at the close of the seventeenth century, before it fell into Kant's hands.

Early formulations of the doctrine of disinterested perception of the beautiful tended to contrast the pleasure of such perception with that of ownership or personal advantage.[3] Joseph Addison, for example, writes of "a man of polite imagination" that "He . . . often feels a greater satisfaction in the prospect of fields and meadows, than another does in the possession."[4] And Francis Hutcheson, who might with some justice be called the father of modern philosophical aesthetics, insists that "this pleasure of beauty is distinct from that *joy* which arises upon prospect of advantage."[5]

It is far more plausible, one suspects, to view these early accounts of what later was called the attitude of aesthetic disinterestedness not so much as defining a special kind of contemplation but merely as explicating a perfectly ordinary thing, *contemplation* itself (the "contemplative attitude," if you will) as opposed to other stances one might assume toward some object of perception or thought. Addison's "man of polite imagination," taking pleasure merely in the "prospect of fields and meadows," is taking pleasure in their contemplation, in how beautiful they look, rather than in their possession, which is not a different kind of contemplation, but rather not contemplation at all. And Hutcheson can be interpreted as contrasting contemplation, in perception, of how an object looks (namely, "beautiful") to a thought process subsequent to or simultaneous with the act of perceptual awareness, in which he thinks about how he can make use of that object to his personal benefit. In the former case he is "merely contemplating" the object; in the latter, something else.

In light of the foregoing, Kant can be seen, in his notion of disinterested perception, as distilling the philosophical essence of the kinds of things writers like Addison and Hutcheson had been saying for nearly a century. That essence is simply this: pure contemplation is completely disengaged from consideration of the object's possible or actual existence. For all other interests in it, beyond mere contemplation, possession, as in the case of Addison, and prospect of advantage, as in the case of Hutcheson, are predicated upon the object's existence: it can neither be possessed nor made use of to one's benefit without *that*. Pure contemplation is by definition the regarding in perception or thought of what is presented to our awareness, without regard to what actually may be the case. In other words, we regard how things look or sound or appear to us in our "mind's eye"; it is all one, whether what looks or sounds or appears *is* the way it looks or sounds or appears, or even "is" at all. When we do that, we are contemplating rather than some other thing, and in so doing we are experiencing beauty, or the lack thereof. As Kant puts it:

> All one wants to know is whether the mere representation of the object is to my liking, no matter how indifferent I may be to the real existence of the object of this representation. It is quite plain that in order to say that the object *is beautiful*, and to show that I have taste, everything turns on the meaning I can give to this representation, and not on any factor which makes me dependent on the real existence of the object. . . . One must not be in the least predisposed in favour of the real existence of the thing, but must preserve complete indifference in this respect in order to play the part of judge in matters of taste.[6]

Kant thinks of the beautiful, quite naturally, as a source of pleasure or delight. And having introduced that delight as delight "apart from any interest," he occupies himself in the rest of the First Moment in explaining its nature by contrasting it with pleasure or delight deriving from two other sources: the *agreeable* and the *good*. In both these other cases, he insists, the delight or pleasure is *not* disinterested. But in showing how that is the case, he obviously hopes to make more plain just what disinterested delight really amounts to.

"*That is* AGREEABLE," Kant says, "*which the senses find pleasing in sensation.*" He uses as an illustration the green color of meadows, the point of which is to distinguish between what he calls *objective* and *subjective* sensation. "The green colour of the meadows belongs to *objective* sensation, as the perception of an object of sense; but its agreeableness to *subjective* sensation, by which no object is represented: i.e. to feeling, through which the object is regarded as an Object of delight (which involves no cognition of the object)."[7] For subjective sensation Kant reserves the term "feeling."

Now the crucial difference between objective and subjective sensation is that in the former, an object is posited beyond the sensation (in the present instance) of greenness, namely the green color, whereas in the latter no object is posited beyond the mere sensation of agreeableness. In this sense the feeling of agreeableness is "subjective" and the sensation of greenness not. Nevertheless, the agreeableness of the green sensation is not, on Kant's view, a disinterested pleasure, because there is a stake here in the real existence of the "object"—again, the green color. As Kant puts his point: "Now, that a judgement on an object by which its agreeableness is affirmed, expresses an interest in it, is evident from the fact that through sensation it provokes a desire for similar objects, consequently the delight presupposes, not the simple judgement about it, but the bearing its real existence has upon my state so far as affected by such an Object."[8]

One presumes that Kant is saying something like this: In the case of the agreeable sensation of greenness, I, of course, wish for the agreeable feeling to continue. But I am not wishing for *any* old agreeable feeling to continue; I am wishing for the continuation of the particular agreeable feeling of greenness that I am now experiencing. And for *this* particular feeling to continue, Kant seems to be claiming, the same cause must remain in place—in this case, the green color. So it then follows that the subject enjoying the agreeableness of the green sensation is enjoying an interested delight, being committed to the continued, therefore real existence of the color. This is in sharp contrast to one experiencing the delight in the beautiful, who is indifferent to whether *what* is represented to him is real or not, *he* being concerned only with the representation itself. *His* sensation is disinterested delight.

From here we can move on to delight in the *good*, which takes two forms, corresponding to the two traditionally recognized kinds of goodness: *instrumental* and *intrinsic*. "We call that *good for something* (useful) which only pleases as a means; but that which pleases on its own account we call *good in itself*."[9]

With regard to the instrumentally good, that which is *good for something*, it is clear that our satisfaction arises, in any particular case, from the fact that the thing is indeed able to do or accomplish what it is supposed to. As for the intrinsically good, it of course has no end in the sense of a *use*. And that is particularly important to emphasize, in the Kantian context, for Kant famously thought that the only intrinsic good was the morally *good will*, which must will not to any beneficial end or consequence in view, either to self or other, but merely out of respect for the moral law as such. Nevertheless, the good will is not "aimless"; it acts rationally, and has a rational "end" in the sense of acting out of respect for the moral law. Thus Kant can assert for both species of the good: "In both cases the concept of an end is implied, and consequently the relation of reason to (at least possible) willing, and thus a delight in the *existence* of an Object or action, i.e. some interest or other." Thus, for Kant, the good, whether instrumental or intrinsic, along with the agreeable, but in sharp contrast with the beautiful, is not a source of disinterested pleasure. Indeed, the title of §4, from which I have just been quoting, is: *"Delight in* THE GOOD *is coupled with interest."*[10]

One can get a fairly clear picture of the interrelatedness of all the key concepts of the First Moment in Kant's succinct and penetrating summary at the beginning of §5, which Kant titles: *"Comparison of the three specifically different kinds of delight."*

> Both the Agreeable and the Good involve a reference to the faculty of desire, and are thus attended, the former with a delight pathologically conditioned (by stimuli), the latter with a pure practical delight. Such delight is determined not merely by the representation of the object, but also by the represented bond of connexion between the Subject and the real existence of the object. It is not merely the object, but its real existence that pleases. On the other hand the judgement of taste is simply *contemplative,* i.e. it is a judgement which is indifferent as to the existence of an object, and only decides how its character stands with the feeling of pleasure and displeasure."[11]

Particularly significant for my purposes is the sentence that directly follows the summary I have just quoted. Kant continues his thought: "But not even is this contemplation itself directed to concepts; for the judgement of taste is not a cognitive judgement (neither a theoretical one nor a practical), and hence, also is not *grounded* on concepts, nor yet *intentionally directed* to them."[12]

As I understand the course Kant is steering here, it is directly *from* the notion that, in disinterested perception, we are concerned not with the real (or possible) existence of what is represented to us, but merely with the representation itself, *to* the notion that (therefore) we are not even concerned, nor can we be, with *what* the representation is a representation *of*, merely with the representation as a pure formal structure or pattern. For if we have no stake, in pure contemplation, in the real or possible existence of what is represented to us, we have no concern with what is represented either, something we would of course have to know to answer or even consider, be concerned with, the existential question.

This result leads us directly to the Second Moment. For that is exactly what it claims, the conclusion being: "The beautiful is that which, apart from a concept, pleases universally."[13]

The philosophical problem Kant poses for us in the Second Moment—the problem which, indeed, persists throughout the Critique of Aesthetic Judgment as its principal theme—is how an *aesthetic* judgment, a judgment predicated merely upon a feeling of delight or aversion, can also be a *universal* judgment, a judgment which demands, or at least anticipates, universal agreement. It can, with some justice, be called the main theme not only of Kant's aesthetic critique but also of Enlightenment aesthetics *tout court,* at least so far as it is an aesthetic epistemology, not solely a philosophy of art.

The problem poses itself for Kant, looked at one way, as the problem of how a judgment based upon delight or aversion, and so notoriously *subjective,* can elicit or demand universal assent, as an "objective" judgment would. Alternatively, it can be framed as the problem of how a judgment *not* based on a concept can elicit or demand universal assent, since the fact that concepts are or should be common coin renders judgments based upon them universally valid.

Our concern is not primarily with the profound and profoundly difficult answer Kant frames to this "antinomy of taste" (as he calls the problem later in the Critique of Aesthetic Judgment). Rather, it lies specifically in the notion that the pure judgment of taste is made *without a concept.* For it is this notion, combined with that, in the First Moment, of the disinterestedness of the delight in the beautiful that, I believe, together provide the basic materials for Schopenhauer's account of what later ages would call the "aesthetic attitude," and for the account of artistic genius for which that attitude provides the model.

It is Schopenhauer's conclusions concerning *genius* that, of course, are our quarry.

From this viewpoint, with Schopenhauer in mind as at least one historical outcome of the Kantian aesthetics, what is most noteworthy is how little Kant says, in either the Second Moment or, for that matter, the entire Critique of Aesthetic Judgment, about *how* one might manage to achieve the conceptless perception or judgment required for the experience of the beautiful. What this strongly suggests is that Kant did not see this in itself as a particular problem. And that, I think, is a very important thing to notice.

As we have seen, Kant intended, in the "Analytic of the Beautiful," to provide a philosophical analysis of a perfectly ordinary human activity, the activity of contemplation. That activity, one has good reason to suppose, is common to all people in all stations of life. And although, undoubtedly, some people are more contemplative than others, we all do have our moments.

This is not to say Kant thought the pure judgment of taste to be unproblematic. With emphasis on *pure,* it can easily be seen that we have here a degree concept; that contemplation can exist in varying degrees of disinterestedness, more or less perturbed by the intrusion of concepts. And this, obviously, leaves open a way to account for the palpable existence of *disagreement* in judgments of the beautiful in spite of Kant's insisting that when "we call the object beautiful, we believe ourselves to be speaking with a universal voice, and lay claim to the concurrence of everyone...."[14]

But whether or not the pure judgment is ever totally pure, whether or not contemplation is rare or frequent, it is, I suggest, *common,* for Kant, in the sense of not exotic—a perfectly ordinary activity in which we engage, or try to engage, whether or not we are paupers or princes. With Schopenhauer, all that is changed. For although Schopenhauer's aesthetic attitude has obvious roots in Kant's "Analytic of the Beautiful" (in particular, the First and Second Moments), it has a distinctly exotic character, and is connected with such far from ordinary individuals as the madman, the religious mystic, the child prodigy, and the *genius.*

There is no need, fortunately, to burden the reader with a detailed account of Schopenhauer's murky metaphysics. We require only some of the most basic distinctions.

Schopenhauer accepted without question or argument the Kantian distinction between the world as we experience it, as "idea" or "representation" (as the most recent translation has it), and the thing-in-itself, the source of this representation. As he says at the outset of his magnum opus, *The World as Will and Representation:* "The world is my representation: this is a truth valid with reference to every living and knowing being, although man alone can bring it into reflective, abstract consciousness." To this he adds: "If any truth can be expressed *a priori,* it is this...."[15]

Our world, *the* world, the world of representation, is known to us, Schopenhauer believes, solely through what he calls (after Leibniz) *the principle of sufficient reason,* which, as he describes it, has a *four-fold root:* space and time, premise and conclusion, cause and effect, motive and action. The forming of our world, the understanding of our world, our actions, our lives in our world are governed by this principle, by these categories of explanation and perception. That is the "normal" state of affairs.

The world as we form and know it through the four-fold root of the principle of sufficient reason is an "objectification," as Schopenhauer calls it, of the thing-in-itself, which, Kant's doctrine to the contrary notwithstanding, he positively characterizes—characterizes, in fact, as *will.* "The will alone is: it is the thing-in-itself, the source of all those phenomena."[16] He describes this insight as "the most important step of my philosophy, namely, the transition from the phenomenon to the thing-in-itself, given up by Kant as impossible."[17]

The metaphysical will, the thing-in-itself, manifests its "objectification" in two ways: as Platonic ideas, and as the world of phenomena, of representation, moderated by the principle of sufficient reason. Furthermore, at the level of idea, the will, the thing-in-itself, and its objectification are in very close, indeed intimate connection.

> The particular thing, appearing in accordance with the principle of sufficient reason, is therefore only an indirect objectifica-

tion of the thing-in-itself (which is the will). Between it and the thing-in-itself the Idea still stands as the only direct objectivity of the will, since it has not assumed any other form peculiar to knowledge as such, except that of the representation in general, i.e., that of being object for a subject. Therefore, it alone is the most *adequate objectivity* possible of the will or of the thing-in-itself, only under the form of the representation.[18]

These very brief remarks give us the bare bones of Schopenhauer's metaphysics, at least insofar as is necessary for an understanding of his concept of genius. I turn now to that concept, which, of course, is our principal concern. In sketching it out, I want to show three aspects: its relation to Kant's theory of disinterested pleasure, the plausibility of seeing it, as I do, as a new version of the Platonic theory of inspiration, and, finally, Schopenhauer's characterization of genius as a kind of childishness. The last mentioned of course is vital to my argument, as it forges the link with Mozart, the new symbol of musical genius: the swing of the pendulum from the Longinian musical genius, exemplified by Handel, to the new, Platonic one, exemplified by the little man-child from Salzburg.

Before I go on, however, it might be a good idea to put these observations into their appropriate chronology. What I have already said about Schopenhauer, and what I will be saying in a moment, is all based on a reading of *The World as Will and Representation*. The first edition of this compendius work was published in 1819. It was divided into four books, the third devoted to aesthetics and philosophy of art. It is in this third book that Schopenhauer expounds his theory of genius fully for the first time, and I will be drawing heavily on this material in what follows.

A second edition of *The World as Will and Representation* appeared in 1844, in two volumes. The first volume was essentially a reprint of the first edition. But the second volume, longer than the first, contains entirely fresh material, in the form of "Supplements" to each of the four books of volume one. Significantly, for my purposes, one of the supplements to the third book is a chapter devoted entirely to the concept of genius. Significant too is the fact that it is at the close of this chapter that Schopenhauer introduces the notion of genius as a kind of childishness, with Mozart as his chief exemplar (although Goethe is mentioned as well). I will, naturally, be relying heavily on this chapter also. Why it was not until 1844 that Schopenhauer connected his concept of artistic genius, already fully formed in 1819, to Mozart and the childlike, is a question we must ponder along the way, and in the next chapter.

I will now get on with the explication of Schopenhauer's concept of genius, with a reminder to the reader that the task is three-fold: to understand its connection to Kant's theory of disinterestedness; to understand its connection to the Platonic theory of divine possession; to understand its relation to the childlike.

It was Schopenhauer's idea, as it was Kant's, that the concept of genius applies especially to the fine arts: solely, for Kant, and nearly so for Schopenhauer (with philosophy [!] as the other contender). There is no room in either philosopher's system for the notion of scientific genius, or any other kind beyond the above-mentioned. Thus Schopenhauer characterizes "the real nature of genius" as "that quality of the mind which is alone capable of producing genuine works of art."[19] Or, expressed in a slightly different way, he speaks of "the method of genius, which is valid and useful in art alone."[20] Furthermore, art is characterized as exclusively "the work of genius."[21] Why Schopenhauer thought genius to apply almost exclusively to art and the artist we shall see in a moment.

Schopenhauer defines art as "the way of considering things *independently of the principle of sufficient reason,* in contrast to the way of considering which proceeds in exact accordance with this principle, and is the way of science and experience." The definition of genius follows directly from the definition of art. "Only through the pure contemplation described above, which becomes absorbed entirely in the object, are the Ideas comprehended; and the nature of *genius* consists precisely in the preeminent ability for such contemplation."[22]

The genius, then, for Schopenhauer, can be described as that person who is able to and does consistently perceive the world in complete independence of the principle of sufficient reason. When he does so he then is able to perceive the Ideas directly, and, in the special case of the composer, indeed the thing-in-itself, knowledge of which entities he conveys to others through the fine arts. With the exception of music, "the object of art, the depiction of which is the aim of the artist, and the knowledge of which must consequently precede his work as its germ and source, is an *Idea* in Plato's sense, and absolutely nothing else...."[23] Whereas "music is by no means like the other arts, namely a copy of the Ideas, but a *copy of the will itself,* the objectivity of which are the Ideas."[24]

The preeminence of music among the fine arts, for Schopenhauer is clearly of deep significance for my project. It makes it quite understandable why, in the first place, Mozart should be his primary exemplar of the genius-as-child, and why, considering Schopenhauer's influence on Romantic thought, Mozart as child should become, at least for awhile, the very symbol of genius itself.

What is it like to be able to perceive things, as the artistic genius does, for Schopenhauer, independently of the principle of sufficient reason? It takes very little effort to conclude that it is very like what Kant describes as perceiving without interest, *ohne alles Interesse,* in the First Moment of the "Analytic of the Beautiful."

Be it recalled that to perceive the world, which is to say, the world of appearance, through the principle of sufficient reason is to understand it under the concepts of space and time, premise and conclusion, cause and effect, motive and action. At one level this point of view expresses itself in science, at another simply in the perception of the ordinary person in his or her ordinary, practical way of life, be it in a profession or in daily affairs. Thus, according to Schopenhauer:

> we regard houses, ships, machines, and the like with the idea of their purpose and their suitability therefor; human beings with the idea of their relation to us, if they have any, and then of their relation to one another, whether in their present actions or according to their position and vocation, perhaps judging their fitness for it, and so on. We can pursue such a consideration of the relation more or less to the most distant links of their concatinations. In this way the consideration will gain in accuracy and extent, but remains the same as regards its quality and nature. It

is the consideration of things in their relations, in fact *by means of* these, and hence according to the principle of sufficient reason. In most cases and as a rule, everyone is abandoned to this method of consideration; I believe even that most people are incapable of any other.[25]

To be committed to the principle of sufficient reason is to be committed to everything that constitutes the *reality* of objects in the phenomenal world. It is, in a word, *interested* perception, the very opposite of Kantian disinterestedness. But, then, to perceive the world as the genius does, independently of the principle of sufficient reason, just *is* to perceive disinterestedly in something very like the Kantian way. And Schopenhauer makes no effort to cover his tracks in this regard. For he himself describes it in just such terms on a variety of occasions, as, for example, where he writes that "it [genius] considers things without interest [*ohne Interesse*] . . . ,"[26] or, again, where he describes "the common, ordinary man" as "not capable, at any rate continuously, of a consideration of things wholly disinterested [*uninteressierten*] in every sense, such as is contemplation proper."[27]

It seems abundantly clear, then, that Schopenhauer's concept of genius has its modern source in the First Moment of Kant's "Analytic of the Beautiful," although Kant's own treatment of genius, as we shall see, lies in a different direction. No less obvious—perhaps, indeed, even more obvious—is Schopenhauer's evocation of the ancient Platonic afflatus rather than the Longinian genius. Indeed, reference to the Longinian conception, so prominent in the pages of the eighteenth-century writers on genius, is absent from Schopenhauer's book, whereas Plato's theory of poetic inspiration has left its mark throughout.

To work our way into the Platonic aspects of Schopenhauer's artist-genius we had best fill in more fully the picture of disinterested perception that Schopenhauer paints. On Schopenhauer's view, anyone under the discipline of the principle of sufficient reason (which means most of us, most of the time) is completely in thrall to his or her relentless, striving will—and *thraldom* is the entirely proper characterization, as Schopenhauer views the human condition.

All *willing* springs from lack, from deficiency, and thus from suffering. Fulfillment brings this to an end; yet for one wish that is fulfilled there remain at least ten that are denied. . . . No attained object of willing can give a satisfaction that lasts and no longer declines; but it is always like the alms thrown to a beggar, which reprieves him today so that his misery may be prolonged till tomorrow. Therefore, so long as our consciousness is filled by our will, so long as we are the subject of willing, we never attain lasting happiness or peace.[28]

Nor can we obtain liberation from our thraldom by immersing ourselves in the abstract structures and research projects of science; for "science, following the restless and unstable stream of the fourfold forms of reasons or grounds and consequences, is with every end it attains again and again directed farther, and can never find an ultimate goal or complete satisfaction. . . ."[29]

For Kant the disinterested pleasure in the beautiful has the appearance of a perfectly ordinary, mundane affair. Someone contemplates a flower or a pepper garden (Kant's own homey examples), and there it is—no big deal. But just because for Schopenhauer disinterestedness (that is, independence of the principle of sufficient reason) takes the form of liberation from a kind of slavery to will, unsatisfied desire, restlessness of spirit, that is the common lot, it becomes no ordinary, no common thing—indeed, a mystical, religious state open to few to experience. Schopenhauer's descriptions of this state of disinterested, will-less knowing are always ecstatic, as, for example, where he writes: "Then all at once the peace, always sought but always escaping us on that first path of willing, comes to us of its own accord, and all is well with us. It is the painless state, prized by Epicurus as the highest good and as the state of the gods; for that moment we are delivered from the miserable pressure of the will. We celebrate the Sabbath of the penal servitude of willing; the wheel of Ixion stands still."[30]

Nor is Schopenhauer unaware of how close he comes, in his notion of this ecstatic state of will-less knowing, to the Eastern mystics whom, perhaps, he was one of the first, if not the first Western philosopher to appreciate. Thus he writes of the person contemplating nature in such a disinterested state that "he [will] be moved by the consciousness of what the *Upanishad* of the Veda expresses . . . ,"[31] which is to say: "I am all this creation collectively, and besides me there exists no other being."[32]

With this picture of the genius as ecstatic before us, we can now easily draw the Platonic connection; indeed, in places Schopenhauer draws it for us. It consists, essentially, of three aspects shared by Schopenhauer's artist-genius and Plato's poet possessed: madness, the loss of ego or "personhood," and at least the appearance of possession by some external agency, an outside source of inspiration. We have seen all three of these suggested in the *Ion*. It remains for us now to locate them in *The World as Will and Representation*. This is not a difficult task.

The theme of genius as a form of madness, and the resemblance of the genius to the madman, is an almost obsessively persistent theme in Schopenhauer. And it is in this regard that the connection with Plato is explicitly drawn. "It is often remarked," Schopenhauer writes, "that genius and madness have a side where they touch and even pass over into each other, and even poetic inspiration has been called a kind of madness. . . ."[33] There then follows a number of references to ancient Greek and Roman authors, Plato in particular. There is no reference to the *Ion*, but there is to the *Phaedrus*, in which the same doctrine of divine possession is espoused. "Also in the *Phaedrus* (245A), he distinctly says that without a certain madness there can be no genuine poet. . . ."[34]

Although Schopenhauer does not quote the passage from the *Phaedrus* to which he refers, it would be instructive to present it here. Plato has Socrates say, in part: "But he who without the divine madness comes to the doors of the Muses confident that he will be a good poet by art, meets with no success, and the poetry of the sane man vanishes into nothingness before that of the inspired madman."[35]

For Plato, either metaphorically or in reality—I do not know which—poetic madness is a divine gift. For Schopenhauer, however, the madness has become naturalized for a modern age. What the madman and the artistic genius have in common, on Schopenhauer's view, is not possession by the god but, rather, the absence of "common sense," the inability to get along in the everyday world of human affairs. Both are disoriented, both are perceiving the world independently of the principle of sufficient reason. So, in a kind of absentminded disregard of space and time, ratiocination, causal inference, and the normal regard for the motivation of human action, both stumble about the world of ordinary affairs. For the madman it is an affliction, for the genius a blessing. But the appearance they both present to the common sensibility is the same. The genius, "the individual so gifted becomes more or less useless for life; in fact, by his conduct we are sometimes reminded of madness."[36]

The second symptom (if I may so call it) of the Platonic afflatus is the loss of self or personhood. In the *Ion* this is the result of the poet being used by the god as the god's conduit. The god speaks through the poet; so it is not the person of the poet but the "person" of the god that makes the poetry. In the throes of poetic creation the poet is literally no longer himself.

In Schopenhauer's version, again, free of supernatural overtones, the artistic genius, liberated from the will, from *his* will, and from its ceaseless striving within the sufficient-reason principle, ceases essentially to be himself; for it is his will and its striving that constitute his particular ego. As Schopenhauer describes the phenomenon: "the transition that is possible, but to be regarded only as an exception, from the common knowledge of particular things to knowledge of the Idea takes place suddenly, since knowledge tears itself free from the service of the will precisely by the subject's ceasing to be merely individual, and being now a pure will-less subject of knowledge." He continues: "We *lose* ourselves entirely in this object, to use a pregnant expression; in other words, we forget our individuality, our will, and continue to exist only as pure subject, as clear mirror of the object, so that it is as though the object alone existed without anyone to perceive it, and thus we are no longer able to separate the perceiver from the perception, but the two have become one, since the entire consciousness is filled and occupied by a single image of perception."[37] In Plato the poet ceases to be because he becomes the god. In Schopenhauer's

Platonism the artistic genius ceases to be because he becomes the object of knowledge, the Idea. The god speaks through Plato's creator, the Idea through Schopenhauer's. But in both the creator ceases to be.

It is just this loss of self that, in the *Ion*, makes Socrates want to say that the poem comes from outside the poet himself. And it is this very same loss of self that makes Schopenhauer want to say that we have at least the *appearance* of external "inspiration," this being the third of the links between the Platonic afflatus and Schopenhauer's "aesthetic attitude." So Schopenhauer observes that "a *genius* added from outside so to speak, seems to be active here . . . something foreign to the will, i.e., to the I or ego proper."[38] And, again, Schopenhauer writes of the attitude of the artist-genius as "something foreign to human nature," something accruing to "only extremely rare men," so that "what he produces or creates is then ascribed to a *genius* different from him, which takes possession of him."[39] So the final link to the Platonic theory of divine inspiration is forged.

Schopenhauer leaves little doubt that his concept of artistic genius —which is to say, genius *tout court*—is a revival, a modern evocation of the Platonic poet possessed. But to it he adds, in the end, something completely alien to the ancient world, or the Enlightenment, for that matter, and altogether at home in the Romantic era: the genius as the perpetual child. To this notion, crucial to my argument, I now turn.

The connection between the childlike and genius is drawn by Schopenhauer at the very end of his discussion of the latter concept, in 1844, and appears almost as an afterthought, without, so far as I can see, even a hint in the edition of 1819. He begins: "I have still to add here a special remark on the *childlike* character of genius, on a certain resemblance between genius and the age of childhood."[40] But afterthought or no, what he has to say in this regard is perhaps his most original contribution to the subject.

One might, on first reflection, be inclined to suspect that the genius and the child have in common, simply, ineptitude in the world of appearance, the genius because he has put aside the principle of sufficient reason, the child because he or she simply has not yet mastered it. But Schopenhauer has something deeper, more penetrating in mind that, it seems to me, marks an appreciation of childhood and the child that was lacking in the Enlightenment (although Rousseau strikes one as an exception in this regard).

It is not, for Schopenhauer, that the child and the genius share a defect, in their lack of "practical" understanding. Rather, they share a gift, of which the defect (so-called) is a symptom. The gift is freedom from the dominance of the will. In the child this freedom is due to the fact, so Schopenhauer believes, that the intellect develops early, the will late—and this because the will is basically the instrument of sexual desire. Children, "in consequence of that process of development . . . have more intellect than will, in other words than inclination, craving, and passion." Our "mental powers develop much earlier than the needs they are destined to serve . . . ," and so "in childhood our whole existence lies much more in knowing than in willing." And that is "why children in general are so sensible, reasonable, eager to learn, and easy to teach, in fact are on the whole more disposed to and suitable for all theoretical occupations than are grown-up people."[41]

One way of characterizing a genius, then, is to describe him as someone who manages to retain the child's dominance of intellect over will into maturity. The genius, in other words, is simply an old child. "In fact, every child is to a certain extent a genius, and every genius to a certain extent a child."[42]

It is at this point in his argument that Schopenhauer adduces the example of Mozart, of whom it was said "that he remained a child all his life."[43] Note that it is not the child prodigy who impresses Schopenhauer; rather, it is the picture Mozart's early biographers painted of a man who remained forever a child. No doubt, the child prodigy contributed to this conviction that Mozart was a childish person throughout his adult life. But it was the childlike adult rather than the precocious child who dominated Schopenhauer's thinking, apparently. And it is from this myth of Mozart as the perennial child that he draws his final conclusion concerning the nature of genius.

> Therefore every genius is already a big child, since he looks out into the world as into something strange and foreign, a drama, and thus with purely objective interest. . . . He who through-

out his life does not, to a certain extent, remain a big child, but becomes an earnest, sober, thoroughly composed and rational man can be a very useful and capable citizen of this world; but he will never be a genius. In fact, the genius is such through that preponderance of the sensible system and of the activity of knowledge, natural to the age of childhood, maintaining itself in him in an abnormal manner throughout his whole life, and so becoming perennial.[44]

I asked earlier in this chapter why it should have taken so long for the idea of genius as childishness, and the Mozartian embodiment of that idea, to enter Schopenhauer's thinking on the subject. His concept of genius, except for this all important aspect, was already fully formed in the first, 1819 edition of *The World as Will and Representation*. By that time the first biographies of Mozart were available, as well as living memory, to attest to his *alleged* childishness in adulthood. Yet it was only in the second edition, in 1844, that Schopenhauer inserted into his account of genius the idea of the childlike genius, and the image of Mozart as its primary exemplar. Why so?

I venture the following (tentative) hypothesis. That the biographical materials for a childlike adult Mozart were readily available to Schopenhauer in 1819 would cut no ice with him *unless* there was some overwhelming reason to think that that was important. But it could not *be* important to Schopenhauer's account of genius *until* Mozart became recognized, through the growing familiarity with his works, as a towering artistic genius, one of the immortals. And that recognition was slow in coming. Mozart was certainly a curiosity because of his remarkable childhood, an interesting enough figure to have acquired biographers. His prodigy years still existed in living memory. It was not, however, until he achieved the status of transcendent genius that he would have been of significance to Schopenhauer in his account of genius. That Mozart was a childish adult was of no particular philosophical interest until that adult came to be seen as the transcendent, world-class genius that he was. Perhaps 1819 was too early a date for such recognition; but by 1844 Mozart had arrived.

In any case, it is now time to turn from the philosophical foundations of the new Platonic theory of genius to its artistic embodiment in Wolfgang Amadeus Mozart. Whether fact or fiction, or a little of both, it is the Mozart story—the story of the child prodigy and the childlike man—that gave to the early Romantics an image of musical genius, indeed genius itself, very unlike the one that Handel had provided for the British Enlightenment.

VI

The Little Man from Salzburg

There was a certain logical cogency in the course my argument took from the forming of the Longinian concept of literary genius in eighteenth-century Britain to the enshrinement of Handel as the musical embodiment of that concept. Handel's career in England was roughly contemporaneous with the development of that philosophy of genius, as we have seen. His arrival in London coincided almost exactly with the publication of Addison's influential *Spectator* paper on literary genius, his death with the publication of perhaps the culminating document, in England, of the Longinian tradition, Young's *Conjectures on Original Composition*. The composer was there for the philosophy, the philosophy for the composer. How the two were put together by Mainwaring in 1760 is not difficult to comprehend.

With Mozart, and Schopenhauer's philosophy of genius, the logistics are not so easy to make out. For here the order is changed: first the music and then the words.

Mozart died in 1791. Schopenhauer completed his philosophical picture of the artistic genius—in particular, its childlike character, with Mozart as the exemplar—in 1844. Over half a century separated the two events. It was during that time that the Mozart legend was formed and made available to the philosopher. But there is no doubt that it was available well before the appearance of the second edition of *The World as Will and Representation*—indeed, well before the appearance of the first, in 1819. In fact, when Schopenhauer adduces Mozart for his illustration of genius as the perpetual child, he refers to the earliest biographical notice we have, Friedrich Schlichtegroll's, in the *Nekrolog auf das Jahr 1791,* published in Gotha in 1793. By 1798, Franz Niemetschek had published the first separate biography of Mozart— a work that is invaluable to us in obtaining an early version of the Mozart legend: *Wunderkind* and grownup child.

Thus, the legend of Mozart was fully formed, and lay waiting for Schopenhauer long before it was ripe for philosophy. What was needed, as I have suggested earlier, was not the ripening of the legend but growth of the composer's stature as artistic creator. The time was not at hand in 1819—it was in 1844.

Tracing the growth of Mozart's reputation in the first half of the nineteenth century is beyond the purview of this book. What does urgently concern me is the picture of the child-man and man-child that the early nineteenth century formed, and that became the aesthetic symbol of Schopenhauer's Romanticized Platonic genius: the genius not merely as the madman, or the possessed, but as the eternal youth.

I don't think there can be much doubt that Mozart's unique, extraordinary childhood—so well known to the Austrians, Germans, French, Italians, and English because of his extensive travels—had a profound influence on how the early Romantics viewed the nature of artistic creativity, as did the myth, if that is what it was, of the forever childlike adult, which the early biographies were constructing. And as Mainwaring's biography of Handel has served here as an invaluable source for our knowledge of how that composer's genius was seen by his contemporaries and immediate posterity, so Niemetschek's of Mozart can serve us in a similar way for our knowledge of how the early nineteenth century viewed Leopold's miraculous son.

Niemetschek's biography of Mozart stands, in the history of musical biography, between Mainwaring's account of Handel's life and Johann Nicolaus Forkel's pioneering life of J. S. Bach (1802). It is, thus, only the second such attempt at a volume devoted to the life and works of a composer. My discussion of Niemetschek's little book naturally falls into two parts: Mozart the Wunderkind and Mozart the adult. In the case of this remarkable artist, there does not seem to be anything in between.

Niemetschek's account of the prodigy years begins:

> Mozart was just three years old when his sister (then aged seven), had her first clavier lessons, and here the boy's genius first came to light. He would often sit at the clavier of his own accord and amuse himself for hours harmonising in thirds, and when he found them he would play them and was greatly delighted. So his father began to teach him easy pieces; and he saw with delight and astonishment that his pupil exceeded all human expectations; he generally learnt in half an hour a minuet or a little song and then played it with correct expression.[1]

The wonders, many of them no doubt familiar to many of my readers, continue: "By the time he was six he had made such strides with his music that he started composing little pieces for the clavier which his father then had to write down. From then onwards he was totally absorbed by music, and showed no interest in childish pursuits, unless they were combined with music." At about this age, according to Niemetschek,

> his father one day came home from his orchestra with a friend: they found the little musician with a pen in his hand. His father asked him what he was doing.
>
> Wolfgang: "Writing a concerto for the clavier."

Leopold examined the composition. The conversation continues:

> "Look at this, my friend," he said laughingly, "how the whole piece has been composed correctly according to the rules. Only it cannot be performed, as it is too difficult to play."
>
> Wolfgang: "That is why it is called a concerto."[2]

It was about this time that, according to Niemetschek's narrative, Leopold Mozart took his amazing progeny on their first European tour—1762 to be precise. Their destinations were Munich and, later, Vienna, where, Niemetschek relates, "One of the ladies of the court assured me that both children made a very great impression; people could hardly believe their ears and eyes at the performance." Emperor Francis I "was greatly delighted with the little 'magician' (as he was jokingly called)."[3] And so the well-known stories continue.

The visit to England, which, on Niemetschek's reckoning, began on 10 April 1764—Mozart was eight years old at the time—is particularly noteworthy. There was "unusual applause and approval shown by the public everywhere . . . ," Niemetschek tells us, and adds that "In Paris and London, pieces by Handel and [Johann Christian?] Bach were placed before him, which to the astonishment of all experts he was immediately able to perform with accuracy and with proper expression." And: "When he played before the King of England he was given, in some instances, merely the bass, to which he promptly played a charming melody."[4]

What Niemetschek did not know—at least, shows no evidence of having known—about the Mozarts' visit to England was the extraordinary "examination" of Wolfgang that was made by Daines Barrington, Fellow of the Royal Society, written up in the form of a scientific report and submitted to the Royal Society on 28 November 1769. It is an altogether remarkable document, so preeminently English in its tone of disinterested, factual inquiry: an artistic wonder in Vienna, a natural wonder in London.

The opening of Barrington's "case study," addressed to the Royal Society, through its secretary, Mathew Maty, M.D., is striking:

> If I was to send you a well attested account of a boy who measured seven feet in height, when he was not more than eight years of age, it might be considered as not undeserving the notice of the Royal Society.
>
> The instance which I now desire you will communicate to that learned body, of as early an exertion of most extraordinary musical talents, seems perhaps equally to claim their attention.[5]

There follows, then, a careful yet, nevertheless, awestruck account of Wolfgang's extraordinary musical feats, the astonishment all the more impressive considering how intent Barrington is on presenting a scientific, clinical account of his subject, as befits a Fellow of the Royal Society who makes representations to the most prestigious "natural philosophers" in Britain and Europe. To give a full account of this remarkable document would be otiose. But some select examples will help to fill out the image of the prodigy that the Romantics held before their collective eye.

Some of Barrington's anecdotes are second-party testimony. The most interesting are those based on his own observations and "experiments." His comments on them are worthy of note. We must remind ourselves that Wolfgang was eight years old when these events took place.

Barrington proposed to Mozart that he improvise an operatic love song. Here is what happened.

> The boy on this (who continued to sit at his harpsichord) looked back with much archness, and immediately began five or six lines of a jargon recitative proper to introduce a love song.
>
> He then played a symphony which might correspond with an air composed to the single word, *Affeto.*
>
> It had a first and second part, which, together with the symphonies, was of the length that opera songs generally last. . . .[6]

It is of some interest to remark upon how this anecdote is introduced in Barrington's account. Barrington writes: ". . . I told his father that I should be glad to hear some of his extemporary compositions," following which, he reports: "The father shook his head at this, saying, that it depended entirely upon his being as it were musically inspired. . . ."[7]

After the love song Barrington asks for "a *Song of Rage,* such as might be proper for the opera stage. . . . Finding that he was in humour, and as it were inspired. . . ." Wolfgang again complies: "This [rage aria] lasted about the same time with the *Song of Love;* and in the middle of it, he had worked himself up to such a pitch, that he beat his harpsichord like a person possessed, rising sometimes in his chair."[8]

The picture being painted here is clearly of the Platonic genius, inspired and possessed—indeed, nearly mad. That the genius is eight years old completes the picture that Schopenhauer is finally to give philosophical legitimacy to, for his contemporaries, in 1844. Barrington has all the materials in place, with so to speak, "scientific rigor," in 1769.

What is particularly interesting, for our purposes, is how Barrington's report concludes. The comparison, by an Englishman, between the prodigality of Mozart and Handel seems inevitable, if the Englishman is familiar, as Barrington was, with Mainwaring's biography. As evidence of Mozart's "inspirational" kind of genius, Barrington reports, on Leopold's testimony, that Wolfgang "was often visited with musical ideas, to which even in the midst of night, he would give utterance on his harpsichord. . . ."[9] At the end of his report, in making the comparison with Handel, Barrington reverts to this anecdote of Mozart's nocturnal inspirations when a child. "Mainwaring likewise mentions that Handel, when very young, was struck sometimes whilst in bed with musical ideas, and that, like Mozart, he used to try their effect immediately on a spinet, which was in his bed-chamber."[10]

What is remarkable about this comparison of Mozart's "inspiration" with Handel's is that Barrington has, unintentionally, clearly without realizing it, seriously misremembered and misrepresented Mainwaring's text, reading into it the Platonic picture of genius that he is so obviously accepting for Mozart, albeit, perhaps, as metaphor. Mainwaring's well-known anecdote, quoted in an earlier chapter, which Barrington is obviously misremembering, is of "a little clavichord privately convey'd to a room at the top of the house," where Handel "constantly stole when the family was asleep," and engaged in "arduous practice at the hours of rest. . . ."[11] There is no hint in Mainwaring of a nocturnally possessed child-genius repairing to the attic to obey his muse by recording his musical inspirations. Handel routinely spent his nights, the text clearly suggests, *practicing the clavichord*—that is all. But Barrington is obviously taken with the inspirational, ecstatic representation of genius that Leopold's account of nocturnal visitations so neatly fits, and easily transforms the vaguely remembered account of Handel's nocturnal music-making into a parallel instance of the same sort of thing, which it patently is not. Mainwaring made something quite different of Handel's precosity, as we saw earlier.

At this point let us return to Niemetschek's account of Mozart's childhood, not for more of the familiar yet forever stunning anecdotes, but for his picture of the child prodigy's character. For here, in myth, the child is father to the man—*is* the man.

What is perhaps the most notable aspect of Niemetschek's characterization of Mozart, both child and man, is a tendency toward complete absorption in the task at hand—usually, of course, a musical task, be it composing or performing. It is the kind of thing Nietzsche must have been thinking about when he wrote: "Man's maturity: to have regained the seriousness of a child at play."[12] Mozart never had to regain it, for, according to the myth, he never lost it.

Mozart, Niemetschek tells us, "entered into everything with keenness and enthusiasm, due to his very sensitive nature." A case in point: "He would cover chairs, tables and floors with numbers when he was learning arithmetic, and thought and spoke of nothing but arithmetical problems. . . ."[13] The point is put even more clearly—the character trait more accurately identified—in a passage just before, in which Niemetschek writes that

> little Mozart . . . had to be called away from the clavier, sometimes almost chased away, otherwise he might still have been there at daybreak.
>
> This self-forgetfulness, when he was making music, lasted all his life; he would sit at the clavier every day till late at night—a sure sign of the genius by which he was absorbed, to the almost total exclusion of all else.[14]

"Self-forgetfulness" is the key word here. It correctly names both what Niemetschek was describing in the charming anecdote about the child Mozart's temporary preoccupation with arithmetic as well as Mozart's lifelong preoccupation with music. It is one of the colloquial ways of characterizing just that "attitude" commonly ascribed to genius and, furthermore, just that attitude, I suggest, that Schopenhauer is endeavoring to capture in his application to it of Kantian disinterestedness in *The World as Will and Representation*.

THE LITTLE MAN FROM SALZBURG

Indeed, just as we can see almost the complete collection of characteristics associated with the Platonic concept of genius in Barrington's observations on the eight-year-old Mozart, so too in Niemetschek's description of Mozart as child and man that we have just looked at. There is the loss of self that the word "self-forgetfulness" suggests. There is the suggestion, as well, of "possession," of "inspiration" in Niemetschek's phrase, "the genius by which he was absorbed." It is a somewhat obscure phrase. But I understand it to be implying at least a metaphorical separation of Mozart from his "genius," as does the notion of being possessed or inspired by it. What is intriguing in Niemetschek's image is that, rather than being seized by his genius, Mozart is, as it were, enveloped into it. It is a gentler image perhaps: absorbed rather than possessed or grabbed or snatched away. The basic Platonic idea, however, is manifestly there.

Of great importance, as well, is that what we have been looking at in Niemetschek's characterization of Mozart's personality is not an isolated instance or two but persists, in his account, and projects firmly into Mozart's adulthood the abstraction and even childishness that Schopenhauer makes so much of in his philosophy of genius. Thus Niemetschek says of the adult Mozart: "As a dedicated artist he became oblivious of all external considerations"; and, even more to the point: "His imagination was always active, always occupied with music; that is the reason why he appeared absent-minded and forgetful."[15] "His glance was unsteady and absent-minded . . . ," Niemetschek says in another place.[16] Again, we cannot help being reminded, in these descriptions of Mozart's adult mentality, the obliviousness to "all external considerations," his appearing "absent-minded and forgetful," his "glance . . . unsteady and absent-minded," of Schopenhauer's distracted genius, in complete disengagement from the principle of sufficient reason—hence, from all that makes an individual attentive to his surroundings and personal circumstances.

Of the man that remained a child, Niemetschek does not, like the *Nekrolog*, from which Schopenhauer quotes, state the thing outright, in so many words. But it requires little effort of the imagination to see that what he does not express in letter he does assuredly in spirit.

Niemetschek tells us that Mozart as a child "was always very kind and friendly with his playmates and was attached to them with all the affection of his warm nature. . . ."[17] This warm, openness of nature, the direct unguarded expression of affection, is, of course, a common character trait of children. When it is preserved into adulthood it is frequently perceived as a childlike trait in the adult. And Mozart's first biographer does not fail to observe this trait in the grown-up composer. Indeed, he initiates a tradition that ascribes Mozart's "downfall" (so-called) to his childlike, naively trusting nature. "Natural benevolence and rare feelings of good-will were his characteristics. He succumbed to these generous inclinations, and was often deceived because of his instinctive trust of others. In fact, he often gave comfort and hospitality to his greatest enemies and slanderers." Or, in a similar vein: "In fact, even as a child and later as a boy he . . . showed [people] . . . the utter sincerity and warmth of feeling of which his gentle heart was capable. This trait in his character was typical of him when he grew up, and was often his undoing."[18]

Nor does Niemetschek leave us in any real doubt as to his own interpretation of Mozart as a childlike adult. Indeed, immediately after characterizing him as overly trusting and excessively affectionate, he observes that: "Among his friends he was as confiding as a child, full of fun. . . ." Niemetschek adds: "His friends in Prague . . . cannot praise his guileless nature enough."[19] Mozart the man, then, is a guileless, fun-loving, overly trusting, childishly affectionate naif who cannot tell friend from foe.

The characterization of Mozart the adult as "full of fun" deserves special comment, because stories survive of what sort of "fun" this was. They formed a part of the picture of the man-still-a-child that was emerging in the late eighteenth and early nineteenth centuries. It is musical "fun and games," and is supposed, according to the legend, to stretch back to Mozart's childhood. Thus, as Niemetschek remarks, "even in his childish amusements, his keenness on music was shown, and games with music were his favourites."[20]

But according to the perpetual-child legend, the musical games persisted into adulthood. And anecdotes of them (true or false not the issue) constitute one of its most charming aspects. A sampling of them concludes our picture of the Mozart who was a child, and the Mozart who remained one: Schopenhauer's genius as perpetual child.

Mozart, Niemetschek informs us, "was very fond of animals and —particularly—birds."[21] According to one story, the main, rondo theme of the finale of the Piano Concerto in G, K. 453, was based on a starling's song. Mozart records in his expense book the purchase of the bird, for 34 kreutzers, on 27 May 1784. Beneath the entry he writes the theme, and adds, as a critical comment: "That was fine." But the bird proved to be an even shorter-lived composer than its owner, dying three years later. Georg Nikolaus Nissen, Constanza Mozart's second husband, writes that "When the bird died he arranged a funeral procession in which everyone who could sing had to join in, heavily veiled—made a sort of requiem, epitaph in verse."[22]

There is apparently no evidence as to what was sung at this avian funeral. But musical compositions of Mozart's exist, both trivial and profound, that emerged from incidents equally playful and inconsequential. For Mozart, so the myth is telling us, composition itself was a game—mere child's play.

On the trivial side is the comic terzet, "Liebes Mandl, wo ist's Bandl," K. 441, written in 1783, dedicated to Gottfried von Jaquin. As Mozart's great nineteenth-century biographer, Otto Jahn, tells the story:

> Mozart had made his wife a present of a new belt ribbon which she wished to wear one day when she was going for a walk with Jaquin. Not finding it she called to her husband: "Liebes Mandl, wo ist's Bandl?" (Where is the belt, my dear?) They both looked for it in vain till Jaquin joined them and found it. But he refused to give it up, held it high in the air, and being very tall, the Mozarts, both little, strove in vain to reach it. Entreaties, laughter, scolding, were all in vain, till at last the dog ran barking between Jaquin's legs. Then he gave up the ribbon, and declared that the scene would make a good terzet. Mozart took the hint, wrote the words in the Vienna dialect (which is essential for the comic effect), and sent the terzet to Jaquin.[23]

But of equally inconsequential origins, and as musically profound as the Bandl terzet is ephemeral, can be adduced the concert *scena,* "Bella mia fiamma" (K. 528), the chromaticism and modulations of which retain the capability to shock and surprise a twenty-first-century ear. I translate from a Berlin periodical of 1856, which is, apparently, the first source of the anecdote.

> Petranka is well-known as the villa in which Mozart enjoyed staying with his musician friends, the Duscheks, during his visit to Prague, and where he composed several numbers for his "Don Juan." On the summit of a hill near the villa stands a pavilion. In it, Frau Duschek slyly imprisoned the great Mozart, after having provided ink, pen, and paper, and told him that he would not regain his freedom until he had written an aria he had promised her to the words *bella mia fiamma addio.* Mozart submitted to the necessary; but to avenge himself for the trick Frau Duschek had played on him, he used various difficult-to-sing passages in the aria, and threatened his despotic friend that he would destroy the aria if she could not succeed in performing it at sight without mistakes.[24]

The picture of Mozartian genius, then, that the early nineteenth century made for itself, partly through the growing number of written accounts and partly through living memory, was, to begin with, it hardly needs saying, a picture of the greatest child prodigy in music the world had yet seen (or ever seen since). It seems doubtful that the second picture, that of the adult who remained a child, would ever have come to be without the extraordinary, indeed marvelous childhood. Paul Henry Lang correctly observed that, in the process by which Mozart was "enshrined as the symbol of genius in those years": "It was inevitable that his untimely death would arouse interest in the child prodigy, and it was the precocious youngster whom they saw in everything. . . ."[25]

Lang does not venture to say why "it was the precocious youngster they saw in everything." But it is certainly reasonable to suppose or at least conjecture that the philosophy of genius, culminating in Schopenhauer, played a (if not *the*) major role: the philosophy of genius which, through Kant's theory of disinterested perception, made intellectually respectable the commonplace characterization of the genius as distracted, otherworldly, impractical, possessed, slightly mad, self-absorbed, *and* childlike. So in the age of the early Romantics, when such a picture of genius was becoming congenial, it was inevitable that Mozart the child prodigy (who, indeed, scarcely outlived his childhood) should become the paradigm of musical genius, indeed, of genius *tout court*, "the symbol of genius," as Lang put it. Thus was constructed from myth and memory the game-loving, childish, naively affectionate, impractical, distracted little man whom Niemetschek and his contemporaries presented in their biographies.

Before Schopenhauer, both Goethe and Hegel must have been impressed, Goethe deeply so, by the child Mozart, and Goethe, too, by the adult; for Mozart almost invariably is cited by him as the paradigm instance in *Eckermann's Conversations with Goethe* whenever the subject of genius comes up.

Of Mozart the *Wunderkind* Goethe preserved a vivid memory late into his life. Eckermann tells us: "We spoke about Mozart. 'I have seen him as a child of seven years old,' said Goethe, 'when he on going through gave a concert. I myself was about fourteen years old, and I remember still quite clearly the little man in his headdress and sword.' I opened my eyes, and it appeared to me almost a miracle that Goethe was old enough to have seen Mozart as a child."[26]

This conversation took place in 1830, when Goethe was eighty-one years old. Wolfgang gave three concerts in Frankfort in the summer of 1763, which is when the poet must have seen him. *What* he saw we can see for ourselves in the portrait of Mozart, *im Galakleide*, 1762/63 (Figure 2). That Goethe described him as "the little man" is full of significance. For not only is that what we see in the portrait. Mozart was, as an adult, physically small. (He couldn't reach the ribbon when Jaquin held it up.) Aloisia Weber, the sister who spurned Mozart's romantic advances, was asked years after whether she had, during his lifetime, realized he was a genius. She is supposed to have replied that she just thought he was "a little man." Niemetschek says: "There was nothing special about the physique of this extraordinary man; he was small. . . ."[27]

Figure 2. Mozart in gala dress, 1763. Unsigned oil portrait, attributed to Pietro Antonio Lorenzoni. Mozart-Museum der Internationalen Stiftung Mozarteum, Salzburg. © Mozarts Geburtshaus, Salzburg.

THE LITTLE MAN FROM SALZBURG

When Mozart was six he was a little man who composed like an adult and behaved like a child. When thirty-six, he was *still* a little man who behaved like a child and composed . . . the way he composed. That is the image of his genius.

Goethe gives no indication that he was familiar with the stories of Mozart's childishness as an adult or that he extrapolated from the child prodigy to the notion of genius as childlike. But the fact of Mozart's extraordinary accomplishments in childhood certainly led him to think deeply about the nature of music, and of musical genius. And in what he says to Eckermann about these things one can see the Platonic afflatus peeking out.

> "It is remarkable," said I, "that of all talents the musical shows itself earliest, so that Mozart in his fifth year, Beethoven in his eighth, Hummel in his ninth, already astounded their immediate neighbourhood by their play and compositions."
>
> "The musical talent," said Goethe, "can well show itself earliest, while music is something innate, inward, which required no great nutriment from outside and no experience drawn from life. But a phenomenon like Mozart remains always a miracle, which is not to be further explained. How would the Godhead, however, find everywhere opportunity to do his miracles, if it did not at times attempt it in extraordinary individuals, at whom we are astonished and cannot understand where they come from.[28]

The key phrases here, for the Platonic interpretation of what Goethe is saying about Mozart's genius and, one presumes, genius in general, are: "a phenomenon like Mozart remains always a miracle, which is not to be further explained," and, in contemplating the "miracle" of the "Godhead," "we are astonished and cannot understand where they [the "extraordinary individuals"] come from." The message here, in Goethe's words, as in Socrates', in the *Ion* and *Phaedrus,* is that a certain kind of creativity, at a high enough level, is simply inexplicable in the sense of there being no known recipe or explanation for how the ideas come. Hence the suggestion, metaphorical or not as the case may be, of an outside, divine origination. It should always be remembered that, for Plato, poetry was the only human activity on our list of the fine arts requiring a (what shall we say?) *non*-explanation for its occurrence.[29] His is not a "general" account of artistic genius as we would consider it. But Goethe's observations, and Plato's, are of the same inexplicable, "methodless" acquiring of brilliant, original ideas (with, in Plato's case, as in Schopenhauer's, madness in the "method"). And Mozart the Wunderkind is the perfect phenomenon to stimulate such Platonic observations precisely because his marvelous juvenilia were produced before any knowledge or "method" *could* have been acquired, even if there were such, thus proving beyond doubt that no such knowledge or method is necessary, even if available, for creative activity at the highest level.

For Goethe, however, music was a special case, as it was for Schopenhauer (which we have seen) and for Hegel (which we will soon see). It was a special case both for Goethe and for Hegel because of the possibility it held out for early, youthful success. Both had a similar explanation for this: music required no life experience, and so could be pursued at a very high level by children—witness the Mozart phenomenon.

It is noteworthy that the two English translations of *Eckermann's Conversations with Goethe* available to me differ importantly in their readings of the passage where Goethe remarks on music's special status in the above regard. R. O. Moon, whose translation I have been relying on, has it: "'The musical talent,' said Goethe, 'can well show itself earliest, *while* [*indem*] music is something innate, inward, which required no great nutriment from outside and not experience drawn from life.'" But John Oxenford has it, rather, in the crucial place: "for [*indem*] music *is* something innate and internal, which needs little nourishment from without, and no experience drawn from life."[30]

What is interestingly different about these two translations is that Moon suggests music *becomes* dependent upon outside nourishment but *begins* as "innate," whereas Oxenford has it as innate *simpliciter*. The difference turns on how *indem* is to be translated, since it carries either the temporal sense of "during the time that," "whilst," "while," or the explanatory sense of "in that," "since," "because," "as." Moon opts for the former, Oxenford the latter, and it is Moon's translation (far the clumsier, incidentally) that makes a good deal of sense in the case of Mozart. For, one would think, although a ten-year-old *can* master the formal aspects of music and produce quite plausible, performable sonatas and symphonies, as Mozart indeed did, when it comes to writing an opera or other texted work, one needs knowledge and experience of human psychology if one is to represent characters or events believably on the dramatic stage. And it has often been observed that Mozart's mastery of opera came much later than his mastery of instrumental forms, in the sense, at least, that even the earliest of his instrumental compositions remain performable and reward listening. His earliest ventures into opera, on the other hand, are display pieces, startling examples of precocity but hardly worth staging, with the exception, perhaps, of *Bastien und Bastienne,* whose childlike plot and simple characters were easily accessible to the twelve-year-old who composed it.

Hegel, as I have said, shared Goethe's opinion that the composer is the artist in whom talent shows itself at the earliest age because no experience of the world is required, at least when "the principal thing [is] the purely musical structure of his work and the ingenuity of such architecture." In that case: "On account of this lack of material not only do we see the gift for composition developed at the most tender age but very talented composers frequently remain throughout their lives the most ignorant and empty-headed of men."[31]

It is difficult not to think that Hegel had Mozart primarily in mind when he made these remarks.[32] Both elements of the Mozart legend can be detected. The child prodigy, of course, is there. But so also, at least dimly visible, is the immature adult, if "ignorant and empty-headed" can be interpreted that way. However, the note of derision in Hegel's description, which comports well with his low opinion of absolute music, leaves no doubt that he meant to pay musical talent no compliment. One can scarcely, then, expect to find Mozart as a paradigm of true artistic genius in Hegel's philosophy of art.

Goethe, however, is another matter. At least in the *Conversations of Goethe with Eckermann,* Mozart seems invariably to come to his mind when the subject of genius is proposed, frequently as the paradigmatic instance. Thus, for example, when the question arises of whether it is wise for the genius to be self-taught, Mozart is the first to be quoted on the subject—*then* Leonardo (both, incidently, to the contrary).[33]

Goethe speaks of the unattainable in art, toward which men strive. The list of such artists is a short one—Raphael, Mozart, Shakespeare—"that which belongs to nature, the greatness innate in nature."[34]

Again, Eckermann raises the question of the relation between genius and production. "You appear . . . to call productivity that which," he says, "one formerly called genius." No sooner is the word "genius" uttered then the name of Mozart follows.

> "Both indeed are things which live near together," replied Goethe. "For what else is genius but that productive power, by means of which deeds arise, which can show themselves before God, and in nature, and for which reason have results and last? All the works of Mozart are of this kind; there lies in them a productive power which works on from generation to generation and may not so soon be exhausted and consumed."[35]

Of particular interest with regard to the future development of the Mozart legend is Goethe's observation that "Every exceptional man has a certain mission which he is called to fulfill. If he has accomplished it, so is he on this earth and in this form no further necessary, and Providence turns him again to something else." Again, the first example of artistic genius adduced to illustrate this point is Mozart. "Mozart died in his six and thirtieth year, Raphael at the same age, Byron only a little older. But all had fulfilled their mission in the complete manner, and it was well time for them to go so that still something remains over to be done for other people too in this world calculated for long duration."[36]

The premature death, as we have seen Paul Henry Lang observe, is part of the legend of the Wunderkind and childlike man. Historian of ideas William Stafford, in his intriguing book *Mozart's Death: A Corrective Survey of the Legends,* calls this the Mozart Theodicy. "Two hundred years on, we are distressed by Mozart's death, by the thought of all that was lost thereby; this story [the Mozart Theodicy] tells us not to grieve, for all was accomplished."[37] The story was already in place, fully formed by Goethe, as Stafford himself knows, if Eckermann is to be credited. And it is yet another instance, in the *Conversations*, of the pride of place Mozart occupies whenever the poet turns his thoughts to the concept of artistic genius.

How deeply the image of Mozart penetrated Goethe's thinking about genius cannot be more emphatically put than by observing that the very last paragraph of the very last entry in the *Conversations of Goethe with Eckermann*, dated 11 March 1832, begins: "But let one, however, endeavour only and produce with human will and human power something which can be placed by the side of the creations which bear the names of Mozart, Raphael or Shakespeare."[38] Again, the name of Mozart comes first among geniuses. And again note the hint of divine possession. Eckermann's *Conversations* ends, and we can fairly take it as Goethe's last message to the world: "Thus he [God] is continually working in higher natures so as to lead up the lower ones."[39] He died eleven days later, 22 March 1832.

That Mozart had become "enshrined as the symbol of genius" (to use Lang's phrase) in Goethe's mind seems obvious, and that Goethe saw music as a special art no less so. But the way music was special for Goethe lay not in its preeminence over the other arts, rather, merely in its peculiar propensity to manifest itself in the very young—hence, of course, the Mozart connection. Thus there was no reason to elevate the child business into any kind of characteristic of artistic genius *tout court*. Nor did Goethe do so.

It was Schopenhauer who, through his peculiar metaphysics, elevated music to its ascendancy over all the fine arts to make it, indeed, in thought if not in fact, *the* art of the Romantic era. This, together with a philosophy of genius that made the childlike its hallmark, made Mozart the inevitable choice for the embodiment of artistic genius across the board. Whether the Mozart legend was the cause or the effect, or a combination of the two, I cannot say. But that Mozart was enthroned as the symbol of artistic genius in the first half of the nineteenth century there can be no real doubt.

What is surely curious, to return once more to the case of Goethe, at least in the *Conversations of Goethe with Eckermann*, is the almost complete absence of the name of Beethoven. Beethoven died in 1827 —the *Conversations* took place from 1823 to 1832—and had been, for a long time, the dominant musical figure in Europe. Yet in the one place where comment on him from Goethe would seem absolutely demanded, not a word is forthcoming.

Early in the *Conversations,* Eckermann describes a social gathering at which the poet was present. "Schmidt, member of [the] official Council, sat himself at the piano and performed some pieces of Beethoven, which those present appeared to receive with inward sympathy. An intellectual lady then related much that was interesting of Beethoven's personality. And so gradually it became 10:00 o'clock and the evening had passed for me in the highest degree pleasantly."[40]

It seems incredible that Goethe, having listened to music of the most prominent (and controversial) composer of his day, and to remarks about his personality by an "intellectual lady," should not have had comments of his own worthy of being recorded by his Boswell. Yet there are none. When the subject of genius arises, Mozart's name comes first, or in the select company of Raphael and Shakespeare.

Yet Beethoven was, and had been for a long time, a commanding presence. *His* myth was already in the making, the "intellectual lady," no doubt, contributing her bit. "Beethoven the Creator" was waiting in the wings, to swing the pendulum back from the Platonic genius to the Longinian. But before he makes his entrance, we must first set the philosophical stage for the figure of Beethoven as the symbol of genius that, in the second half of the nineteenth century, completely supplanted that of Child Mozart and the Platonic afflatus.

VII

Giving the Rule

In previous chapters I have tried to show how Schopenhauer made Kant's theory of disinterested perception into a theory of genius with clear affinities to Plato's, and how the early Romantics applied it to the myth of Mozart, the eternal child, which surrounded that extraordinary prodigy, and his premature death. I now lay before you Kant's *own* theory of genius, and argue that it, rather, is to be characterized as a reexpression, albeit in highly original terms, of the Longinian concept, which we will then see, in the next chapter, was well-suited to the figure whose towering musical powers dominated late-nineteenth-century thinking about what the creative intellect is like, in its loftiest manifestations—namely, Ludwig van Beethoven.

But before we get to Kant, it would be useful to backtrack a bit and pick up the strands of genius theory in late-eighteenth-century Britain. For Kant owes much, in his philosophy of art, to the aestheticians of the British Enlightenment. He took, he rejected, he transformed — and his theory of genius is no exception to that.

We left the theory of genius in England at what I described as the culmination of the Longinian phase: the year was 1759; the work, Edward Young's *Conjectures on Original Composition*. But the British had, at this point, by no means lost interest in the concept. Rather, the Longinian craze had about run its course, and the theory of genius was already in the process of taking a different direction. The major player in this new turn of events was the Scottish philosopher Alexander Gerard.

Gerard published in 1759 *An Essay on Taste,* which proved to be one of the most widely read and admired aesthetic treatises of the so-called Scottish Enlightenment, a period rich in such speculations. By 1780 it had appeared in a third edition, with substantial new material. What is of particular interest for us is that the first edition of Gerard's *Essay* already contained a brief section called "Of the Connexion of Taste with Genius," in which Gerard sketched an account of genius, expanded in 1774 into a full-blown theory. This theory, very different in spirit from the Longinian tradition, was laid out in excruciating detail in a book of 434 pages, titled, not surprisingly, *An Essay on Genius.* Fortunately, it will be necessary for us to master only the general principles of Gerard's view. But before we do that, we will have to get at least a vague idea of what the basic foundations were of his general aesthetic theory—that is to say, where he was "coming from." For the theory of genius bears a direct relation to the "school" of aesthetic philosophy to which Gerard belonged, and of which he was one of the founders (or at least early practitioners).

Gerard's work in aesthetics and the philosophy of art makes extensive use of the principle of the "association of ideas," which, by the time he came to publish his *Essay on Taste* in 1759, had had a one-hundred-year-old history in British philosophy, starting as early as Thomas Hobbes, if not before. The principle was made available to eighteenth-century Britain in the fourth edition of the *Essay Concerning Human Understanding,* to which John Locke added a chapter (in Book II) called "Of the Association of Ideas." The use to which the principle was put, in the early years of the century, was what might be called a "negative" one. That is to say, if one thought that some object or other was, say, "naturally pleasing" to mankind, and if it were observed, to the contrary, that Miss Smith or Mr. Jones found it *displeasing,* one could always appeal to the personal history of Smith or Jones—the particular, idiosyncratic associations that Smith or Jones might have formed with the object in question which made it displeasing to *them,* although pleasing to humanity at large.

One of Locke's own examples will do nicely to introduce the idea. Honey is naturally pleasant to the taste. But "A grown person surfeiting with honey no sooner hears the name of it, but his fancy immediately carries the sickness and qualms to his stomach, and he cannot bear the very idea of it. . . ."[1] Thus: honey naturally pleases; I get sick eating too much honey; sick feelings become "associated" in my mind with the idea of honey; honey, in thought or in taste, becomes repugnant *to me.* That is the general drift of the argument.

The negative use of the association of ideas very quickly made its way into aesthetics and the philosophy of art through Francis Hutcheson's *Inquiry Concerning Beauty, Order, Harmony, Design* (1725), arguably the first full-length philosophical study in that new-made discipline. Hutcheson was famous in both aesthetic and moral theory for his notion of internal "senses." In aesthetic theory he postulated a "sense" of beauty, or harmony, that was "naturally" pleased by objects exhibiting what he called *uniformity amidst variety.*

Hutcheson was quick to see that one implication of his view seemed to be that, just as people generally agree what is red or not, because they have in common the sense of sight, they should generally agree what is beautiful or deformed, because they have in common the "sense of beauty." But, notoriously, people do *not* agree on matters of beauty and ugliness—hence cannot have, in common, an innate sense of those things.

Ready to hand, however, to rescue the internal sense theory of beauty was the association of ideas, in its negative use. For the association of ideas is just the mechanism by which the "naturally" pleasant can be made unpleasant. If it works for the external, bodily senses that way, then why not for the "internal," mental ones as well? Thus, Hutcheson argued, we all *do* start off with an internal sense of beauty the operation of which would produce aesthetic agreement were it not for the deflecting influence of the association of ideas, which works for Hutcheson in two different ways.

If the perception of the beautiful is the feeling of pleasure in the sensible presence of uniformity amidst variety, then displeasure rather than pleasure can be the result, "deformed" rather than "beautiful" the judgment, where the opposite should have occurred, in two different but related ways. If Smith and Jones look, say, at a house, and Miss Smith sees part of it as larger than it really is because of certain personal associations with it, her object of perception may well be a different one from Mr. Jones's, his possessing uniformity amidst variety, hers not. Hence the pleasure of beauty accrues to his perception, the displeasure of deformity to hers, even though they both have the internal sense of beauty in common. Or, alternatively, Mr. Jones may associate a certain unpleasant feeling with the house because, perhaps, he suffered some misfortune in it, whereas Miss Smith has no such association. So, where *she* feels the pleasure of beauty in perceiving the house, and pronounces it "beautiful," *he* feels an uneasy, even painful sensation, owing to prior associations, which he *mistakes* for the feeling of deformity, also an unpleasant sensation, and pronounces the house "not beautiful at all." In both cases the associations operate negatively, to pervert what should have been a uniform feeling and judgment, issuing from a commonly held aesthetic sense.[2]

It was in this negative way that the association of ideas operated in British aesthetic theory until about mid-century, by which time a profound change had taken place in the way the principle was viewed by philosophers and critical theorists. Gerard's *Essay on Taste* was the first major work to reflect this change in aesthetics and the philosophy of art, although not the first to give hints at least of an associationist account of beauty and related concepts.

In its negative use, as we have seen, the association of ideas explains how what is "naturally" pleasant can come to be experienced as unpleasant (and vice versa). But a moment's reflection will suggest that things might be turned on their head. Why not say that what is "naturally" pleasant or unpleasant only *appears* to be "naturally" so; that, through *forgotten* associations, what appears to be "naturally" pleasant or unpleasant was originally the opposite, or neutral, and has acquired its present hedonic tone from something else that *is* naturally pleasant or unpleasant? But *why* say it? Why go from the negative use of association to the positive?

In aesthetics and the philosophy of art, the rise of association as a positive (or constructive) principle was due, no doubt, to a growing unease with the tendency of "innate" senses to breed like rabbits in response to newly acknowledged aesthetic qualities. Hutcheson had postulated a sense of beauty. But what of the growing passion for the sublime? Would that require a "sense" as well? Where would it end? Gerard recognized seven "internal senses" in the *Essay on Taste:* the senses of novelty, sublimity, beauty, imitation, harmony, ridicule, and virtue. Surely this appears to be the faculty psychology run amok.

But Gerard, clearly, was aware of the danger, as was Edmund Burke, who, two years before invoked the principle of parsimony in this regard when he wrote in the *Enquiry into the Sublime and Beautiful:* "To multiply principles for every different appearance is useless, and unphilosophical in a high degree."[3] For what Gerard calls "senses" are not, as in Hutcheson's scheme, innate faculties. They are, rather, *acquired* dispositions to feel pleasure (or displeasure) — acquired, that is to say, by the association of ideas. They "may," Gerard avers, "with the greatest propriety, be reckoned senses, though they be derived faculties. . . ."[4] Functioning together, they constitute "taste."

There is no need, for present purposes, to give a full account of Gerard's aesthetic-sense philosophy. But there may be some use in suggesting just how things go with it, by adducing an example of the principle of association at work, in its positive, constructive mode in the *Essay on Taste*. Perhaps most characteristic is the treatment of Hutcheson's central concept: uniformity amidst variety. On his view, the pleasure of beauty is caused directly by the presence of uniformity amidst variety to the internal sense of beauty; it is a purely innate reaction. For Gerard, however, things go quite differently. What *is* innately pleasing to us is not uniformity amidst variety but the mental quality of wisdom — ultimately, the wisdom of God. Anything we *associate* with that, which is to say, anything making us think of that gives us pleasure because we *are* thinking of *that*. But unity and variety, together, *are* associated in our minds, through experience, with wisdom because we know through experience that wisdom or intelligence is their cause. They are "indications of design, wisdom, and contrivance; qualities of mind which we never fail to survey with pleasure," or, more precisely, "uniformity and variety artfully blended in the same object, by excluding both chance and mechanism, put it beyond doubt, that . . . design, and wisdom, and art, have been employed in uniting these opposite qualities so skilfully; . . . we take pleasure in conceiving the excellence of the cause, and by this the delight is heightened which we find in beholding the effect that suggests that excellence."[5] Other of the traditional pleasures of art and natural beauty are treated in similar fashion.

In sum, then, Gerard's idea is that taste, our faculty for enjoying and making critical judgments about art and natural beauty, is an amalgam of seven internal senses, each an *acquired* propensity to associate aesthetic and moral qualities with a few basic, innate pleasure principles. Taste, then, when well developed, is a tendency toward wide and extensive associations of ideas. Artworks of the better kind are objects that are suited to facilitate such associations in the person of taste.

The tradition, in Enlightenment thinking on these matters, is that *taste* is the faculty of artistic appreciation and judgment; *genius,* of course, the faculty of artistic creation when at the highest level. And if, as Gerard is suggesting, taste is the propensity to experience extensive associations of ideas, when confronted with objects well suited to excite these associations, it seems the next logical step to suggest that genius is the propensity to *spontaneously* experience extensive associations of ideas, without the aid of artworks, which are then fashioned into works that can excite these associations in persons of taste. The person of taste is capable of extensive associations of ideas, but only through the instrumentality of artworks. The genius, on the other hand, is capable of giving birth, without the midwifery of fine art, to wide associations of ideas that he or she can then work up into artworks; these artworks, in turn, capable of producing associations in the appropriate perceivers. That, I say, is the next logical step; and Gerard took it in the one brief section devoted to genius in the *Essay on Taste.*

Here is Gerard's initial characterization of what he takes artistic genius to be, although in the *Essay on Taste,* as in the later *Essay on*

Genius, it is clear that artistic genius, unlike in the case of Kant and Schopenhauer, is not the only kind of genius recognized. Gerard writes: "The first and leading quality of genius is *invention,* which consists in a great extent and comprehensiveness of imagination, in a readiness of associating the remotist ideas that are any way related. In a man of genius, the uniting principles are so vigorous and quick, that, whenever any idea is present to the mind, they bring into view at once all others that have the least connexion with it."[6]

So, consistent with the notion that the appreciation of artworks consists of a chain of acquired associations that artworks are specifically designed to generate, is the notion, as Gerard formulates it, that genius—the ability to create, at a high level, artworks that are suited to generate such associative trains—must be a propensity, to a large degree involuntary, to experience such associative trains without the aid of artworks. That it *is* spontaneous and involuntary is *not* so clear in the *Essay on Taste* as it is in the later *Essay on Genius,* where Gerard makes it quite explicit. "We cannot," he says, "call up ideas, as it were, by name, we can only cast ourselves into the roads in which they are likeliest to occur; and if fancy [which is to say, the pump of genius] be not powerful enough to bring them into view, we must remain without them."[7]

But, as Gerard puts it, the propensity to experience associative trains spontaneously, without the aid of artworks, is only the "leading quality" of artistic genius. For if genius is the ability to *create* great works of art, not just imagine them, it is necessary not only to experience, on one's own, extensive associations of ideas, but to be able to embody them in works of art that can excite these associations in others. Thus, Gerard points out in his *Essay on Taste:* "A genius for the fine arts implies, not only the power of invention or design [i.e. extensive, spontaneous association of ideas], but likewise a capacity to express its designs in apt materials. Without this, it would not only be imperfect, but would for ever lie latent, undiscovered and useless."[8]

Finally, the creator, like the appreciator, must possess *taste.* For the spontaneous and extensive train of associations that is the prerequisite for genius cannot simply be left uncontrolled or it will run wild into free fantasy. As well, taste is required to judge, in the making of a work, whether it will or will not have the intended effect. In Gerard's words, genius "needs the assistance of taste, to guide and moderate its exertions.... [W]e acquire much ampler assurance of its rectitude, when taste has reviewed and examined both the design and execution. It serves as a check on mere fancy; it interposes its judgment, either approving or condemning; and rejects many things which unassisted genius would have allowed."[9]

Gerard's picture of artistic genius, then, as it was sketched in broad strokes in the *Essay on Taste,* is of an amalgam of these attributes. The "leading quality" of genius is the propensity for experiencing, more or less spontaneously, extensive associative trains of ideas. When combined with the ability to embody those trains in art objects that can excite them in others, and the capacity of judgment, called *taste,* which keeps out the extraneous and tells the possessor when the job has been rightly done, artistic genius is the result.

This picture, as I have said, was already fully formed in the *Essay* of 1759. The compendious *Essay on Genius* of 1774 merely (if that is the right word) spells it out in systematic detail. I do not mean to suggest that the latter work lacks interest or significance for the history of the concept. Far from it. But it holds no interest for us in the present context. For the theories of genius that dominated nineteenth-century German thought and gave rise to the images of genius that Mozart and Beethoven provided were Schopenhauer's, as we saw, and Kant's, as we are about to see.

Why, then, bother with Gerard's animadversions on the subject? I have not done so merely to close the book on the British adventure. For, although Kant both knew and rejected Gerard's concept of genius, he was, I shall argue, deeply influenced by it. Understanding what he rejected in Gerard will help us understand what he accomplished himself.

What had Gerard really done with the concept of genius? Returning to our theme: Was he a Platonist or a Longinian? The answer is: Neither, and both. That is to say, he paid homage to neither, but was probably consistent with both. For his project, a characteristically eighteenth-century one, was to provide a *mechanistic* account of genius; to lay bare, in other words, its *mental machinery*. For mental machinery was just what the philosophers of the British Enlightenment represented the associationist psychology as being. The associationists were "Newtons of the mind." And the machinery was consistent with the appearance of genius both as "natural talent" and as "inspiration." As a psychological mechanic of genius, Gerard would hardly have found reason to reject the reality of the former; and as the Professor of Divinity in King's College, Aberdeen, he would hardly have been troubled by inspiration from above either. The association of ideas, as a mechanical explanation of what goes on in the mind of the genius, was obviously not seen by Gerard to be inconsistent with constituting part of God's Creation, any more than was Newton's machinery of the Cosmos so seen; but nor need it have been seen by Gerard to be inconsistent with divine intervention, in the form of artistic inspiration. For, presumably, Gerard, as a theologian, could hardly have shared Hume's skepticism in regard to the possibility of the miraculous; and if miraculous was what divine inspiration was, then so be it.

Kant, as I have already remarked, knew Gerard's account of genius and was unsympathetic to it. We can be certain of both because he says as much in one of his manuscript *Reflexionen*, mentioning Gerard by name: "Genius is not, as Gerard would have it, a special power of mind . . . but a principle of animation of all the other [mental] powers. . . ."[10] Whether Kant had in mind, here, the *Essay on Taste* or the *Essay on Genius,* or both, I cannot say. Both had been translated into German by the end of the 1770s. Nor am I clear as to what the exact nature of Kant's difficulty with Gerard is in this respect. Gerard, after all, thought of genius not as a single power but, as we have seen, as an amalgam of acquired powers, including taste. In the *Critique of Judgment,* most likely written well after this manuscript jotting, Kant too makes taste a requirement of genius. But it is worth noting that the connection of genius with what Kant calls (in my translation) "the animation of all the powers [of mind]," is a notion distinctive of his mature, "critical" thinking about the concept. So this jotting, this *Reflexion,* suggests a fairly well advanced stage in Kant's aesthetic thought.

Kant's real difficulty with Gerard comes out, I think, far more clearly in his mature discussion of genius in the third *Critique:* it is by implication, without mentioning the Scottish philosopher by name, where Kant speaks of the way in which genius *frees* us from the law of association. But that is getting ahead of ourselves. So let us begin, systematically, to examine the Kantian concept of genius. I will argue that it both comes out of Gerard's, in an important aspect, and is, at the same time, a rejection of him—in particular, a rejection of the mechanistic association principle as the leading quality of genius. I argue, further, that it is a reexpression of the Longinian concept, in uniquely Kantian terms, to be sure, even though a vital part of what I take to be the Platonic insight remains.

Kant's account of genius takes up §46–50 of the Critique of Aesthetic Judgment, and we shall work our way through it step by step. I begin by quoting the very first, pithy paragraph of the account, in which Kant essentially "defines" the concept. He writes: "*Genius* is the talent (natural endowment) which gives the rule to art. Since talent, as an innate productive faculty of the artist belongs itself to nature, we may put it this way: *Genius* is the innate mental aptitude (*ingenium*) *through which* nature gives the rule to art."[11]

The leading ideas here are those of genius as the faculty of producing artworks, genius as a natural endowment, and, most intriguing, genius as *giving the rule to art.*

To start with, as Kant makes clear in his initial definition of genius, it is the productive faculty for fine art, *exclusively*. This is in sharp contrast to Gerard, who, in his *Essay on Genius,* says that "Genius is properly the faculty of *invention;* by means of which a man is qualified in making new discoveries in science, or for producing original works of art."[12] It is noteworthy that Gerard is already using the term "science," in the *Essay on Genius,* to mean what we mean by it, and what his predecessors called "natural philosophy." This is apparent from the fact that Newton is his most frequently cited example when "scientific" genius is the topic. So, in sharp contrast with Kant, and later, Schopenhauer, as we have already seen, Gerard characterizes genius, quite rightly, one would think, as covering a far wider range of human activities than merely the fine arts, including not only the theoretical sciences but the practical as well. Just *why* Kant so circumscribed the concept of genius we shall see later on.

The notion of genius as natural endowment is the first of two that seem clearly in harmony with the Longinian tradition, the second being the notion of genius as rule-giver, not rule-follower. That Kant rejected the alternate Platonic route of "inspiration" is already apparent in another of the earlier manuscript *Reflexionen,* where he wrote that "Genius is perhaps not a Daemon, whose inspiration and revelation illuminate."[13] Having said this much about genius as natural endowment, there seems little more to detain us at this point. The more intriguing notion of genius as rule-giver beckons.

Art in general, Kant points out, seems to require some kind of method. In the case of crafts and techniques this is obvious, as Socrates was so fond of reminding all and sundry. "For every art," Kant says, "presupposes rules which are laid down as the foundation which first enables a product, if it is to be called one of art, to be represented as possible." But the fine arts, which is to say, the arts of beauty—*schönen Kunst,* in German—cannot be produced by an ordinary, statable method or set of rules just because the production of fine art is, ipso facto, by definition, the production of beauty. And we know from the "Analytic of the Beautiful" that beauty is that which pleases without a concept—hence cannot have a concept, or set of concepts as the method of its production. "The concept of fine art, however, does not permit of the judgement upon the beauty of its product being derived from any rule that has a *concept* for its determining ground, and that depends, consequently, on a concept of the way in which the product is possible."[14]

But although no method of production is possible for the fine arts—no system of rules or recipes because they are *fine* arts, arts of *beauty*—nevertheless they *are* fine *arts, arts* of beauty, not beautiful objects of nature. They are artifacts, and cannot therefore be without some sense of systematic, intelligent, intentional production. What can that be, on Kant's view? Kant writes, in this regard: "But since, for all that, a product can never be called art unless there is a preceding rule, it follows that nature in the individual (and by nature of the harmony of the faculties) must give the rule to art, i.e. fine art is only possible as a product of genius."[15]

What exactly does all of this mean? Kant sums it up in four explanatory precepts. All seem to encapsulate basic, common intuitions about genius and the arts.

The first precept is that genius cannot be "an aptitude in the way of cleverness for what can be learned according to some rule and that consequently *originality* must be its primary property."[16] In other words, originality, which had become a leading and admired characteristic of genius in the Longinian tradition, follows, on Kant's view, directly from his definition of beauty as being without a concept, and genius, therefore, the producer of beauty, as not susceptible of methodization.

Kant's second observation is that originality is not a sufficient condition for artistic greatness; for "there may also be original nonsense. . . ." (An insightful remark, that!) So there must be something about original artworks that makes their originality valuable. It is, Kant concludes, that they can serve as exemplary models: "and, consequently, though not themselves derived from imitation, they must serve that purpose for others, i.e. as a standard or rule of estimation."[17]

Again, Kant is enunciating here a concept that is part of the Longinian view, although it is expressed with a philosophical depth and systematicity that are new, and peculiarly his. What it means, then, to give the rule to art is not to make up a rule or rules for others to follow, but to create a work, or, perhaps more accurately, a body of works from which, after the fact, a set of rules can be extracted for others to follow — as, for example, Aristotle did in the *Poetics,* for Greek tragedy, or Fux, in the *Gradus ad Parnussum,* for strict counterpoint. The following of such rules would, of course, produce not original works of art but derivative ones. Kant writes of the genius, later on, in pursuing this thought, that

> for other clever minds his example gives rise to a school, that is to say a methodical instruction according to rules, collected, so

far as circumstances permit, from such products of genius and their peculiarities.

And to that extent, fine art is for such persons a matter of imitation, for which nature, through the medium of genius, gave the rule.[18]

But there must be more to "giving the rule" than this: more, that is, to the role that great artworks play as exemplars. For so far I have talked only of their influence on those who, with talent rather than genius, use the rules and methodologies the exemplars spawn to create artworks of less than genius quality. But the history of art, after all, is, in the main, the history of genius's influence on subsequent genius. That cannot work through propagation of rules, since, by definition, genius does not follow them.

Kant is not unaware of the obvious art-historical fact that works of genius are *a* if not *the* prime mover in the work of subsequent geniuses. And he has this to say about it: "the product of genius . . . is an example, not for imitation (for that would mean the loss of the element of genius, and just the very soul of the work), but to be followed by another genius—one whom it arouses to a sense of his own originality in putting freedom from the constraint of rules so into force in his art, that for art itself a new rule is won—which is what shows a talent to be exemplary."[19]

The thought here, I take it, is that the influence of a work of genius on another *genius,* if it is to bear real fruit, cannot be through imitation or the following of rules derived from the work, because that would, of course, result not in another work of genius, even if produced by one, but merely in a derivative, unoriginal exercise. What must happen, rather, Kant conjectures, is that the work of genius somehow awaken in the other an awareness of his own powers, and so to incite him to free creation. Kant, wisely, does not try to tell us how *exactly* this takes place. How could he? Should he provide an associative mechanism, like Gerard's, or some other such explanation, he would be providing for the operation of genius concepts which, ex hypothesi, it cannot, qua genius, operate by. Kant, steady to his text, remains silent. But this too, I think, matches our intuitions. We *do* believe that works of genius stimulate the creative juices of their genius successors. But for all our talk about "influences," what do we really know? A sensible person leaves it there.

The third characteristic of genius, for Kant, is that "It cannot indicate scientifically how it brings about its product, but rather gives the rule as *nature*." It is here that Kant comes closest to the Platonic view. It was Plato's great insight, as I suggested at the outset, that there is no "decision procedure," no instruction manual for writing great poetry, as there is, for example, for making shoes or navigating ships. Even the poets themselves didn't know how they did what they did. Plato's insight into poetry was extended, of course, by Kant's time, to all the fine arts. That insight is what Kant is enunciating here in regard to genius. As he continues the thought: "Hence, where an author owes a product to his genius, he does not himself know how the *ideas* for it have entered into his head, nor has he it in his power to invent the like at pleasure, or methodically, and communicate the same to others in such precepts as would put them in a position to produce similar products." And he concludes, with a nod to the Platonic afflatus, that we sometimes picture genius "as the peculiar guardian spirit given to a man at his birth, by the inspiration of which those original ideas were obtained."[20]

Notwithstanding the reference to "inspiration" (*Eingebung*), however, the tenor of the passage is, as a matter of fact, more Longinian than Platonic. For what Kant is saying is that genius, when spoken of in this way, is nonetheless, *natural* talent, "given to a man at birth"; and talk of it as inspiring a person throughout life as a "guardian spirit" is just a picturesque way of representing the fact that one's inborn talent, one's genius, while it endures, continues to produce original ideas. Furthermore, that the Kantian account of genius includes the Platonic insight that there is no *techne,* no methodology for the production of original poetic, or, later, artistic ideas, is after all an insight that the latter-day Longinians and Platonists share, so is not in itself a defection to the Platonic view.

Kant concludes this four-part characterization of genius with the limitation on it that it appertains to the fine arts alone, and nothing else—and, most emphatically, *not* to natural science. "Nature prescribes the rule through genius not to science but to art, and this also only in so far as it is to be fine art."[21]

It is not for me to linger long here over this extraordinarily misguided view of original scientific discovery. But I cannot notice it without at least discussing it briefly. Here is how Kant expands his thought in this regard:

> all that *Newton* has set forth in his immortal work on the Principles of Natural Philosophy may well be learned, however great a mind it took to find it all out, but we cannot learn to write in a true poetic vein, no matter how complete all the precepts of the poetic art may be, or however excellent its models. The reason is that all the steps that Newton had to take from the first elements of geometry to his greatest and most profound discoveries were such as he could make intuitively evident and plain to follow not only for himself but for every one else. On the other hand no *Homer* or *Wieland* can show how his ideas, so rich at once in fancy and thought, enter and assemble themselves in his brain, for the good reason that he does not himself know, and so cannot teach others.[22]

Perhaps there may be another interpretation of this passage than my own, more charitable to Kant. But as I am obliged to read it, he seems clearly to be confusing a method of displaying with a method for *making* discoveries. Kant, in other words, has mistaken Newton's shop window for his workshop. We know from the historical record that the order in which Newton presents the theorems in the *Principia* is not the order in which they "came to him." Frequently the proofs came long after Newton had come "intuitively" to believe them. And he could no more tell you *how* they came to him, or how you could make such discoveries yourself, than Homer or Wieland could tell you "how his ideas ... enter and assemble themselves in his brain...." The leap of imagination must be there for the scientist as well as for the poet or composer, or anyone else who has a "good idea."

So far, we have seen how Kant characterizes the artistic genius. I now turn to the question of how he characterizes the product of that genius: in particular, how we perceive the work of genius as differing from the work of the mere imitator, or person of taste, no matter how gifted or well schooled. This will round out our discussion of Kant as well as draw the promised connection with Gerard.

Kant says (to get right to the heart of the matter): "Of certain products which are expected, partly at least, to stand on the footing of fine art, we find they are *soul*less; and this, although we find nothing to censure in them as far as taste goes."[23]

I take it that here, as in the foregoing discussion, Kant is trying to capture, philosophically, some common intuition we all have regarding the concept of genius in art. The present case is one which I am sure we have all experienced at one time or another. When confronted with a painting, say, of one of the lesser seventeenth-century Dutch portrait painters or a superbly worked out "academic" fugue, we admire the mastery of technique and tasteful detail but "feel" there is something lacking that we can't quite put a name to. "It's lifeless," we say, or, "It lacks the 'spark' of genius." It is that experience, that intuition that Kant is trying to get at. An earlier age would have called it the *je ne sais quoi,* and left it at that. Kant tries, philosophically, to pin it down, although he is wise enough to know where he must stop.

Kant's notion is that the life or spirit—*Geist* is his word for it—that genius imparts to the work of fine art consists in what Kant calls "aesthetic ideas." An aesthetic idea, in an artwork, is "that representation of the imagination which induces much thought, yet without the possibility of any definite thought whatever, i.e. *concept,* being adequate to it, and which language, therefore, can never quite get on level terms with or render completely intelligible."[24] The imagination is given "an incentive to spread its flight over a whole host of kindred representations that provoke more thought than admits of expression in a concept determined by words."[25] Or, again, the aesthetic idea serves "the proper function . . . of animating the mind by opening out for it a prospect into a field of kindred representations stretching beyond its ken."[26]

It is not inaccurate to characterize what Kant was describing here as a train of ideas or thoughts. That, of course, is the connection with Gerard. I think Kant was well aware of the connection, and that anyone familiar with the Scotsman's theory would both draw it and, perhaps, mistakenly think that Kant was just appropriating, at this point, the well-known (and well-worn) psychological principle of the association of ideas that Gerard had exploited for his own theory of genius. That is why, I am certain, Kant was so quick to distance himself from the traditional doctrine of association *as soon as he introduced his own*. Thus he wrote, with direct reference to the "aesthetic idea . . . which induces much thought," which is to say, ideas of a mental train, "By this means we get a sense of our freedom from the law of association (which attaches to the empirical employment of the imagination), with the result that the material can be borrowed by us from nature in accordance with that law [of association], but be worked up by us into something else—namely, what surpasses nature."[27]

What Kant is saying, here, I take it, is that the train that the aesthetic idea sets up, the train of "more thought than admits of expression in a concept determined by words," may begin with a perfectly ordinary, "empirical" association, or train of them, governed by the empirical "law" of association. But then, in a work of genius, it will "spread its flight," as Kant puts it, and becomes that rich and ineffable train of thought that imparts "spirit" to the work, and gives us intimations of "what surpasses nature"—something, Kant obviously thought, Gerard's empirical association of ideas could never do. Indeed, Kant obviously was suggesting, I think, that the association of ideas is a deterministic psychological mechanism. Hence the image of the work of genius, through its spirit, its Geist, giving us "a sense of our *freedom* from the law of association"—presumably, then, a sense of our freedom of will, which is, indeed, in a distinctly Kantian sense, something that "surpasses nature."

One more step, now, and we have the complete Kantian doctrine of genius, if only in an abbreviated form. For we have yet to see what genius, Geist, the aesthetic idea, the ineffable train of thought have as their ultimate payoff. It is nothing less than beauty and the satisfaction thereof.

In Chapter V, you will recall, where I laid the Kantian foundations for Schopenhauer's Platonic rendition of genius, we came to understand that the pleasure of the beautiful issues out of what Kant characterized as disinterested perception. I left that theory dangling there because we did not need the rest of it for our understanding of Schopenhauer. But we need it now to complete our understanding of Kant's Longinian concept of genius.

It is necessary to be reminded that in the "Analytic of the Beautiful," Kant posed to himself (and to us) the problem of how a judgment—in particular, the pure judgment of taste, of the beautiful—could be, at the same time, merely based upon pleasurable feeling and yet be justly claimed by those who pronounce it as universal in scope. How, that is, one has a right to make a judgment, based merely on one's pleasurable subjective state, and demand or expect the agreement of all others, just as if he were making an "objective" statement about the external world. His answer, briefly, is that, to begin with, we all share the same concepts and cognitions. Our cognitive judgments, based on our concepts held in common, are hence paradigm instances of universal, "objective" judgments. But Kant also thought all our cognitive judgments have, as their prerequisite, so to say, a special relationship between the two human cognitive faculties, understanding and imagination, which Kant called their *harmony* or their *free play* or, sometimes, their *quickening*. When the cognitive faculties are in this relationship, a pleasurable state results. It is a pleasurable state universal among us (under the proper conditions) because we all share these faculties, and the possibility, therefore, of this pleasurable state occurring.

But it is disinterested perception, that is, perception of the beautiful, which puts the cognitive faculties of understanding and imagination into this universally shared harmony, free of any concept. This is established in the Second Moment of the "Analytic of the Beautiful." In Kant's words: "As the subjective universal communicability of the mode of representation in a judgement of taste is to subsist apart from the presupposition of any definite concept, it can be nothing else than the mental state present in the free play of imagination and understanding (so far as these are in mutual accord, as is requisite for *cognition in general*). . . ."[28] This mutual accord amounts, for Kant, to a "common sense" of beauty among us; hence, judgments of the beautiful, pure judgments of taste, *can* be both based on feeling alone, independent of concepts, and yet be universal for all of that. As Kant elegantly puts the conclusion: "We are suitors for agreement from everyone else, because we are fortified with a ground common to all."[29]

But how, you are perhaps beginning to wonder, does this return to unfinished business in the "Analytic of the Beautiful" connect with our present business, which is the doctrine of genius? A brief summation of that doctrine, as we so far have it, will show us how to fit in this final piece of the puzzle.

Genius, Kant tells us, is the innate ability to create works of fine art. The special contribution of genius to fine art is Geist, or spirit, which is what distinguishes fine art in its highest manifestations from art that is merely the product of talent or emulation—perhaps not *literally*, then, fine art at all, but fine art–like. Spirit consists of a chain or process of thought, of extreme richness and depth, for which we can find no adequate description in language: something ineffable.

Genius, then, to repeat, is the faculty that produces fine art in its exemplary form. But recall the German for fine art: *schöne Kunst,* or *beautiful* art. If genius is the ability to create fine art, then it is, eo ipso, the ability to create beauty. And, as we have just seen, a necessary condition for the perception of the beautiful is that the cognitive faculties of understanding and imagination be put into harmony. Fine art, *beautiful* art, must therefore, because it is beauty, do that too. On Kant's view, indeed it does. That is the office of Geist. Spirit, the train of ineffable thought, eventuates in just that harmony of the cognitive faculties Kant has already described in the "Analytic of the Beautiful." As Kant puts it, where poetry is the fine art in question: "In a word, the aesthetic idea is a representation of the imagination, annexed to a given concept, with which, in the free employment of the imagination, such a multiplicity of partial representations are bound up, that no expression indicating a definite concept can be found for it—one which on that account allows a concept to be supplanted in thought by much that is ineffable in words, and the feeling of which quickens the cognitive faculties. . . ."[30] The connecting up of genius, then, to beauty, completes the account of genius, insofar as present purposes require; and that connection to beauty is made complete with the bringing in of the free play, the harmony of the cognitive faculties, referred to here as their "quickening."[31]

It is time now for me to make my conclusion. I began this chapter with the claim that Kant was drawing us a picture, essentially, of the Longinian genius, albeit with original, characteristically Kantian lineaments. But by now, I guess, the attentive reader who recalls that claim will be beginning to have some doubts. For the Longinian concept of genius, from Longinus to Young, has always directly connected genius with the sublime; that has been an ever-present theme. Kant, in contrast, connects genius directly with the beautiful; in our entire account of Kant on genius there has been no need to mention the sublime at all. Surely this anomaly needs to be confronted.

To begin with, it must be observed that Kant associates the sublime most closely with nature, not art (although he allows that some genres may possess it: tragedy and oratorio, for example). Thus, since genius is a faculty of *creation,* of *artistic* creation, it follows that the beautiful will be the principal product.

Nevertheless, Kant's views on the sublime *do* more or less compel him to connect genius principally with the production of the beautiful. Does not this of itself, once and for all, disassociate Kant from the Longinian tradition? I claim not.

I rest my case for a Longinian connection in Kant's theory of genius on two of its pervasive themes: *nature,* and *giving the rule to art.* So pervasive are they, and such powerful images for even the casual reader of the third *Critique,* that (the disassociation of genius from the sublime notwithstanding) I am completely confident that my case rests on the firmest of foundations and is beyond reasonable doubt.

Of course the themes are connected. Genius gives the rule to art, and genius is a natural endowment—hence it is *nature,* in effect, that gives the rule: "Nature prescribes the rule through genius . . . to art."[32]

Now as I pointed out earlier, these two themes, genius as *natural* genius rather than divine inspiration, and genius as somehow, to put it vaguely at first, "free" of the rules, emancipated from their tutelage, as it were, are clearly Longinian ones.[33] But as they stood, in that tradition, their connection was left obscure or, if explored at all, left without much philosophical enlightenment behind. That, if you are "doing what comes naturally," you are liable to inadvertently make mistakes in "grammar" is true enough, yet this is completely absurd as an explanation for a Handel or a Beethoven.

What Kant did in binding together these two notions of genius as natural and genius as "giving the rule" was to make the connection deep, inevitable, and philosophically enlightening. Furthermore, in joining nature with the concept of artistic genius as the imperious lawgiver, Kant was exploiting two of the later nineteenth century's most cherished concepts. They dug deep into the Romantic consciousness.

Without question, the most quotable passages in Kant's aesthetics are those to the effect that genius is what gives the rule to art. It has gained the status of a *bon mot;* if anyone but a philosopher is asked what he or she can remember about Kant's discussion of art and beauty, dollars to donuts that will be what is quoted.

My point is that Kant's assembling together of genius, nature, and the rule of art as the rule of nature constituted a philosophical image so vivid, so commanding, that it made as nothing, really, the disassociation of genius from the sublime. And it was, quintessentially, a Longinian image, not a Platonic one: the genius as possessor of the law, not possessed by the god; the genius of action and power, not the passive genius to whom creation was a "happening," a "seizure," different from a pathological affliction only in that it had a fortunate outcome in the work of art.

Nor should we underestimate the influence this Kantian image imposed on nineteenth-century thought. We have lived through a time in which Kant's *Critique of Judgment* and, particularly, the part that deals with what we would call "aesthetics" was rescued from relative philosophical obscurity, in comparison with the philosopher's other well-known works. But in the nineteenth century, far from being a forgotten work, it was perhaps Kant's most admired and influential: a link to the "supersensible" that the *Critique of Pure Reason* could not provide, so the Romantics saw it, and a worthy starting point or foundation for future philosophy of art.

Thus Kant's philosophy of genius was a commanding presence. And it was so just at the time when a musical genius—indeed, our most potent and long-lived image of musical genius—was gaining absolute ascendancy. I am speaking, of course, of Beethoven, whose glowering visage has dominated our thoughts about what musical genius, indeed, genius itself, must be like in its highest manifestations—what, even, it must *look like*.

Kant's elaborate yet easily "epigrammed" concept of the genius as nature's rule-giver to art seemed to be made for the imperious figure of Beethoven, as his contemporaries and immediate posterity saw him. Or was the figure made for the philosophy? In any case, the two were certainly joined. And it is no surprise that Beethoven's music was closely associated with the sublime, thus rejoining in his person and creations the Kantian theory of genius with the aesthetic category of the sublime, from which Kant had sundered it.

The pendulum was about to swing from the Platonic back to the Longinian, from Mozart the eternal child, chosen by God, Amadeus, to the Longinian Beethoven, power incarnate, the very personification of Nature with a capital "N," that the Romantics so revered. So let us now turn to the imposing figure of Beethoven the Creator, with Kant as our philosophical patron.

VIII

An Unlicked Bear

It was once claimed that Wagner had generated more scholarly literature than any other human being in the history of arts and letters. Apparently Beethoven is not far behind.[1] Material on which to build a picture of Beethoven as the Longinian genius, in the Kantian mode, is therefore not wanting. On the contrary, it is overabundant.

Ironically, the need to paint this picture is inversely proportional to the availability of the materials necessary to do so. For no image of genius in the history of the Western world is more familiar to the ordinary person than that of Beethoven, with the possible exception of Albert Einstein. And in the case of Einstein it is merely the visual image, not the character of the man, that is known, whereas the Beethoven legend of the deaf, distracted, rumpled, and unruly creator is common coin. So to tell this aspect of the Beethoven story is, in a way, only to remind the reader of what he or she already knows.

In redrawing this familiar picture, however, I mean to place it in a philosophical setting. In so doing, I intend to interpret it in ways that will both continue the argument of this book as well as convey to the reader something deeper than the mere amusement or sympathy that such anecdotes are usually designed to do. The story may be familiar, but its philosophical significance, at least as I see it, remains to be revealed.

But if the story is familiar, and if the point of telling it is neither to evaluate its historical accuracy nor to amplify it with newly discovered evidence, then the daunting quantity of the materials need not intimidate us. To tell the familiar story, all that is required is the familiar, readily available sources, and it is those on which I shall rely. What I have to contribute is not a new or amplified story of Beethoven the Creator but my own philosophical interpretation of the old one.

The genius myth that was built up by the German and French Romantics around the figure of Beethoven has, naturally enough, two separate but interrelated aspects: a characterization of the man and a characterization of the music. They are interrelated, of course, because the myth infers the man from the music and the music from the man—or, to put it in a slightly different way, how the Romantics perceived the man influenced how they heard the music, and vice versa. Integrated though the man and the music may be, however, in the myth of the genius, it is necessary for purposes of exposition to separate them out. So I turn first to the Romantic picture of Beethoven, the Longinian genius, as painted by his contemporaries: those who knew him in Vienna. I rely a great deal (but not solely) on O. G. Sonneck's invaluable little volume, *Beethoven: Impressions by His Contemporaries*. I will present this picture in pieces; then, in the end, I will try to put them together into a whole characterization of what I call the Longinian genius in the Kantian mode.

BEETHOVEN WAS A SLOB

No aspect of Beethoven's life in Vienna is more familiar to the casual reader of program notes than the description of Beethoven's slovenly appearance and the deplorably untidy, even dirty conditions in which he lived, in various dwellings in Vienna and its environs. Thus, of Beethoven's abode, Carl Czerny remembers: "The room presented a most disorderly appearance; papers and articles of clothing were scattered everywhere, some trunks, bare walls, hardly a chair, save the wobbly one at the Walter forte-piano (then the best)...."[2] Worse yet is J. G. Prod'homme's description: "Picture to yourself the dirtiest, most disorderly place imaginable—blotches of moisture covered the ceiling; an oldish grand piano, on which the dust disputed the place with various pieces of engraved and manuscript music; under the piano (I do not exaggerate) was an unemptied *pot de nuit*. . . . The chairs, mostly cane-seated, were covered with plates bearing the remains of last night's supper. . . ."[3] And so on.

Of his slovenly manner of dress, composer Louis Schlösser provides this touching account:

> At this encounter I had been surprised at the very outset to find Beethoven, usually so careless about his attire, dressed with unwonted elegance, wearing a blue frock coat with yellow buttons, impeccable white knee-breeches, a vest to match, and a new beaver hat, as usual on the back of his head. . . . I could not resist telling my teacher Mayseder, who lived in the neighborhood, about the striking metamorphosis of Beethoven's elegant appearance, an event which, however, caused Mayseder far less surprise than it had caused me, for he said with a smile: "This is not the first time that his friends have taken his old clothes during the night and laid down new ones in their place; he has not the least suspicion of what has happend and puts on what lies before him *with entire unconcern.*"[4]

The key to the legend of Beethoven's slovenliness both with regard to his surroundings and personal appearance is given by Schlösser in his concluding phrase: *with complete unconcern*. Beethoven was completely oblivious to his physical surroundings, so took no notice that his rooms were dirty and his clothes rumpled. *His mind was somewhere else,* and this connects up with or is a special case of a second quality of Beethoven's character as genius.

BEETHOVEN WAS AN ECSTATIC

He was "distracted." When he was so, it was because he was in the throes of creation.

Here is Ferdinand Ries's account of an afternoon walk with the master.

Throughout our walk he had hummed and, in part howled, up and down the scale as we went along, without singing any individual notes.... When we entered the room [in Döblingen] he ran to the piano without taking off his hat. I sat down in a corner and soon he had forgotten me. Then he raged on the keys for at least an hour. At last he rose, was surprised to see me there and said: "I cannot give you a lesson today; I still have work to do."[5]

Another walking companion, an English visitor, Edward Schulz, tells us that Beethoven "seemed quite lost in himself, and only hummed in an unintelligible manner."[6]

Anton Schindler, Beethoven's wannabe amanuensis and notorious maker of fabrications, gives us perhaps the most vivid picture we have of the ecstatic genius in the throes of musical composition.

> In the living-room, behind a locked door, we heard the master singing parts of the fugue in the *Credo* [of the *Missa Solemnis*]—singing, howling, stamping. After we had been listening a long time to this almost awful scene, and were about to go away, the door opened and Beethoven stood before us with distorted features, calculated to excite fear. He looked as if he had been in mortal combat with the whole host of contrapuntists, his everlasting enemies. His first utterances were confused, as if he had been disagreeably surprised at our having overheard him.[7]

I mention that Schindler was well known for his inaccuracies and even downright inventions to remind the reader that historical *truth* is not the issue here. Indeed, the less truth there is in the stories, the more they support my thesis, which is that the Beethoven legend, like the Handel and Mozart ones, is theory-driven: a philosophy or ideology of genius lies behind it, namely, the Longinian, as reinterpreted by Kant. And if the facts do not entirely fit the theory, it is the facts that must be altered to suit.

Furthermore, the picture of Beethoven the composer as Beethoven the ecstatic, essentially "absent from the premises," spills over, not surprisingly, into Beethoven the performer. For the performer as improviser made a deep and lasting impression on Beethoven's contemporaries. Prod'homme averred, "unless one has heard him improvise well and quite at ease, one can but imperfectly appreciate the vast scope of his genius."[8] And, of course, the improviser is the genius-performer in the act of *composition,* of artistic *creation,* whom Bettina von Arnim portrays in this wise, at the piano: "Suddenly his surroundings were completely forgotten, and his soul expanded in a universal sea of harmony."[9]

That Beethoven was distracted, "absent from the premises," was also described—and note the way ordinary language puts it—as his being "absent-minded." Thus Ries observes that "in the taverns which he was most accustomed to frequent, all came to know his oddities and his absent-mindedness, and let him say and do what he wished, even permitting him to leave without paying his bill."[10] Why was his mind absent from the premises? The assumption was, of course, that it inhabited, in those times, the "place" where he created.

But could there have been a more prosaic reason for this apparent forgetfulness and inattention? Of course there was one; it, however, was not allowed to remain prosaic, and became, in time, a major component of the sublime Longinian genius that Beethoven was in the process of evolving into in the eyes of his contemporaries and immediate posterity.

BEETHOVEN WAS DEAF

If the ordinary citizen knows *anything* else about Beethoven besides the fact that he was a composer, it is at least *that.* A deaf composer: forever a startling, awe-inspiring image! Beethoven himself used his purported absentmindedness as a coverup for his deafness, Ries says. "He was so sensitive about his incipient deafness, that one had to be very careful about calling his attention to his deficiency by talking loudly. When he did not understand something he usually blamed absentmindedness to which he really was subject in the highest degree."[11]

Of course it is easy to confuse absentmindedness with deafness, for deafness seems sometimes as if to absent one from the company. Ries affirms that Beethoven truly was absentminded. But did the impression of absentmindedness feed on the growing deafness (with a little help from Beethoven)? Actually, it doesn't much matter, because the deafness itself, even more than the absentmindedness, became an essential, integral part of the Longinian genius myth that Beethoven was coming to embody—indeed, its most important part.

The image of the deaf Beethoven now joined that of the blind Homer (another "sublime," Longinian genius) as somehow symbolic of the artistic enterprise at its very highest level. In a wonderfully Romantic film called *Eroica* (1949), there is a moving scene in which Beethoven is depicted trying to conduct a rehearsal of one of his works. The camera becomes his eyes, so we can see what the conductor sees, and the soundtrack is *silent,* to tell us what he *hears*—which is to say, *nothing.* The ensemble breaks down, and the composer becomes disconsolate. A friend (Amenda) consoles him. God, of course, has taken away his physical hearing so that his immaterial ear can hear spiritual sounds that no one else has heard and bring them down to us. As Victor Hugo paints the picture, in the most vividly Romantic colors: "The symphonies of Beethoven are emissions of [cosmic] harmony, and these gleaming, tender, and profound symphonies, these marvels of euphony, have sprung from a head whose ear is dead. It is as if we saw a blind god who creates suns."[12]

But however comforting it may be to think your affliction is meant to be a blessing rather than a curse, in human terms, nevertheless, it is something that must be overcome. And in the case of a deaf composer the challenge could hardly be greater to the task at hand. It is, indeed, a *heroic* overcoming.

BEETHOVEN WAS A HERO

Certainly, the most well-known written document of Beethoven's life, the so-called *Heiligenstadt Testament* of 1802, expresses, along with a quite understandable and to be forgiven strain of self-pity, a truly heroic resolve to overcome.[13] Of his affliction he wrote: "How could I admit the weakness of a sense, that, in me, should be keener than in most,—a sense that at one time I possessed in full perfection,—a perfection such as few in my profession have ever enjoyed."[14]

The suicidal impulse is certainly here, along with the self-pity. Both are overcome, however, by the heroic resolve: ". . . I was on the brink of taking my life," the composer tells us; "Art alone hindered me. It

AN UNLICKED BEAR

seemed inconceivable that I should leave this world, without having produced all that I felt I must. And so I go on, leading this miserable life. . . ." Thus Beethoven characterizes himself in heroic terms: a man "who in spite of all natural obstacles has striven to keep his place in the ranks of worthy artists and men."[15]

The *Heiligenstadt Testament* is not the only "document" of Beethoven's authorship that connects him directly with the heroic. The other is, needless to say, the Third Symphony, the *Eroica:* "about" a hero, originally dedicated to one, and "heroic" in "content" and "stature." It is the most important work in the evolution of Beethoven's style, and one of the most important in the history of Western art music. As the late Paul Henry Lang said of it, "one of the incomprehensible deeds in arts and letters. . . . [T]he Eroica simply dwarfs everything in its boldness of conception, breadth of execution, and intensity of logical structure."[16] An incomprehensible deed, to be sure—also, one wants to say, a *heroic* deed.

Furthermore, from the *Eroica* onward, Beethoven's music comes to be seen by the Romantics as particularly expressive of the heroic as no other music before. Indeed, the so-called middle or second of the three periods into which Beethoven's work is still divided, at least in the popular musical literature, more often than not is referred to as the *heroic* period.

Schlösser saw Beethoven as "the insuperable tonal hero, accorded the most devoted reverence by all classes, whose genius, by striking the shackles from the infinity of the psychic had called into being a new era of culture. . . ."[17] And Prod'homme was so exultant over having been granted an audience by the unapproachable, morose, and solitary genius that he crowed: "I took my leave, feeling prouder than Napoleon when he entered Vienna. I had made the conquest of Beethoven!"[18] He conquered the hero whose one-time hero had conquered Europe, and it is a measure of the two heroes that the former conquest was deemed the greater.

But a hero must, by and by, die a hero's death. So indeed does Beethoven Hero (to appropriate Scott Burnham's title).[19] Anselm Hüttenbrenner, who claimed to have been an eyewitness to the deathbed scene, conveyed this description to Beethoven's great biographer,

Alexander Weelock Thayer, in 1860. It is theatrical, heroic in the extreme—and very hard to credit—at least in its more hystrionic details. But historical truth, after all, is not our quarry—a philosophy of genius *is,* and that philosophy is most vividly highlighted by this most Romantic of Beethoven anecdotes. It is, after all, a quintessentially Romantic philosophy.

> After Beethoven had lain unconscious, the death-rattle in his throat from 3 o'clock in the afternoon till after 5, there came a flash of lightning accompanied by a violent clap of thunder, which garishly illuminated the death-chamber. . . . After this unexpected phenomenon of nature, which startled me greatly, Beethoven opened his eyes, lifted his right hand and looked up for several seconds with his fist clenched and a very serious, threatening expression as if he wanted to say: "Inimical powers, I defy you! Away with you! God is with me!" It also seemed as if, like a brave commander, he wished to call out to his wavering troops: "Courage, soldiers! Forward! Trust me! Victory is assured!" When he let the raised hand sink to the bed, his eyes closed half-way. . . . The genius of the great master of tones fled from this world of delusion into the realm of truth. . . .[20]

It is almost impossible to avoid the impression that the author of this purple passage has merged the figure of Beethoven, the commander of tones, into his one-time hero, commander of armies (or is it, by this time, the *other* commander who, after all, prevailed in the end?). In any case, it need hardly be argued that what is depicted here is the death of Beethoven Hero.

One wonders why thunder and lightning were not enough. They were enough for Beethoven's attending physician, Dr. Wawruch, who describes the last moments in this wise: "Toward six in the afternoon came a flurry of snow, with thunder and lightning—Beethoven Died.—Would not a Roman augur, in view of the accidental commotion of the elements, have taken his apotheosis for granted?"[21] Why the clenched fist raised in defiance of God almighty?

Well, if the heroic mold into which Beethoven is being poured is the Napoleonic one, and that seems the most reasonable candidate,

AN UNLICKED BEAR

then it is a *rebel* hero whom we are talking about. Beethoven Hero is Beethoven Rebel, which comports well with both the man and the composer.

BEETHOVEN DEFIANTLY DISOBEYED "THE RULES"

That Beethoven was seen as a musical law-breaker by his contemporaries and immediate posterity I will say more about when we turn from the man to the music. What concerns us now is Beethoven's "heroic rebellion" in his personal life. It seemed to express itself in two ways: socially and politically. He would not observe the social conventions. When this involved his equals or inferiors, it was merely social rebellion; but when directed against the aristocracy, of course, it took on political significance.

Not to put too fine a point on it, Beethoven was uncouth. Luigi Cherubini called him "an unlicked bear."[22]

But there was also a sense of superiority, not merely toward people of the "lower orders"—his servants never lasted very long on the job—but apparently toward his social equals as well. Because of this, as is well known, his relations with Haydn were strained. "His youthful arrogance was particularly hard to be borne by a man of Haydn's age and the older master used to refer jokingly to Beethoven as 'that Great Mogul.'"[23]

By far the most significant manifestation of Beethoven's rebellion against the customs and mores of society was his treatment of the Viennese aristocracy, and surprising in the extreme was the willingness of this company to acquiesce in it. Beethoven got away with murder. Concerning the former, the composer Anton Reicha wrote of Beethoven: "to give you an idea of how careless he is of convention it will suffice to tell you that the Empress. . . . sent him a request to visit her one morning; he responded that he would be occupied all day, but would try to come the day after."[24] And in the latter regard, Ferdinand Ries wrote:

> Etiquette and all that etiquette implies was something Beethoven never knew and never wanted to know. As a result, his behavior when he first began to frequent the palace of Archduke

Rudolph often caused the greatest embarrassment to the latter's entourage. An attempt was made to coerce Beethoven into the deference he was supposed to observe.... One day, finally, when he was again, as he termed it, being "sermonized on court manners," he very angrily pushed his way up to the Archduke, and said quite frankly that though he had the greatest possible reverence for his person, a strict observance of all the regulations to which his attention was called every day was beyond him. The Archduke laughed good-humoredly over the occurrence, and commanded that in the future Beethoven be allowed to go his way unhindered; he must be taken as he was.[25]

Such stories of Beethoven's rudeness to his "betters" constitute, by far, the largest class of anecdotes of his personal life—at least, that is my impression. And whether or not they are exaggerated, in retrospect, by his friends and acquaintances, they tell us something very important about the figure of Beethoven Hero, the Romantic version of the Longinian genius: he is a child of the Revolution; his "rudeness" is ideological, not merely the bumptiousness of an untamed Caliban.

It would be tedious to multiply these anecdotes of aristocrat-bashing, but the picture would not be complete if the most famous and most revealing of them were absent. According to Bettina von Arnim, Beethoven and Goethe were walking in Teplitz when

> there came towards them the whole court, the Empress and the dukes; Beethoven said: "Keep hold of my arm, they must make room for us, not we for them." Goethe was of a different opinion, and the situation became awkward for him; he let go of Beethoven's arm and took a stand at the side with his hat off, while Beethoven with folded arms walked right through the dukes and only tilted his hat slightly while the dukes stepped aside to make room for him and all greeted him pleasantly....

When Goethe catches up, Bettina quotes Beethoven as saying to him: "... I've waited for you because I honour and respect you as you deserve, but you did those yonder too much honour."[26]

If this story is true—and Bettina von Arnim is not a paragon of reliability—it may have elicited the following comment from Goethe, in a letter to Zelter (a musician whom Beethoven highly respected): "I made the acquaintance of Beethoven in Teplitz. His talent amazed me. However, unfortunately, he is an utterly untamed personality, not at all in the wrong, if he finds the world detestable, but he thereby does not make it more enjoyable either for himself or others."[27]

Regardless of the politically revolutionary aspects of Beethoven's convention-breaking behavior, the image of the unlicked bear, or, as Goethe put it, the "untamed personality," has perhaps another implication, and connects up with another of Beethoven's frequently documented character traits. Beethoven, the unlicked bear, the untamed personality, might also be characterized as William S. Newman does: "a wild but innocent child of nature."[28] The unlicked bear sought its natural habitat.

BEETHOVEN'S ORIGINAL MUSICAL IDEAS CAME TO HIM IN THE OPEN AIR AND NATURAL SURROUNDINGS

Beethoven, so the stories go, loved nature. He was an inveterate walker. There was, of course, nothing extraordinary in that. It was a sign of the times: a harbinger of Romanticism. Just as Handel's environment was the opera house and the streets of London and Mozart's the Prater, Beethoven's was the Vienna woods.

What *is* extraordinary in the stories about Beethoven's nature walks is that they tell us his musical ideas came to him primarily in the open air, on these daily excursions into field and forest. Thus, his very first biographer, Johann Aloys Schlosser, claimed (1827–28), ". . . Beethoven liked to compose outdoors: there he could best find ideas. When they came, he treasured them as the inspirations of the moment but did not concern himself with developing them immediately. While still outdoors, however, he would commit them to paper and would continue them on his way home and once at home."[29] And Louis Schlösser quotes Beethoven himself as to the source of his musical ideas: "I could almost grasp them in my hands, in Nature's open, in the woods, during my promenades, in the silence of the night, at earliest dawn."[30]

What is extraordinary about these stories is that it should matter whether a *composer* receives his musical ideas out of doors rather than in his study. If we are told that one painter works in her studio and another in the open air, we would take the remark not merely as anecdotal but as possessing aesthetic import. It is clear why it makes an artistic difference whether an artist paints wildflowers in sunlight or an arranged still-life indoors. But what possible artistic difference could it make if a composer thought of a theme while looking at a copse of trees or at lined music paper?

Most of the anecdotes about Beethoven's open-air composing do not make anything more of it than an interesting quirk of the master. But the connection between nature loving or even nature worship and the Romantic ideology of genius is too important for us to think that these tales of Beethoven's rambles in the woods, growling melodies to himself (as one companion pictures the composer[31]), are merely anecdotal and not philosophy-driven.

We shall return later on to the role Nature, with a capital "N," plays in the Romantics' Longinian picture of Beethoven Genius. But at this point we now have enough facets of the composer's supposed personality in place for me to make a preliminary, general assessment of the picture they combine to project, and to ask how consistent that picture so far is with the Longinian one, as we understand it from our previous account. Of course, the Romantics are going to ring some changes on it, although it will, I trust, remain recognizable and intact.

The first three character traits of Beethoven on my list are, it should be noted, consistent *both* with the Platonic, inspiration picture of genius, and with the Longinian, "natural," sublime one. Beethoven's untidy, even squalid living quarters and his rumpled, careless attire bespeak a complete lack of interest in those "mundane" conditions of ordinary life. But such disregard could just as well be the result of possession by the god as the flight of the sublime genius to regions too difficult and inaccessible for mere mortals to attain. And since the distraction that that disregard betokens is merely a special case of the ecstatic state, that Beethoven *was* an ecstatic is also compatible with either Platonic inspiration or Longinian concentration. In either case, the genius is "absent from the premises."

But likewise the deafness. Without in the least denying its reality (although how deaf Beethoven was at any given time, and when or if it became total, are still disputed questions), the deafness became for the Romantics a powerful metaphor for the composer's musical genius. And the deafness, per se, could function either as a Platonic or a Longinian metaphor. The gist of the metaphor is that Beethoven's outer ear being closed, he was able to hear with an "inner ear" the otherwise inaccessible but marvelous sounds that he then recorded in his sublime compositions. With the tumult of worldly cacophony no longer present to distract him, the master could hear what no one had heard before. What *did* he hear? Perhaps he was thus enabled to hear the still, small voice of God, which the sounds of this world deny to others: the Platonic reading. Or perhaps his deafness liberated him from the sounds of this world so that "With this music we enter a new world, which he was to conquer triumphantly":[32] the Longinian trope. The deafness metaphor can go either way.

However, the second trio of Beethoven's character traits is unequivocally Longinian. Beethoven is a hero. He fights to create, overcoming all enemies and obstacles. Beethoven Hero is an active creative agent, the inspired Platonic artist, a passive instrument of the god. Beethoven Hero is the epitome of the Longinian.

So too is Beethoven the scofflaw. We will know that for a certainty when we come, in a moment, to the description of Beethoven's works by his contemporaries and immediate successors. For our scofflaw, at this point, is merely the social and political rebel, not the musical one. But the man in the myth is prelude to the music, and Beethoven the *musical* scofflaw, a vital part of the Longinian picture, is waiting in the wings.

Finally, the peculiar notion of Beethoven's ideas coming to him in the outdoors while he communes with nature is not exactly inconsistent with the Platonic model, but, at the very least, it seems completely *irrelevant* to it. The whole point of the inspiration theory is that the god can take possession of you anywhere, anytime—in the bathtub or in the barbershop. So why *particularly* in natural surroundings? There must be something else at work here, and the fact that the Longinian concept of genius is "natural genius" gives us a hint to follow up on.

To summarize these preliminary sketches of Beethoven's mythic character, the first three traits are consistent with both the Platonic and Longinian pictures of genius, the second three only with the Longinian one. In the interest of consistency, though, it would be reasonable for us to give a Longinian spin on the first three as well, thus reaching the tentative conclusion that the mythic Beethoven was a thoroughly Longinian character.

However, when we press on, now, to a consideration of Beethoven's music as understood by his contemporaries and early enthusiasts, we will see that, far from being a tentative conclusion, the idea that Beethoven and his creations were seen in the Longinian mold is supported by overwhelmingly conclusive evidence, making the evidence for a Longinian Handel or Platonic Mozart, convincing though I think it was, paltry in comparison.

To begin with the most obvious evidence, descriptions of Beethoven's music abound with the two key words "sublime" and "grand." Thus Balzac refers to the "sublime productions" of Beethoven.[33] Berlioz describes a passage from the Fourth Symphony as "this sublime page of the giant of music."[34] Poet Alfred de Vigny says: "Sublime flight toward unknown worlds becomes the habit of his soul."[35] "Sublime divagations" and "sublime lamentations" are terms in which the critic Henri Blaze de Bury describes Beethoven's works.[36] And, perhaps needless to say, the descriptions transfer to the man himself. He was "The great man, with his head suggestive of Olympian sublimity . . . ,"[37] "the most sublime of them all, Beethoven,"[38] and so on.

Such examples could be multiplied indefinitely, to no useful purpose. But, to indulge in just one more, it is of some interest to us to observe that not only are the words and concepts of sublimity and grandeur still in place and available to characterize Beethoven's productions, but the distinction between the sublime and beautiful, so characteristic of the Longinian craze in the eighteenth century, was still at least implicitly appealed to after Beethoven's death, one of the most revealing instances of this being the following passage from Schlosser's biography, in which, significantly enough for our argument, Mozart the Platonic genius takes on the mantle of Beethoven's opposite number: thus, Beethoven the sublime, Mozart the beautiful.

Schlösser writes: "it seems natural to compare Mozart and Beethoven. The former delights us by the perfection of execution; the latter excels by the grandiose concept of his creations."[39]

Far more important, though, than that the word "sublime" surfaces with boring regularity in descriptions of Beethoven's music is how it is described when the "S" word is absent. For it is then that we see just what the sublime had become for the Romantic movement.

It is, of course, not surprising that Beethoven's compositions were almost invariably described as large and powerful, whether or not "sublime" or "grand" was part of the description. In his funeral oration, Grillparzer spoke of the many instances in which "the force of his creations overwhelms you like a rushing tempest . . .";[40] and of his improvisations, conductor Ignaz Seyfried wrote:

> When once he began to revel in the infinite world of tones, he was transported also above all earthly things; his spirit had burst all restricting bonds, shaken off the yokes of servitude, and soared jubilantly into the luminous spaces of the higher aether. Now his playing tore along like a wildly foaming cataract, and the conjurer constrained his instrument to an utterance so forceful that the stoutest structure was scarcely able withstand it. . . .[41]

The large, the powerful, the tempestuous, the dangerous, the terrifying are, of course, common coin in eighteenth-century concepts of the sublime, from Addison to Burke. What is remarkably new in the Romantics' descriptions of the Beethovenian sublime is the "astronomical"—the size, the power, and the rest now reached, in Beethoven, "astronomical proportions." It becomes a commonplace to describe Beethoven as dwelling among stars, suns, and celestial spheres, bringing their harmony back with him to earth in his sublime compositions. Furthermore, it is but a small step, for the Romantics, as for the rest of us, from the astronomical to the infinite. As Leo Schrade noted, "The romantics it was who 'discovered' the infinite."[42] "It is in Beethoven that this element seems first to have revealed itself to the French romantics, and it was Berlioz who first discovered it there."[43] In Berlioz' words, "His glances are directed into space; and he flies toward the suns, singing the praises of infinite nature."[44] Or, again, in the words of another great figure of the Romantic movement, Victor Hugo, "This deaf man heard the infinite."[45]

Now it is the argument of this book not only that Handel, Mozart, and Beethoven, respectively, came to symbolize Longinian genius, Platonic genius, and Longinian genius yet again, but also that these incarnations of the genius myth were driven by philosophy: in Handel's case, the British philosophers' version of Longinus on the sublime, in Mozart's case Schopenhauer, in Beethoven's Kant. So it must be my task, in this chapter, to show not merely that Beethoven was seen during his lifetime and after his death as a genius in the Longinian mold, but also that this interpretation of the man and the music has upon it the trademark of Kant. I say this now because, as we shall see, that the Beethovenian sublime is the *infinite* sublime makes a crucial connection to the third *Critique*. Readers familiar with that work will have already seen this connection. Others will see it soon enough, when I present my argument for the Kantian implications of the Beethoven genius myth. But before I undertake that argument, there remain some missing portions of the picture to paint.

What goes hand in hand with the notion of the sublime artwork, we recall, is the flawed artwork: the genius of the sublime is negligent of the rules of "correct" composition. No artist that I know of more perfectly exemplifies this than Beethoven; for no artist that I know of was more vilified in his lifetime, or more admired afterward, for breaking the artistic commandments, of which music, perhaps, has more than its fair share.

That Beethoven was a social and political scofflaw we already know. That this rebellious attitude was also seen to express itself in his compositional practice is not very hard to document.

The difficulty that Beethoven's early auditors had with his "unruly" music is well known. Composer Johann Wenzel Tomaschek complains: "Harmony, counterpoint, eurythm, and particularly musical aesthetics, he did not seem to have overly much at heart; hence his larger works are defaced by occasional trivialities."[46] And a far better, more renowned composer than Tomaschek, Louis Spohr, writes of Beethoven's late works: "His constant endeavour to be original and to open new paths, could no longer, as formerly, be preserved from error by the guidance of the ear."[47]

The early French critics were particularly offended by Beethoven's breaking of the rules. Paul Scudo upbraids the composer for being negligent of the "essential laws of harmony" and paying too little attention to "proportions of the parts."[48] The artist Delacroix, too, shared Scudo's distaste for the composer's lack of "correctness" and "rigorous proportions."[49] Such misjudgments are the stock in trade of the anecdotal literature and are well documented (with purposeful emphasis on the negative) in Nicholas Slonimsky's humorous classic, *The Lexicon of Musical Invective*.[50]

Far more important—indeed, of the essence—is the *positive* spin that the Romantics and other early enthusiasts of Beethoven's genius put on his breaking of the rules. That there were grammatical mistakes in Handel's "sublime" compositions was a continual *complaint* of his contemporaries, and such lapses were seen as regrettable, even by his admirers, although necessary in the circumstances. Beethoven, however, very early on in his posthumous "appreciation history," was *admired* by his more advanced listeners for his rule-breaking, even while others were still clucking over his musical "ain'ts." This marks a new philosophical outlook, and Kant, as I shall argue, provided the foundations for this Romantic attitude.

The late works were, of course, the difficult ones to accept even for listeners who had managed to assimilate those of the early and middle periods. They were seen, more than any of Beethoven's other compositions, as flouting the accepted rules of musical grammar and form. But there were also listeners who saw these compositions as the more awesome and admirable for their breaking of what might just as well be thought of as oppressive constraints on originality. After all, rebellion was in the air.

Schrade, in this regard, tells of musician J. B. Sabattier's valiant defense and sponsorship of the later quartets.

> At the very time when Scudo condemns the later works, J. B. Sabattier pleads for the last quartets. Some have found it con-

venient, he says, to assert that the "sublime chief works" are "baroque." The form of these compositions is indeed too free, too far beyond scholastic rules not to astound all those who had trouble even in understanding Beethoven's earliest chamber music. Sabattier blames the petty "spirit of routine" that despotically rules all contemporary arts; the spirit of going along in the good old ways.... He [Beethoven] was forced to "break the rules," for "always the form must be subordinate to the idea."[51]

That Beethoven the man was, self-consciously, a social and political nonconformist—a subverter of the rules and customs of ordinary human intercourse, even between commoner and aristocrat—the myth makes clear. That the music at times flouted the laws of musical syntax and form is obvious enough as well. That Beethoven the artist was quite aware of what he was doing when he departed from musical "decorum" is a crucial aspect of the story as well.

Two anecdotes about Beethoven's expressed attitude toward his breaking of "the rules" are particularly relevant. The first, perhaps my favorite of all Beethoven stories, comes from Thayer, quoting Czerny. Pianist and composer Anton Halm

> "once brought a sonata of his own composition to him [Beethoven]," says Czerny, "and when Beethoven pointed out a few errors, Halm retorted that he (B.) had also permitted himself many violations of the rules. Beethoven answered: 'I may do it, but not you.'"[52]

The second story is told by Ferdinand Ries:

> Once, while out walking with him, I mentioned two perfect [parallel?] fifths, which stand out by their beauty of sound in one of his earlier violin quartets, in C minor. Beethoven did not know of them and insisted I was wrong to call them fifths. Since he was in the habit of always carrying music-paper about him, I asked for some and set down the passage in all four parts. Then when he saw I was right he said: "Well, and who has forbidden them?" Since I did not know how I was to take his question, he

repeated it several times until, much astonished, I replied: "It is one of the fundamental rules." Again he repeated his question, whereupon I said: "Marburg, Kirnberger, Fuchs, etc., etc., all the theoreticians!" "And *so I allow them!*" was his answer.[53]

The two punchlines, "I may do it, but not you," and "so I allow them," provide, of course, the aesthetic morals of these two stories. They are different but related morals, and, I shall argue, they are both Kantian morals: they provide another link to Kant's theory of genius and constitute my second promissory note in that regard, to be paid in full at the conclusion of this chapter. However, two more pieces of the Longinian puzzle must be put in place before we can get to that.

First of all, it will be recalled that in Longinus' text, as in subsequent theories more or less derived from it in the eighteenth century, the power of the sublime genius was frequently analogized to the power of a god: the sublime genius was a godlike being, bringer and breaker of the law. This, of course, follows from both rule-breaking and the power trope. In Beethoven, the analogy becomes exaggerated to an extreme degree through superheated Romantic rhetoric: it is almost as if in Beethoven's case, the god*like* creator has become a god in fact.

Berlioz' favorite image of Beethoven is "the indefatigable eagle": "How he hovers and balances in his harmonious sky! He dives into it, soars, descends again, disappears; then returns to his starting place, his eye more brilliant, his wings stronger, intolerant of rest, quivering, *athirst for the infinite.*"[54] For Victor Hugo, Schrade relates, ". . . Beethoven became an inhabitant of the infinite, dwelling in the spheres, being part of them. . . ."[55] And Berlioz' friend Joseph d'Ortigue simply declares ". . . Beethoven a supernatural being."[56]

Beethoven's devoted friends and casual acquaintances openly worshiped the master. Ludwig Rellstab describes "the hope of seeing Beethoven" as "the greatest of all"; and when he finds himself at the composer's door, it is "the sacred threshold," "the sacred portal" of the being he "so profoundly reverenced."[57]

Wilhelmine Schröder-Devrient, Beethoven's Leonore of 1822, wrote of "the veneration I have vowed and shall continue to vow his lofty spirit as long as I live."[58] He was "accorded the most devoted reverence by all classes . . ." said Louis Schlösser,[59] and tenor August Röckel, Beethoven's second Floristan, stated that ". . . I was ready to kneel at his feet."[60]

What is truly remarkable, indeed unique in the Beethoven genius myth is the role played by the composer's visual appearance, represented in the graphic arts and in sculpture, both during his lifetime and in the century following. I know of nothing else even remotely like it in the history of arts and letters. One can quite literally *see* the progress from Beethoven the man to Beethoven the hero to, finally, Beethoven the god. Beethoven becomes, in the process, a work of art himself. As William S. Newman remarks in his brief but pithy visual history of what he calls "the Beethoven mystique," "If it was the critics and philosophers who created and defined [it], . . . it was the painters and sculptors who gave it its sense of immediacy."[61]

It would be going beyond the limits of this study to treat the visual history of Beethoven Genius in any thoroughness or detail. But at least an idea of the progress from man to superman can be conveyed in the following three figures. In the first, a portrait by Isidor Neugass (circa 1806), we see a conventional representation of the successful, thirty-six-year-old composer (Figure 3). If there is a hint of genius, it is only, perhaps, in the intensity of the gaze. The dress is, one presumes, conventional for one in Beethoven's social status and class.

But now regard the portrait by Joseph Carl Stieler (1819–20). The composer is now fifty, the score of the *Missa solemnis* in his left hand (Figure 4). The intensity of the gaze remains. But gone is the suggestion of conventional, middle-class "success in one's profession." We now have the two visual symbols that made the face of Beethoven the face of genius itself: the wild, electric hair and the world-shattering frown—the most famous frown in the history of art.

This is Beethoven Hero: not, mind you, a knight in shining armor on a white charger, but the rebel at the barricades, the barbarian at the gates. You don't want to cross this man. He can destroy you with one withering glance. The Viennese were genuinely afraid of him, and many were the petitioners at his door who could have said, along with

Figure 3. Portrait of Beethoven by Isidor Neugass, circa 1806. By permission of the Beethoven-Haus Bonn, Collection H. C. Bodmer, photographer.

Figure 4. Portrait of Beethoven by Joseph Karl Stieler, 1820. By permission of Beethoven-Haus Bonn, Collection H. C. Bodmer, photographer.

AN UNLICKED BEAR

Ludwig Rellstab, "as I stepped timidly over the sacred threshold, I could hear my heart beat."[62]

Deification came later, after a decent interval of mannerist exaggeration. And one has little trouble in choosing the artist who placed Beethoven decisively in the ranks of the immortal gods. It was sculptor Max Klinger, whose statue of Beethoven on his throne, with his eagle at his feet (1902), requires no words to argue the point (Figure 5).

But Beethoven the god was not, in the myth, Beethoven God. If he was *a* god, he wasn't God. What was his relation to the Deity? Where did Beethoven stand in the Romantic theology? The answer to this question will put the finishing touches on our picture of Beethoven Genius and will, as well, answer a question left outstanding early on: Why does Beethoven Genius get his musical ideas in the open air, communing with nature?

Who or what *was* the Romantics' God? That is hardly a difficult question to answer. For many, He (or She?) was Nature with a capital "N." Pantheism and Nature worship were staples of the Romantic movement. It was the Romantics, after all, who rediscovered Spinoza, that enigmatic figure in Western philosophy: atheist to the Enlightenment, God-intoxicated to them.

Indeed, at least one of Beethoven's contemporaries, Anton Schindler, although (as I have remarked before) a less than impeccable authority, suggested that Beethoven had a kind of "Nature Religion." "It may be said with some measure of certainty that his religious beliefs were based less on church dogma. . . . Without visualizing any artificially made theory, he yet all too plainly recognized God in the world and the world in God. His theory in this connection shaped itself up for him in nature as a whole. . . ."[63] Such a religion as Schindler sketched for Beethoven comports well, of course, with the latter's frequently remarked upon love of nature. And whether this really was Beethoven's religion, or one of Schindler's many fabrications, it is just the religion that Beethoven ought to have had, according to the philosophical theory driving the Romantic characterization of his genius. For our purposes, furthermore, it is what philosophy demands of Beethoven's religion, not what history determines it to be, that is of the essence.

Figure 5. Statue of Beethoven, 1902, by Max Klinger. Photograph by Christoph Sandig.

Now if I am correct in characterizing the Beethoven myth as in the Longinian mode, it should come as no surprise that in reference to Beethoven, the word "inspiration," and its surrounding concepts, are infrequently applied. For they are, of course, part and parcel of the Platonic tradition, not the Longinian one. Nevertheless, these Platonic notions were also rife among the Romantics. As Schrade says,

"The romantics looked upon the musician, the poet, the artist, as beings possessed by a god. Inspiration was derived from a supernatural, divine source. Thus the musician was fancied to be in constant conversation with divinity."[64] And, not surprisingly, Goethe, devoted to the "inspiration" metaphor, *was* one of those who applied it to Beethoven. To Bettina von Arnim, Goethe wrote of the composer, "before that which is uttered by one possessed of such a daemon, an ordinary layman must stand in reverence, . . . for here the gods are at work strewing seeds for future discernment. . . ."[65]

But put it the case that Beethoven *is* possessed by the god. What is the god possessing him? Surely it is not implausible in the present context to suggest that it is the Nature-god, given the pantheistic leanings and reverence of the Romantics for Nature. In other words, to be "inspired" by God is to be inspired by Nature. Furthermore, this, then, makes it understandable why Beethoven gets his musical ideas in his communion with Nature. For in communing with Nature he is communing with God; he is God-possessed.

As well, in an intriguing way, this Romanticized, Naturalized Platonism is perfectly consistent with the Longinian picture of genius. For the Longinian, genius is a natural gift; for the Platonist, an inspiration from the gods. But where God and Nature are one, an inspiration from God *is* a natural gift, a natural gift an inspiration from God. In a sense, then, the Romantic version of the Longinian genius becomes indistinguishable, metaphysically, from the Platonic, although the Longinian vision of Beethoven the man and of his music is still as distinct from the Platonic picture of genius and its products, as Homer from Virgil or Handel from Mozart, in the pre-Romantic period.

Our Longinian picture of Beethoven Genius is now complete. It remains for us to draw the crucial Kantian connections.

I begin with the obvious. One of Kant's singular contributions to Enlightenment aesthetics, and to the succeeding Romantic movement, is his theory of the sublime. Certainly this theory grows out of previous exemplars, especially Edmund Burke, for whom Kant expresses considerable admiration in the *Critique of Judgment*. But Kant adds something to it that (it is clear from, among other things, their characterizations of Beethoven's sublimity) the Romantics were deeply impressed by, namely, the concept of the infinite.

Like so much in the third *Critique*, Kant's thinking on the sublime is fraught with difficulties and has supplied material for interpreters galore. Nor is it to the present purpose to explore this large body of work. All that is necessary to make my point here is simply to observe that in both of Kant's concepts of the sublime—what he calls the "mathematically sublime" and the "dynamically sublime"—the *infinite* is the defining idea.

Kant characterizes the mathematically sublime in this way: *"that is sublime in comparison to which all else is small."*[66] But, clearly, the *only* thing in comparison to which *all* else is small must be the infinitely large. Thus: "Nature, therefore, is sublime in such of its phenomena as in their intuition convey the idea of their infinity."[67]

Of the dynamically sublime Kant writes: "Nature considered in an aesthetic judgement as might that has no dominion over us, is *dynamically sublime*."[68] Now, for Kant, the imagination "finds nothing beyond the sensible world to which it can lay hold. . . ." But in the experience of the dynamically sublime, "this thrusting aside of the sensible barriers gives it a feeling of being unbounded; and that removal is thus a presentation of the infinite."[69]

So, for Kant, Nature can present itself to us as infinitely large or as infinitely powerful, which is to say, either as mathematically or dynamically sublime. In both cases, it is not merely a large magnitude but an infinite one that we (subjectively) experience. It is this Kantian notion of the sublime that, I suggest, underlies the Romantics' characterization of Beethoven's sublimity as revelatory of the infinite. It is a link to Kant too plain to be missed.

Reverting now to Kant's theory of genius, it bears repeating that its most distinctive feature is the notion of genius giving the rule to art: Kant's peculiar spin on the traditional notion, stretching back all the way to the Longinus text itself, of the sublime genius as negligent of correct composition. It seems to me to fit so well with Beethoven, the "Great Mogul," as to make it beyond doubt that the Romantic myth of the sublime genius in general, and Beethoven in particular as its primary exemplar, are both driven by the Kantian formulation rather than anything that had gone before. (The name of Longinus has all but dropped from the literature.) So let us return to Beethoven the law-breaker for the purpose of viewing that aspect of his genius through Kant's eyes. That is to say, let us look at Beethoven, the "Great Mogul," as *giving the rule to art*.

In the first of the two stories I have related—of Beethoven's imperious attitude toward "the rules"—you will recall that the punchline was, "I may do it, but not you." In other words, Beethoven may break the rules but lesser composers may not. How shall we understand this response?

I take it for granted that Beethoven was supposed, in this anecdote, to be aware of his superiority—in other words, of his genius. So the content of his response is that a genius may break the rules, but a lesser mortal may not. Why not?

Let us suppose that Beethoven knows the rules he breaks, is aware of breaking them, and Halm breaks the rules out of ignorance. In that case, I presume the suggestion would be that Beethoven knows why he is breaking the rules—that is to say, he has an aesthetic reason for breaking them, a musical effect he wants to achieve—whereas Halm simply breaks them by accident. Therefore, the cash value is: you can break the rules only if you know what your are doing thereby. Beethoven knows what he is doing, Halm does not; so he, Beethoven, may break the rules, but not Halm.

The problem with this interpretation is that it has nothing to do with the vast gulf between Beethoven and Halm, the gulf between genius and lesser forms of creativity, which, I am assuming, is implied by Beethoven's retort. For it is certainly within Halm's powers to learn the rules, if he is ignorant of them; and once he does, then he has as much right to break them as does Beethoven, on this interpretation. This really leaves unanswered the question of why Beethoven may do it but Halm may not.

But suppose, rather, that both Beethoven and Halm know the rules they have broken, and why. In that case, the reason Beethoven may break them and Halm may not rests squarely in the fact that Beethoven is a genius and Halm is not. What is it, then, that allows genius this license and denies it to others? The answer, it seems to me, becomes clear only when the Kantian interpretation of genius is put on Beethoven's retort.

Beethoven, in that case, can be understood to be saying something stronger than (to change the wording slightly) "I may do it but you may not": rather, it is "I *must* do it, you *must* not." From what does the imperative strength of the "must" derive? The Kantian formulation of the genius concept provides a ready answer.

The Kantian genius *cannot* follow the rules—which is to say, follow established models—for if he did he would not, in so doing, ipso facto, *be* a genius. To be a genius is to be a formulator of models for *other* people, nongeniuses, to follow. That is what Kant means by the genius as one who gives the rule to art. He gives lesser men the works they must try to emulate. To emulate is to follow the rules.

So, qua genius, Beethoven *must* break the rules. If he does not, he ceases to be "genius." But Halm, on the other hand, *must not* break the rules. For *his* only means of creating worthy compositions is to follow existing models that the genius has laid down for such limited talents. Not being a genius himself, he cannot break the rules; for if he does, he will produce worthless stuff. Not being a genius, he requires the guidance of the rules, which is to say, the models that genius has provided.

Of course breaking the rules is not a *sufficient* condition for genius. If it were, then Halm could become a genius simply by intentionally (or even accidentally) breaking the rules. Rather, to make things clear, we must understand "genius" in both a *dispositional* and an *occurrent* sense. Because Beethoven is a genius in the dispositional sense, he can also be a genius in the occurrent sense, which is to say, when he gives the rule to art. But Halm, not being a genius in the dispositional sense, cannot become a genius in the occurrent sense by doing what a genius does: by breaking the rules. Beethoven, however, though a genius in the dispositional sense, *can,* in composing, *not* be a genius in the occurrent sense. That would happen, for example, when he is composing a counterpoint exercise for Albrechtsberger, or honing his contrapuntal skills by writing an "academic" fugue after a model from Bach, or, for that matter, in long stretches of compositional "working out."

AN UNLICKED BEAR

So, to sum up, the first of the rule-breaking stories seems to make the most sense if it is given a Kantian interpretation: that is to say, an interpretation that assumes the interchange between Beethoven and Halm to be that between a genius and a nongenius in the Kantian sense. Let us now turn, then, to the second of the rule-breaking anecdotes, and see what it yields.

Ferdinand Ries, you will recall, confronts Beethoven with an instance of parallel fifths in one of the latter's string quartets (Op. 18, No. 4). Beethoven demands to know who has forbidden them, to which Ries responds: "Marburg, Kirnberger, Fuchs, etc., etc., all the theoreticians!" To which the Great Mogul imperiously replies: "And *so I allow them.*"

Now the first thing we must assume about this story is that Beethoven knows perfectly well who has forbidden parallel fifths and why. Every beginning counterpoint student knows these things, and it is impossible to believe Beethoven did not.

In the story, therefore—and, remember, its truth or falsity is irrelevant—Beethoven is making a *point* by asking (repeatedly) who forbids parallel fifths: he wants it out front that it is the theoreticians, which is to say, those who, after the fact, derive rules from the models laid down by genius—in the present case, one presumes, Palestrina and his contemporaries. And the point Beethoven is making is that *because* the theoreticians make the rules, he breaks the rules; their rules forbid fifths, so—*therefore—he allows them*. What is the real meaning of this tale? Why the "therefore"? Again, the Kantian notion of genius makes it clear.

The theoreticians, in this sense, are the compilers of counterpoint texts. These texts are, in a sense, models, reduced to rules and recipes. To follow these texts *is* to be guided by the models. The texts are a shortcut. Someone else has put the models in easily usable form. The counterpoint texts are a distillation of the models—the models in a concentrated dose.

But if you follow these rules, then, you are in effect emulating the models. Furthermore, in so doing, you would *not* be a genius in the occurrent sense. So, that the theoreticians have forbidden something implies that you, qua genius, *must* allow it, or at least *can* allow it *when it pleases you to do so.* Thus, Beethoven's answer to Ries is the Kantian answer: that something is forbidden by the rules obligates the genius to allow it, or suffer the consequence of ceasing to be genius (in the occurrent sense). For the genius is, by definition, not the follower of rules but the giver of rules: the one who gives the rule to art.

I have tried, in this chapter, to present the picture of Beethoven, the Longinian genius of the sublime, as it was painted by his contemporaries and by the later Romantics. And I have argued, at the end, that this picture was patterned not on the traditional model of the Longinian genius, as fashioned by the early and middle Enlightenment thinkers, but on Kant's in the *Critique of Judgment*.

When the pendulum of genius swung from the Platonic Mozart to the Longinian Beethoven, it had, in the space of not more than fifty years, occupied the Longinian position twice, the Platonic once: Handel to Mozart to Beethoven. But when the pendulum swung to Beethoven, the clock got stuck. Indeed, the image of Beethoven, the glowering, all-powerful liberator, the man who freed music, the musical and social rebel, Beethoven the deaf, the distracted, has endured to our own times. His Fifth Symphony was our victory theme and battle cry during the Second World War. He was our cartoon genius when we were laughing at Romantic pretensions, and our movie genius, when we were celebrating them. If you wanted to get a good laugh or a good cry from the "long hairs," Beethoven was your man. Indeed, for all I know, he was the original "long hair." Mozart was still wearing a wig or a pigtail.

Thus the hegemony of Beethoven Genius lasted well over a century. Indeed, it is only in recent memory that that hegemony has been challenged. The clock has apparently got unstuck, and the pendulum has made another oscillation to the Platonic Mozart. That at least is what I shall attempt to show in the following chapter.

IX

Mozart's Second Childhood

Mozart was thoroughly "Beethovenized" in the first half of the twentieth century, culminating in 1956, the bicentennial of his birth. By that I mean that his *music* was Beethovenized, which is to say, the music of Mozart's that became most admired was just that music that could be seen to exhibit not the childlike or the playful but all those qualities of power and the infinite that Beethoven's music was seen to exhibit in the Romantic characterization of his genius. In particular, it was Mozart's compositions in the minor mode that were singled out—the C-minor and D-minor Piano Concertos, the G-minor Viola Quintet and G-minor Symphonies, the C-minor Serenade for Winds, the D-minor Quartet, the great unfinished C-minor Mass, and, of course, the Requiem—and the favorite word to characterize these works became "daemonic."

The connection of Mozart's music with the "daemonic" was first strongly made, as far as I know, by Søren Kierkegaard, in his overwrought analysis (if that is the right word for it) of *Don Giovanni*, the work of Mozart's that Kierkegaard most venerated, and which he thought most epitomized the composer's genius. The choice of subject was itself significant, for Kierkegaard characterized the Don

Juan story alone, in somewhat mystifying terms, as "the expression for the daemonic determined as the sensuous. . . ."[1] Indeed, Kierkegaard seems to have been the lone holdout, in the nineteenth century, against the dominance of Beethoven as the symbol of genius, championing Mozart above all others, and *Don Giovanni* above all other works of music. "Through his *Don Giovanni*," Kierkegaard writes, "Mozart becomes one in the order of these immortals, one of these visibly transfigured ones whom no cloud ever takes away from the sight of men; with his *Don Juan* he stands foremost among them."[2]

What I have called the Beethovenizing of Mozart's music seems to have put Child Mozart as an aesthetic symbol or universal symbol of genius more or less on the back burner. Talk of Mozart's childhood feats and childlike behavior as an adult became somewhat out of fashion, although still a presence here or there. In all respects Mozart was to be seen as a grown-up: a hardworking composer and family man like Bach. He even made sketches, like Beethoven; and Alfred Einstein devoted a chapter to them in his influential book on the composer.[3]

So by 1956 Child Mozart had finally grown up. And about time, too—it was, after all, his two hundredth birthday.

But Child Mozart was not long in returning: first, in somewhat altered fashion, by way of psychoanalysis; second, in a complete replay of the eternal child, possessed by God, from an unexpected source, and in a rather remarkable fashion. I am interested primarily in the latter reincarnation; but Mozart on the couch deserves at least passing mention.

The relationship of Mozart to his father has been a perennial subject of discussion both among scholars and the laity. Was Leopold an overbearing tyrant or a nurturing parent, wanting only the best for his child? It was inevitable that the Freudians should get hold of the subject.

Putting dead citizens on the psychoanalytic couch has its well-known pitfalls, and skeptical detractors abroad, among whom I count myself. But in the case of Mozart, father and son, and our proceedings so far, doing so yields some interesting results. And if—as in the case of so much that has been said about Handel, Mozart, and Beethoven by their contemporaries—we engage in some willing suspension of disbelief, we can extract the philosophy from the psychoanalysis, while staying neutral as to whether we are dealing here with a modern myth or psychological reality.

Mozart remained a child his entire life: that is the genius myth surrounding him, and that was given theoretical expression in Schopenhauer's philosophy of genius. But what does remaining a child all of one's life consist in? Well, as the Mozart myth has it, and this is, I imagine, pretty much as "common sense" has it, you retain childish "innocence": you play games, you joke, you are not very practical, you don't manage your affairs very well, you are naive in your trust of other people, unguarded in your expressions of emotion, and so on. This was what Mozart was like as an adult, according to the myth of the child-genius.

But was Mozart *really* like this? And, anyway, are those traits *really* what characterize "never really growing up"?

Ample research done on Mozart in recent years casts grave doubts on this picture of the supposedly childlike adult, or, at the very least, suggests that the picture is highly exaggerated through apocryphal anecdote.

But, after all, the modern psychologist may claim, these "commonsensical" characteristics of adult immaturity surely do not withstand expert scrutiny. They are, that authority will tell you, neither necessary nor sufficient conditions for the diagnosis of "juvenile adult." Mozart could well have possessed them and *not* been a "man-child" and (more important) *not* have possessed them (as modern scholarship seems to suggest) and yet still correctly be described, as the Mozart myth does, as someone who remained a child all his life. To see this we need merely turn to the relationship between Wolfgang and Leopold.

A normal, "grown-up" adult, so at least one modern psychological theory goes, is someone who has freed himself of his father's authority—that is to say, "revolted" from it—but who also has eventually become reconciled with the father. Thus, Papa wants you to become a physician and follow in his footsteps, eventually taking over his lucrative practice, but you want to be a physicist. He pulls, you pull, and finally you wrest yourself free of him. A physicist you become. For a while there is ill feeling between father and son. But in time, Papa starts talking to his friends about "my son, the physicist," parental pride triumphs over hurt pride, and familial harmony is restored. Thus, forget about fun and games and the rest. If you have successfully negotiated the alienation and reconciliation process with your old man, you are a mature adult, whether or not you still like to play with electric trains and talk gibberish.

But, on the other hand, if you have not successfully achieved the alienation-reconciliation thing, you will be judged, on that account alone, as remaining a child all your life, even if you are "sober as a judge" and never crack a joke from cradle to grave. And just so Mozart, according to Brigid Brophy, in her heavily psychoanalytic study of Mozart's operas. He never really made the break; he never really was reconciled. "The influence of Leopold Mozart for ever driving Mozart to rebel, and for ever pulling him back on the strings of filial piety, could not be resolved by physical distance (which was bridged by letters) or even finally by Leopold's death. The father was indeed eternal—in the son. And equally Mozart was eternally a son: a personality, an Ego, whose existence was physically possible only in and through the filial relationship."[4]

For starters, how *could* Wolfgang *avoid* going into his father's line of work? As Brophy observes: "Artists' biographies often read: His father intended him for the law/the church/medicine/commerce, but after studying/practising for a year or two, he broke away, to his father's displeasure. . . ." But Leopold too was a musician. Indeed, "Leopold was both the real father and the master of the apprentice." So "There was no question of his being displeased by his son's choice of profession: it was his own choice, both for himself and, more important, for his son."[5]

In short, Mozart never could, never did manage the break with his father that maturity requires, nor, necessarily, the subsequent reconciliation. "Mozart's was a double burden: his own identification with Leopold, and Leopold's with him. Leopold had chosen to pursue his own career through his son's. He demanded the right to supervise and control Mozart's career as well: the talent was not Mozart's but *theirs*."[6] So, regardless of Mozart's actual or supposed childish behavior as an adult, he remained a child all his life, in the psychoanalytic sense, by never having been able to negotiate the separation from his father and the ultimate reuniting that real maturity requires. Child Mozart has returned via the psychoanalyst's couch.

But does the Freudian Child Mozart (if Freudian *is* what he is) have anything specifically to do with either the Platonic concept of genius possessed or, for that matter, any concept of genius whatever?

It seems that, for Brophy, the "unconscious" plays something like the role of "possession" in the Platonic account of genius. The problem is that being "possessed," being "inspired" by one's unconscious, as Brophy herself admits, is characteristic both of genius *and* "the mere fluent fantaisiste who may be equally 'inspired'—that is, equally dependent on an unconscious impulse and unconscious material."[7]

So being "possessed," or, to use Brophy's word, "inspired," by the unconscious is not a sufficient condition for "genius": that is to say, artistic production at the highest, Mozartian level. But that is exactly what the Platonic metaphor of divine possession is meant to capture. Mozart's divine music is divine because it is *divine:* the music of the gods. The gods do not take possession of men and women to make them produce garbage. They inhabit mortals so that mortals can produce what, unaided, they never could produce. And the unconscious cannot sit in for the divine just because the unconscious is the property of us *all*. God singles out Mozart from the rest of us. The unconscious singles out no one from anybody else.

But what of Mozart as the eternal child, in the psychoanalytic sense? Does *that* provide any stand-in for Schopenhauer's reexpression of the Platonic metaphor? Again, the answer must be No. For it is precisely the ordinary childlike qualities—the play, the impracticality—that mark out the character of the "possessed one," the one free of the principle of sufficient reason. Not having successfully separated from your father marks out no one in particular. Again, as Brophy herself remarks in this regard: "The elements we can pick out as the unconscious sources of Mozart's supreme creativity are just those we would have to pick out as the unconscious sources of the peculiar behaviour of dozens of neurotics or hysterics."[8]

Of course, as not successfully separating from your father is hardly a sufficient condition for genius, neither are the usual childlike characteristics attributed to Mozart by his contemporaries, and adduced by Schopenhauer. The point is that the latter, *in the Platonic package*, are *supposed* to be—that membership is what gives them their power as part of the Platonic genius metaphor. And, of course, it may well be that as part of a "Freudian package," the eternal child as "unseparated son" might serve a similar purpose to the childlike qualities in the Platonic one. That, however, is a subject for other books and other heads than mine. I will simply conclude with Brophy's own estimate of the Freudian package (if that, indeed, is what she is offering): "We do not, of course, possess a 'solution' to the puzzle of an artistic personality."[9]

I have not, then, brought up Brophy's Freudian picture of Mozart as the son unsuccessfully separated from the father for close examination or critique. For a truly masterful treatment of that subject, one is recommended to the work of Maynard Solomon.[10] I merely suggest that it is the first symptom of a return of the Platonic genius myth, featuring, yet again, Mozart the eternal child as its most potent symbol. And, no doubt, Maynard Solomon must have this in mind, too, when, in writing of the general return *he* sees of the myth of Mozart's eternal childishness, he says: "The most venerable tropes have recently been revived, and to them we are even now adding new perceptions of Mozart the child, albeit now as the rebellious-patricidal-oedipal child or the polymorphous child of his bawdy letters to his cousin, the Bäsle, whom he loved so tenderly."[11] The pendulum is now about to swing from Beethoven, the genius of the Longinian sublime, to Mozart, the Platonic genius possessed.

The return of Child Mozart as aesthetic symbol is remarkable in a number of respects. It is remarkable, first, for its source: not philosophy, psychology, art theory, musicology, or any other "academic" discipline, but a play, a piece of theater (in the best sense) that has had great popular appeal.

It is remarkable, second, because of the extent of the popularity the play and its myth have achieved; witness the fact that as a motion picture, it has been disseminated to a wide range of audiences beyond those of the legitimate stage and across national boundaries.

It is remarkable, finally, for the *extremity* to which the Platonic metaphor has been taken. The child has become the idiot savant (Figure 6).

Figure 6. Mozart. Publicity photograph from the film *Amadeus*. © 1984 The Saul Zaentz Company. All Rights Reserved.

None of my readers will have failed to recognize that the new evocation of the Platonic Mozart myth to which I have been referring is Peter Shaffer's widely known play and movie, *Amadeus*. Because it emanates from a work of art, the new Mozart myth is extraordinarily vivid and alive. But because it emanates from a work of *fiction*, we must be very circumspect in drawing conclusions to the effect that Peter Shaffer is presenting *his* view of what Mozart was really like, or what *genius* is really like. And I shall make no such inferences here. The picture of Mozart and his genius that I present is Antonio Salieri's picture: not Antonio Salieri, the Italian composer who lived from 1750 to 1825, but "Antonio Salieri," a character in Peter Shaffer's fictional play, *Amadeus*.

But I will say this for the epistemic claims of Salieri's picture of Mozart and his genius. Were the picture *not* one that at least seriously appeals to the artistic and philosophical imaginations of our times, it, and the play in which it has such a major role, would not have had such a powerful impact and such a widespread one. It therefore behooves us, in the end, to ask why this image of genius should appeal to us as even plausible, let alone true, *now*—in this time and this place.

The entrance of Mozart—his first appearance in Shaffer's play—is observed by Salieri, seated, unseen by Mozart, in "a grand high-backed winged chair." This is what Salieri observes: Constanze, Mozart's fiance, enters, "pretending to be a mouse.... Suddenly a small, pallid, large-eyed man in a showy wig and a showy set of clothes runs after her and freezes—centre—as a cat would freeze, hunting a mouse. This is Wolfgang Amadeus Mozart." Shaffer puts a period to this description of Mozart—Salieri's vision of him, I want to emphasize—with: "and he is possessed of an unforgettable giggle—piercing and infantile."[12]

It surely is belaboring the obvious to say that Mozart is made to seem, right from the start, through Salieri's eyes and, through them, our own, as childish almost to the point of idiocy. Nor is it the charming, gentle, lovable childishness of the old Mozart legend. This is not Christopher Robin, and just to make sure we do not miss the point, it is made all too obvious to us when, directly, the childishness turns both erotic and scatological. "*She giggles delightedly, lying prone beneath him.* You're trembling! . . . I think you're frightened of puss-wuss. . . . I think you're scared to death! (*Intimately*) I think you're going to shit yourself."[13]

It is this childish, unpleasantly childish scrap of humanity that God, as Salieri sees it, has chosen for His divine musical utterances. And music *is,* Salieri believes, especially God-like among the arts. "Music. Absolute music! A note of music is either right or wrong—*absolutely.* Not even Time can change that. Music is God's art."[14]

That Salieri fully endorses a Christianized Platonism with regard to musical genius is made abundantly clear throughout the play. There's no doubt that, in Salieri's mind, it is divine possession that makes the difference between Mozart and him. As for himself: "at night I prayed for just one thing. (*He kneels desperately.*) Let your voice enter me! Let *me* be your conduct. . . . *Let me!*"[15]

But what sort of a man and artist is Salieri? In his own eyes a *deserving* one. He has totally dedicated himself to *music,* to *work,* to *God.* Of himself, he says, in his diatribe against the Godhead that closes the first act: "Until this day I have pursued virtue with rigour. I have laboured long hours to relieve my fellow men. I have worked and worked the talent you have allowed me. (*Calling up.*) *You know how hard I've worked!*—solely that in the end, in the practice of the art which alone makes the world comprehensible to me I might hear Your Voice!"[16]

But through whom does God choose to speak? Not, alas, through the deserving, *hardworking* Salieri. "I was frightened. It seemed to me I had heard a voice of God—and that it issued from a creature whose own voice I had also heard—and it was the voice of an obscene child."[17] That "creature" is, of course, Amadeus: "Spiteful, sniggering, conceited, infantine, Mozart!—who never worked one minute to help another man!—shit-talking Mozart with his botty-smacking wife—*him* you have chosen to be your sole conduct!"[18]

God *should* have chosen Salieri: the *hardworking* Salieri. *He* deserved it. Isn't it written that "God helps those who help themselves"?

It is a recurring theme in *Amadeus,* based, of course, on various stories of Mozart's prodigious mental powers, that composing for him was quick and easy—completely effortless, like liquid poured from a container. As Maynard Solomon describes this traditional picture of Mozart's creative process:

> Mozart's music was scrubbed of the labor that went into its creation, cleansed of the blood and pain that had been sublimated

in it. Mozart's creativity came to be considered as the product of forces external to him; he was regarded as a receptive, neutral instrument or vessel of a vital, perhaps divine force; he was thought to have written music automatically because that was his instinctive nature, to make music as a silkworm spins silk, to shake masterpieces out of his sleeve without conscious effort or volition.[19]

Salieri, surmising from something Mozart has said that *Zauberflöte* is already composed, asks Mozart, incredulously, "You mean it's finished? So soon?" To which Mozart replies: "Oh, yes—music is easy: it's marriage that's hard."[20] Composing is easy for Mozart; but Salieri has to work at it. That is what infuriates him. "Tonight at an inn somewhere in this city stands a giggling child who can put on paper, without actually setting down his billiard cue, casual notes which turn my most considered ones into lifeless scratches."[21]

Why should God not reward hard work with "inspiration"? Why should He simply bestow it on someone as a gift, without *any* services rendered?

It will be recalled that when I first presented the concept of genius in the early chapters of this book, it was as an answer to what might be described as the problem of why some people get "bright ideas." Why should two people, equally intelligent or talented, equally well-trained, equally accomplished and hardworking, be such that one of them gets "bright ideas" and the other doesn't? The answer: one of them has that "extra" thing, "genius," either by divine possession (the Platonic view) or by natural endowment (the Longinian). But in both cases it was assumed that the genius must work at and learn about whatever the subject of his or her genius is. Even the oracle must prepare for her visitations. They do not just come unbidden.

During the eighteenth century, when these "theories" of genius were being forged in their modern form, nature *and* nurture were always presented as together necessary and sufficient conditions. Or, to put it another way, whether genius was bestowed by divine possession (or its appearance) or by natural gift, art, craft, science were required in addition, or nothing tangible could come of it. It was proverbial that "genius" was a necessary condition for great achievements in the arts, but not a sufficient one. Even Homer had to hone his skills.

But what Salieri offers us is a picture of genius that consists in divine possession alone. It pushes the theory to its outer limits. Creativity at its highest level can occur, then, in the absence of all craft and science whatever. God may choose as his voice *anyone*. And, after all, why should God's voice have to know anything? God is pulling the strings. What need to assign a "second cause"? The Deity needs no help from His oracle. The piano did not write the concerto. There is no evidence in *Amadeus* that Salieri thinks Mozart ever practiced the clavier or took a counterpoint lesson. The idiot savant, after all, does not learn addition.

Notice that only the Platonic, possession theory will serve Salieri's purpose. The Longinian theory will not do, for *it* emphasizes the power of the artist himself as maker and giver of the laws. Nature must give him the gift of genius. But *he* must use that gift. He must *learn* to use it by mastering his "art" or "craft." God does not do that for him.

Of course the saying "God helps those who help themselves" is an expression of the Christian work ethic. And there is no reason why God could not make it a moral prerequisite of His inspiration that His conduit make herself worthy of it by labor. But in Salieri's eyes that is not what has happened in God's relationship to Mozart. Salieri has done the work, and that idler Mozart, who composes with billiard cue in hand, has reaped the rewards. The unworthy vessel has been filled.

Thus the picture of genius that we are presented with through Salieri's eyes is the possession theory in its most extreme form. It says that creativity at the very highest level can occur anywhere, anytime, with no preparation or premonition, practice or participation. Mozart, in Salieri's eyes, is the epitome of the unworthy recipient of God's largesse. He is unworthy, apparently, *both* in his moral character (or lack thereof) and in the fact that he has not merited his inspiration by "hard work." It just "comes to him," unbidden. There isn't even devotion to his muse.

CONSTANZE [to Salieri]   Wolferl would rather play at billiards than anything. He's very good at it.
MOZART   I'm the best. I may nod occasionally at composing, but at billiards—never!²²

Thus, Salieri's Platonized Christian version of the possession theory of genius is a metaphor for the notion that genius is an absolutely spontaneous effusion. It plays no favorites with rank, station, moral character, education, training, application, labor, or even devotion to one's vocation. No one deserves it; it just happens. And it is one hundred percent inspiration, zero percent perspiration. If you want to write great music, you might just as well, like Mozart, perspire at billiards.

With this revival of Child Mozart and the possession theory of genius before us, in its most extreme form, it behooves us, as I said before, to consider why it should have surfaced in this time and this place. In so doing, there is no need to attribute this view of genius to Peter Shaffer, or to anyone else. But it is on display, so to speak, in *Amadeus,* and is, I presume, to be taken seriously. And that is what I intend to do.

I begin with one of the premises of the theory that is merely tangential to the question at hand, but nevertheless worth considering. I think it is probably false. It is an assumption about the relationship of Salieri to Mozart: that Salieri clearly recognizes his own mediocrity and the other's transcendent genius. If it is meant as a generalization of how things usually are in such matters, I think it is way off the mark. Only in retrospect is it plainly apparent that Mozart is the transcendent genius, Salieri the mediocrity. (Bach, remember, was third choice for Leipzig, after Telemann and Graun!) Nor is there any reason to believe that it was obvious to the real Salieri. That Mozart was the greater performer, that he could compose "in his head," that he could compose faster than anyone else, that he was a child prodigy—none of this convinced any of his contemporaries that he was a better composer than Haydn or Paisiello or Salieri, all of whom he surpassed in all of those skills.

Nor was it obvious to Mozart's contemporaries, as it is to us, that his music was superior to theirs (Haydn, of course, excepted). That it was more complicated, more harmonically daring, displayed greater contrapuntal skill, all marks of his superiority to *us,* certainly were not necessarily to them (although they *were* marks of his "learning," "science," "skill"). For it could always be replied (and was) that such complications were "Gothic," "Baroque," in the negative senses of the word; that simplicity, clarity, and beauty of unadorned melody, in the Italian style, Salieri's style (!) were the marks of great musical composition. As is well known, Joseph II said of *Die Entführung aus dem Serail* that it had "too many notes," and the Empress of Bohemia pronounced *La Clemenza di Tito* to be "German trash" (*una porcheria tedesca*)—a less polite way, I imagine, of saying the same thing, since "German" and "complicated" would be musical synonyms for her.

Thus, how Salieri sees Salieri, as mediocrity to Mozart's genius, I find a doubtful representation of how these things generally go in the history of art. And that is a point deserving further discussion. But, after all, my subject is not Salieri's mediocrity (as seen by Salieri), it is Mozart's genius—genius that is *all* inspiration and *no* work. Why are we ready for such a picture of genius? Or are we? I think we are; and here is why I think we are.

Let me adduce two very famous and, to philosophers, very familiar events in the history of twentieth-century art. Many other such, both imaginary and real, are chronicled in Arthur Danto's brilliant and intriguing writings, theoretical and critical, on the sometimes "strange" art objects of our times.

The first case is that of Marcel Duchamp's so-called ready-mades, which were exhibited during and shortly after the First World War as part of what came to be known as the dada movement. Among these was an ordinary urinal, signed "R. Mutt," titled *Fountain,* and hung upside down. Another was simply an undistinguished snow shovel displayed as a sculpture and titled *In Advance of a Broken Arm.* Both are now generally accepted as works of art—indeed, milestones in the modernist movement.

Of course, such works were greeted with scorn and outrage (and, of course, that was Duchamp's intention). And in expressing one's outrage, then as now, one might be moved to say, "Why, a *child* could do *that*."

The second, more recent event, was the "performance" (if that is the right word for it) of John Cage's notorious *4′33″* (4 minutes, 33 seconds). In this performance, distinguished pianist David Tudor walked onto the stage, formally attired in the customary manner of the classical performer, sat down in front of a grand piano for four minutes and thirty-three seconds, and then walked off. An irate customer came up to Cage afterward and said, angrily, "*I* could have done *that*," to which Cage's pregnant reply was: "Yes, but you *didn't*."

In what sense *could* a child do what Duchamp did, or *anyone* do what Cage did? Well, clearly, in the same sense in which a child could *not* paint *The Polish Rider* or a nonmusician compose *The Art of the Fugue*. It takes no skill, learning, craft to pick up a snow shovel and put it in an exhibition; it takes no skill, learning, craft to "compose" *4′33″*. Craftsmanship has nothing to do with these artworks, and many more such of various kinds that were produced in the twentieth century.

But there is another sense in which a child could not possibly have done what Duchamp did, or just anyone do what Cage did. And Cage, in his reply to the man who claimed *he* could have done what Cage did, clearly perceived this. "But you *didn't*." Why not? Because *you* didn't, couldn't have gotten the bright *idea* of doing such a thing. It was "a stroke of genius": a stroke of genius, to be sure, that required no skill or craftsmanship to execute—and that, of course, is the point.

Similarly, a child has all the skill and craftsmanship required—which is *none at all*—to "make" a ready-made sculpture. But to think of doing such a thing, and to think of the title *Fountain* or *In Advance of a Broken Arm*—to get such bright ideas—*that* is a stroke of genius.

The contemporary art world is full of examples, of all kinds, where skill and craftsmanship simply play no role and have nothing to do with why the works of art are admired (if they are). There are, of course, other contemporary genres in which they do. But the existence of art objects like *In Advance of a Broken Arm* and *4′33″* where, so to speak, inspiration is all, skill and science nothing at all, makes us receptive to precisely the picture of genius that Salieri's Mozart presents.

Danto has taught us that the art world must be "ready" for the things that are its artworks. Furthermore, this is true not merely of our own times but of times past, although it is only in our own times that this has become so apparent. *Steamer in Snowstorm* could no more be a work of art in Raphael's time than *In Advance of a Broken Arm* could be in Turner's. In our own times, however, in a process that Danto has felicitously called "the transfiguration of the commonplace," ordinary objects like snow shovels and silence can be made works of art, through no skill or craft at all.[23] An art world ready for *that* is an art world ready for a picture of genius that has been cleansed of all but the "inspirational" part: ready for Salieri's Mozart, billiard cue in hand, giggle on his lips.

Salieri's Mozart, then, is genius at the extreme end of a continuum that has at its middle point the mixture of "inspiration" or "natural gifts" and "science" or "craft" thought essential by the eighteenth-century philosophers and theorists for the production of original masterpieces. This suggests that at one end of the continuum there might be a picture of genius in which "genius" or "natural gifts" has been distilled completely out and only labor remains: in other words, the mirror image of the all inspiration—no work picture is the all work–no inspiration picture. Has such a notion of genius ever been seriously considered? Indeed it has. And although it has never been an equal player to the possessor and the possessed, it has something interesting to tell us. It is worth a brief look.

X

Odd Men Out

Any musical reader of the foregoing pages will not have failed to notice that two towering musical figures are absent from my narrative of the concept of musical genius in modern times. These are, of course, Johann Sebastian Bach and Franz Joseph Haydn. Why does our story so far not include these two familiar names?

I think that musicians—which is to say, performers, theorists, and historians alike—are in agreement as to the foundations of the classical repertory, whether in the concert hall, the opera house, or the classroom. The first historical period from which this repertory is drawn extends from the first quarter of the eighteenth century through the first quarter of the nineteenth, and there is no doubt among both experts and the laity about who the composers are that constitute the historical foundation. They are Bach, Haydn, Mozart, and Beethoven: the big four, with Handel hovering somewhere around the peripheries, his reputation due (largely, in the modern concert repertory) to the enormous popularity of *Messiah* and the continued presence, particularly in England, of some of his other oratorios.

What, then, accounts for the absence of Bach and Haydn from our story, despite universal agreement as to their towering stature? How, in particular, can the name of Johann Sebastian Bach, arguably *the* greatest musical genius of the modern era, be absent from the story of musical genius, as an aesthetic, philosophical concept in modern intellectual history? Surely, the answer must be that Bach and Haydn, in their lives and persons, cannot be made to fit the profile of either of the two dominant genius myths: the possessor or the possessed. That is certainly a hypothesis worth exploring.

The life of J. S. Bach was the life of the middle-class artisan. As most music lovers know, he belonged to a musical family that produced six generations of composers. His sons became distinguished composers in their own right. Indeed, the genius of the family, the generation after Bach would have said, was Carl Philip Emmanuel, not Johann Sebastian, as much as the latter was admired for his virtuosity, learning, and musical "science."

His days and nights were filled, of course, with music. But how he found time to compose the stuff is hard to know, considering that he had to teach, train an orchestra and choir, discipline little boys, and carry on, it seems, protracted disputes with his employers and those worthies of the town of Leipzig with whom he came in contact in performing his official musical duties. He also taught Latin.

The documents of his life have little to do with the glories of art. He thanks one man for a haunch of venison, another for some wine. He petitions—indeed, almost begs—for orchestral forces that constitute an ensemble so pitifully small, they could play in my kitchen (and I live in Manhattan). He writes testimonials for his students, much like the letters of recommendation I must write for mine when they get their doctorates and go out on the job market.

The closest Bach's life comes to the kind of glory in the big world of art that Mozart projected in his letters, or that Handel and Beethoven had projected for them by their early biographers and contemporaries in London and Vienna, is the account of his trip to Potsdam to visit Frederick the Great in 1740. So keen was the Great King to meet the master, so Bach's first biographer, Nicolaus Forkel, tells us, that he didn't even permit his visitor to change from his traveling clothes— certainly a serious lapse in courtly manners. But even this charming story is somehow short of the mark. On learning of Bach's arrival,

Frederick announces to his assembled entourage, "Gentlemen, old Bach is come." *Old Bach!* It is as if some antique curiosity is being trotted out—admirable indeed in learning and skill, who is immediately set a daunting musical task to undertake: improvising a fugue on the king's rather difficult, rather left-footed theme.[1] But this is hardly the description one gives of the arrival of a sublime musical genius. Imagine the prospect of a Viennese nobleman announcing to his guests that "Old Beethoven is come." Imagine what "Old Beethoven" would have done if he had heard the announcement.

Of Bach's estimation of himself, Forkel tells us: "When he was sometimes asked how he had contrived to master the art [of music] to such a high degree, he generally answered: 'I was obliged to be industrious; whoever is equally industrious will succeed equally well.' He seemed not to lay any stress on his greater natural talents."[2]

Here is how Citizen Bach looked to his contemporaries in later years (Figure 7). It is the most well-known portrait, by Haussmann. There are six authentic portraits of him, and to my eyes, at least, none of them looks very much like any other. They look like six different Bachs. But five of the six look like the same *kind* of man: your solid, German Burger. The earliest shows, rather, a very attractive young man, even handsome—a man one might well believe would make music with a "stranger maiden" in the organ loft and earn, thereby, the censure of his superiors (Figure 8). But for the rest, we have no hint of the flame of genius burning within, anymore than we do in the humdrum routine of the Cantor of Thomaskirche. Were he from Hamburg, his name would have been Johann Sebastian Buddenbrooks.

The epitaph one is tempted to read over the life of Johann Sebastian Bach, arguably the greatest pure musical genius in our history, is: "He went into the family business." How do you make genius, in either of its two familiar forms, out of that?

The story of Haydn's life can, no more than Bach's, well be made into either the myth of the Platonic prodigy or the Longinian superman. He was Papa Haydn to his contemporaries, and the sobriquet has stuck.

Haydn's first biographer, G. A. Griesinger, said in 1810: "Haydn's life is marked by no great event; but it is the story of a man who had

Figure 7. Johann Sebastian Bach in 1746. From a painting by Elias Gottlieb Haussmann.

Figure 8. Johann Sebastian Bach. Painting probably by Johann Ernst Rentsch the Elder. Studisches Museum Erfurt.

to struggle under manifold pressures from without, and who solely by the strength of his talent and by tireless exertion happily worked up to the rank of the most important men in his field."[3] Furthermore, even though, as we saw at the very beginning, Haydn gave the customary credit to God, he said of himself, according to Griesinger: "I was never a fast writer, and always composed with deliberation and industry."[4] Beethoven supposedly had an engraving on his wall of the humble dwelling in Rohrau, Lower Austria, where Haydn was born, and would remark, pointing to it, to this effect: "Learn from that how one can come up from nothing." This is not a man that Peter Shaffer's Salieri could feel threatened by, or see as the voice of God.

There is, indeed, a myth in the person of Haydn, and in his life—but not that of the possessor or the possessed. It is, however, a myth familiar to us all, a quintessentially American myth. It is, of course, the Horatio Alger story. The problem is that it is hard to see *genius* there.

Look at the portrait of 1792, of Haydn at the height of his creative powers (Figure 9). What do you see? If you did not know that what he grasps is a musical score—because you know that it is Haydn—might it not just as well, even more appropriate to the face depicted, be the account books of a prosperous merchant? It is as hard to see genius here as it is to see it in the story of the man and his life—far easier to see hard-won prosperity.

We can well imagine a railroad tycoon or financier achieving fame and fortune through "tireless exertion," "deliberation and industry." But that is hardly the exciting stuff out of which genius myths are made. The genius story requires being chosen as God's voice, or being endowed by Nature with the primal power to create in defiance of artistic and worldly constraints. And because Haydn seems to us a Horatio Alger character rather than the voice of God or the personification of Nature's inexorable powers, we cannot take him, for all of his musical greatness, as part of our genius mythology.

One antidote to this unfortunate prejudice is to try to free ourselves from overpowering devotion to these two pictures of what genius must be like. Could there perhaps be something to a "just plain

Figure 9. Haydn, oil painting by Thomas Hardy, 1792.

hard work" picture of genius? Call this the "workaholic theory." There have been men of genius who have borne witness to it.

Graham Greene, in an interview, said: "I have no talent. It is a question of working hard, being willing to put in the time."[5] And every schoolchild knows what that authentic American genius Thomas Alva

Edison—a Horatio Alger character if there ever was one—said about genius: "Ninety-nine percent perspiration, one percent inspiration." However, I think the most intriguing endorsement of the workaholic theory of genius comes from the great Issac Newton, who not only gave it credence but at least suggested what kind of a workaholic the genius is—what the nature of the ninety-nine percent perspiration might be. Newton is supposed to have said something to the effect that he was not more intelligent than other men but that he merely possessed the power to hold a problem before his mind for a very long time. For Newton, then, the ninety-nine percent perspiration, the obsession, if you will, that makes a genius is what we customarily call "extraordinary powers of concentration."

The notion that genius in general (and Newton's in particular) lies in "extraordinary powers of concentration" is deep and nontrivial. It should not be dismissed merely as a kind of false modesty. Indeed, two distinguished writers on Newton take it very seriously indeed.

In his biography of Newton, Edward Andrade has this to say about the nature of Newton's genius:

> when he was asked how he made his discoveries, he said, "By always thinking unto them," and on another occasion, when he seems to have been rather more talkative, "I keep the subject constantly before me and wait till the first dawnings open little by little into the full light." Even for great men of science it is hard to keep the mind concentrated on a problem, to the exclusion of everything else, for more than an hour or two: I believe that Newton, however, could sit for hours with the whole powers of his mind fixed on whatever difficulty he was concerned with.[6]

In a similar vein, John Maynard Keynes wrote of Newton, in an essay called, "Newton, the Man,"

> I believe that the clue to his mind is to be found in his unusual powers of continuous concentrated introspection.... His peculiar gift was the power of holding continuously in his mind a purely mental problem until he had seen straight through it.

> ... Anyone who has ever attempted pure scientific or philosophical thought knows how one can hold a problem momentarily in one's mind and apply all one's powers of concentration to piercing through it, and how it will dissolve and escape and you find that what you are surveying is a blank. I believe that Newton could hold a problem in his mind for hours and days and weeks until it surrendered to him its secret.[7]

Could "extraordinary powers of concentration" be all there is to genius? Andrade and Keynes at least make the concept seem a rich and a deep one. It has more to recommend it than the more general "just hard work," because it is a *kind* of hard work that we can imagine only a few being capable of to the degree of a Newton or a Bach—in other words, *to the degree of a genius*. We all, to be sure, have powers of concentration to some degree or other. But few of us can hold before our minds—for hours, for days, for weeks—the problem of planetary orbits or the elaborate structure of a quadruple fugue. When powers of concentration attain that degree, then they are far beyond the general run, as genius is far beyond "mere talent."

But the workaholic theory of genius, even in its more interesting form, as the "extraordinary powers of concentration" theory, is, we must admit, a boring myth. It has none of the panache, none of the zip and zing of the Platonic genius possessed or the Longinian genius-god. So if it fits Bach the man and Haydn the man, Bach the creator and Haydn the creator, it makes them, alas, boring geniuses—not the stuff of which the metaphors we live by are made, although it does have *something* to teach us about genius, as we shall see in the final chapter of this book.

Being a boring theory, a boring myth, the workaholic concept of genius, quite understandably, has not been a perennial favorite, as have been the Platonic and Longinian ones. So it is quite understandable, too, why Bach and Haydn, who seem to fit the workaholic picture far better than the Platonic or Longinian, have never emerged, at least in the popular or philosophical consciousness, as genius-symbols, although they may indeed occupy such a position among many music lovers and musicians.

Nor is the workaholic genius a symbol for our times. It is not a symbol for the avant-garde because it is the opposite side of the coin to the symbol that *is:* the Mozartian symbol, in Peter Shaffer's version, of all inspiration, *no work at all.* Furthermore, it favors craftsmanship, as the all inspiration symbol does not, because work suggests mastery of some recalcitrant material or other, whether it be the physical material of the painter and sculptor or the abstract material of Newtonian physics.

As well, the workaholic theory of genius will be no more congenial to the general population than to the avant-garde. We live in the age of the "quick fix," not the Judaeo-Christian work ethic. Instant gratification is what we crave, hardly the kind of labor-intensive occupations that may have their payoffs years in the future.

Nevertheless, there *is,* I think, a sense in which the workaholic theory of genius *is* of our times, not because of what *it* is, not because of its content, but because of the *kind* to which it belongs. Let me dilate upon that for a moment.

According to the Platonic, inspiration account of genius, geniuses are different in kind from the rest of us. They have something we don't have: the voice of God.

According to the Longinian account of genius, too, geniuses are different in kind from the rest of us. They have something we don't have: natural gifts.

The workaholic account of genius, however, can be construed in quite a different way from the theories of the possessor and possessed. For it seems to be telling us not that geniuses are different in kind from the rest of us, that they have something we don't have, rather, that they have something we *do* have, but to a degree orders of magnitude beyond us. We *all* have the ability to work; we all have powers (more or less) of concentration. They, however, the geniuses, have them to the n-th degree.

One might, then, describe the workaholic theory of genius as "reductionist." Genius isn't something—it's something *else.* Genius is "really" a very high degree of concentrational powers; not something additional to the mental powers we all have, but simply *one* of those powers in an exceptionally large amount. To use a contemporary buzz word, the workaholic theory of genius is a "deconstruction" of the concept as it has been known previously. And thus it is a theory for our times just because it is a deconstruction of genius, a concept that many find, for one reason or another (usually moral or "political") an objectionable one. It surely is *un*fashionable to suggest that genius is *work*. What is *fashionable* is to suggest that genius "reduces" to something else—something, indeed, that is not very terrific. The "deconstruction" of genius is deflationary.

Of course, to show that something "reduces" to something else is also to achieve one of the most admired of explanatory goals, associated intimately with the scientific enterprise. It is, as well, to satisfy Ockham's Razor, or the law of parsimony, which adjures us to assume no more principles in our explanation than the phenomena to be explained require. The deconstruction of genius depletes the number of mental faculties—however many the theorist might think there are—by *one,* the "faculty" of genius itself. Genius is extra baggage. The workaholic theory unloads that baggage onto the "faculty" of concentration or the propensity for obsessive labor.

However, the deconstruction of genius, in our times, takes forms far more fashionable and modern than the workaholic deconstruction, which, after all, has the imprimatur of Newton and is venerable with age. Furthermore, the form in which I shall examine it, in the next chapter, features as its protagonist none other than the "unlicked bear." So my theme of the pendulum's swing has yet one more variation to play out. And it is, I think, of some philosophical significance that the deconstruction of genius we are about to examine *does* have Beethoven as its "hero" (if Beethoven as *hero* can really survive the deflationary process), and does *not* feature Mozart. These matters we will now take up.

XI

Beethoven Again

We all know people who have positions or reputations we do not think, on the basis of their real talents and abilities, they truly deserve. We say "She was in the right place at the right time," "He knew the right people," or "She had political connections" but that someone else, or five other people, deserve the job or reputation more. This is a common, everyday distinction—it is "common sense."

Perhaps it was "politics" or "the right connections" that made the musical reputations of Telemann and Graun greater than that of J. S. Bach. Both were offered the job at Leipzig before he, in what must be the greatest case of artistic misjudgment in music history. *Clearly* Bach was the best man, and history has vindicated him. For Telemann and Graun are now seen merely as men of talent, Bach as a towering genius—"Nicht Bach, oder Meer," as Beethoven said.

Now I am not saying it *was* politics or not having the right connections that did Bach in at Leipzig, until the third round—but it is, at least, not a silly hypothesis. And if this is a bad example, there surely are others that aren't. Sometimes an artist (or someone else) does have an overblown reputation based on politics or the right connections or good PR. We all know cases like that—cases where it's all politics, "a put-up job."

But, to revert to our example again, what about *Bach*'s reputation? Might not that *also* be a matter of politics, connections, good PR? Granted, Bach has won out over Telemann and Graun in the reputation derby, in the fullness of historical time. Does that mean his reputation is more merited than theirs? Does that mean that he is a genius, in some "objective" sense, and that they are not? What *is* genius, anyway? Maybe it's *all* a put-up job. It's just that Telemann and Graun had better political connections in the eighteenth century, Bach better ones in the nineteenth and twentieth. Maybe, to paraphrase the lady's answer to Bertrand Russell when he asked her what the turtle rested upon, which, so she claimed, was the resting place of the earth, "It's politics all the way down."

One is reminded here of the puzzlement about dreaming in the first *Meditation*. Having made the ordinary, commonsensical distinction between being conscious, while awake, of doing something and dreaming that one is doing it, Descartes then asks the question: How do I know I'm not *always* dreaming, even when I think I'm awake? After all, in my dream, I think I am awake, doing what I dream I am doing. Perhaps that is always what is happening. Perhaps, even when I am "awake," I'm *really* just dreaming I'm awake. Perhaps it's dreaming all the way down. There is a stock answer to this puzzlement which at least suggests there is something fishy going on here. Descartes first distinguishes between dreaming and being awake, on the basis of sometimes knowing he is awake and sometimes knowing he is dreaming or has dreamed. He then goes on to conclude that there is no way of knowing, in any given case, whether he is awake or just dreaming. But this skeptical suggestion is premised on the distinction between being awake and dreaming, and that distinction is premised on the assumption that one sometimes knows one is awake and sometimes knows one is not. Thus, the skeptical stance seems to assume what it denies. Or, to put it another way, where did we get the distinction, in the first place, between being awake and dreaming if we didn't sometimes know we were awake and sometimes know we were dreaming?

The notion that genius is politics all the way down, too, seems to partake of the same paradoxical strategy. First one makes the ordinary distinction between genuinely being a genius and merely having the politically hyped reputation for being one. Then one falls into the skeptical fear (or desire?) that maybe it's *all* political hype. But the thesis that "It's politics all the way down" is predicated on our having the prior distinction between cases of real genius and cases of phony, politically constructed genius, and that distinction is predicated on our sometimes knowing that we are in the presence of a real genius and sometimes in the presence of a phony, PR one. But this is getting ahead of the game—so for starters, let me tell you what the game is.

I am going to begin by stating some precepts and propositions of what I take to be the "commonsense" notion of musical genius, although it can be extended, one presumes, to genius *tout court*. It is the notion that each in its own way the images of the possessor and the possessed were supposed to capture.

I am then going to examine what might, as I see it, be called a sociological and political reduction or deconstruction of this notion—in particular, a reduction or deconstruction of Beethoven's genius.

Finally, I am going to argue that this reduction or deconstruction is supported by fallacious arguments and inadequate data, which is to say, not supported at all.

Notice that I have purposely avoided suggesting any intention to refute the socio-political deconstruction of genius. It cannot be refuted—which is, indeed, one of its problems. And in any case, it is impossible to prove the negative. If one wants to insist that the world is flat and has no compunctions about providing ad hoc assumptions at will to defend the doctrine, there is nothing reason can do with the flat-earther. But it appears to me that the burden of proof, in the case of musical genius, and Beethoven's genius, is upon the enemy of common sense. So showing that the socio-political deconstruction of commonsense genius I am about to examine has no substantial foundation entitles me to the commonsense concept until, at least, a successful reduction or deconstruction comes along. (In the final chapter I will suggest why we may have a very long, if not interminable, wait.)

According to the commonsense notion of genius, Beethoven was a genius if ever there was one. That means, he simply had something extra: as one of my friends used to put it, a "circuit" the rest of us don't have. And whether you think, like the Longinian, that it is a gift of nature or, like the Platonist, that it is at least analogous to divine possession, it is *something*—some *thing*. It is a fact, a hard fact, an objective fact that someone is a musical genius and someone else is not, even though it is a fact that many take a long time to discover or recognize.

But musical genius is not something that can be read off someone, like the color of her hair or her blood pressure, or the strength of her biceps. It is a "dispositional" property, and, ordinarily, one knows that the disposition is present by its being "expressed." We discover that something is soluble in water by seeing it dissolve in water. And we know that Beethoven was a musical genius because we know that, during his lifetime, he created musical works upon which we place the highest possible musical value. Thus, musical genius, on the commonsense view, is the "disposition" to consistently produce musical masterpieces.

Two very important points now emerge about the commonsensical view of musical genius. It implies, and rightly so, that genius is an evaluative concept, and, because genius is a disposition, that there are conditions under which it will *not* be realized. Both these implications are of the utmost importance to what follows; I therefore pause to discuss them briefly.

Genius is an evaluative concept, both "internally" and "externally." By being "internally" evaluative I mean that genius is seen as a disposition to produce supremely valuable products within the field of endeavor in which the genius functions. Thus, a musical genius is one who produces supremely valuable musical works, a scientific genius one who makes supremely valuable discoveries or theories, and so on. We do not call someone a genius unless, within her discipline, she produces at the highest possible level.

But genius is also evaluative in an "external" sense. By that I mean that we don't call someone a genius unless we put the highest possible value on the discipline or field in which she works. We recognize people as musical geniuses not merely because we place a high value on their works, within the discipline of musical composition, but because we place a high value on *music*. We recognize people as scientific geniuses not merely because we place a high value on their discoveries and theories within the discipline of natural science, but because we place a high value on *natural science*. However, even though we may think, as I do, that Mrs. Edwards makes better fried eggs and waffles than any one else in the United States, we would not call her a genius, because we do not, at least at this time, value that enterprise at the level at which we value science or music. (And, it will be recalled, there was a time when *music* was not so valued.)

As well, genius is an evaluative concept in that it demarcates abilities that are both difficult and (therefore) rare. What is easy to do, everyone can do. So even if we do value activities that are both easy and (therefore) widespread among us, we would not call those who engage in such activities geniuses. Geniuses are rare because they can do things the rest of us cannot do at their level.

Furthermore, like any other dispositions, genius can express itself only when the appropriate conditions obtain. Sugar dissolves in water within a certain range of physical conditions; if these physical conditions do not obtain, it will not dissolve when placed in water. Gold is soluble in aqua regia, but not in orange juice. And musical geniuses are able to express their genius in great musical works only in the proper social and political environment, with the requisite institutions in place. On the commonsense view, Beethoven would not have written great musical works (or any musical works at all) if he had been transported as an infant to Australia and had lived out his life in a community of aborigines. But common sense, I dare say, also holds that he would have produced musical masterpieces of the highest order even though he had remained in Bonn all his life and never moved to Vienna. Thus, the commonsense notion of genius is not a notion of genius as disconnected from the social and political institutions in which Western music flourishes, any more than any other disposition is disconnected from the conditions which make its realization possible.

It follows from this dispositional account of genius that there must be and have been more geniuses than there are or have been *fulfilled* geniuses. A more melancholy result, of course, is that disenfranchised groups have been rendered unable to express their genius, not because the social and political institutions necessary to facilitate it did not exist in their "neighborhoods," but because they were systematically denied participation in them, as well as assured by "authorities" that they were not capable of participation, were it granted them. This, as we all know (or should know), has been the fate of the African American in the United States, and of women in world history. The latter, of course, is what the "feminist critique of genius" is directed at, and shall be taken up in the next chapter.

But it might be well to mention at this point that on the "commonsense" view of genius as I construe it, there is no reason in the world why women or African Americans, to name but two traditionally disenfranchised groups, are not possessed of the same percentage of geniuses as white European or Anglo-Saxon males. Indeed, it takes a good deal of "uncommon sense" or bad theory to come to the opposite conclusion.

I have now completed my sketch of what I take to be the basic, commonsensical view of what could be called the "logic" of the concept of genius and, I think, genius in general. I must only add that it is compatible with both pictures of genius that the ancient world bequeathed to us, and that the eighteenth and nineteenth centuries formed into philosophical systems for the fine arts. In other words, both the Platonic possession theory and the Longinian theory of genius as natural gift, are meant to mythically and, later, philosophically, show what makes the commonsense truths of genius possible. So, with this preliminary sketch of "commonsense" genius in place, I turn now to its socio-political "deconstruction."

The work of deconstruction, or reduction, that I will be discussing, I hasten to say, at the outset, presents a carefully researched picture of political and social structures in Beethoven's Vienna, relevant to its musical life, that I have no wish to cast aspersions on or to contest. I am certainly not denying that there *are* social and political structures in the musical world and that the study of them has something interesting and valuable to tell us. What I *am* contesting are the philosophical conclusions about genius, and other art-theoretic concepts that the author draws from the sociological and political data adduced. These conclusions, I shall argue, are completely unsupported by the proffered evidence.

The work I have been alluding to above is by sociologist Tia DeNora. It is called: *Beethoven and the Construction of Genius: Musical Politics in Vienna, 1792–1803*.

One can learn a good deal about DeNora's project by thinking a little about the title of her book. What the title tells us, straightaway, is that it is about how Beethoven's genius was "constructed." A believer in the commonsense view of genius who wished to pursue a commonsense version of her project would have called the book, perhaps, *Beethoven and the Discovery of Musical Genius* . . . or *Beethoven and the Recognition of Musical Genius* . . . or even *Beethoven and the Dissemination of the Reputation for Musical Genius* . . . , implying, of course, or at least allowing for the possibility that Beethoven *was* a musical genius, had that extra circuit, and that if anything was "constructed," it was not his genius but his reputation for having it.

But DeNora's title, *Beethoven and the Construction of Musical Genius* . . . , implies something quite different (and quite *un*commonsensical). It implies that Beethoven's genius was manufactured, fabricated—in a word, *constructed*. Before this was accomplished, Beethoven didn't have genius. After it was accomplished, he did. And it was accomplished by Viennese musical politics, between 1792 and 1803.

What exactly was it that was constructed? Well, *genius*, of course. Beethoven was a genius, and his genius, contrary to popular belief, was not a gift, not an inborn or god-given super-talent; it was something that politics constructed. It was a social or political artifact. However, what immediately strikes one about the discussion of genius in DeNora's book is that the word frequently appears in what philosophers call "scare quotes." (Indeed, I have never read a book in which so many words and phrases are in scare quotes.) Thus, it was not genius that was constructed, but "genius." What are we to make of this?

Scare quotes are used by philosophers and others to flag "dangerous words"—words to be wary of for one reason or another. And one of the most common purposes of placing a word in scare quotes can be illustrated by the following assertion: In Salem they burned "witches," which, I take it, can be paraphrased: In Salem they burned witches (so-called). The person, then, asserting, In Salem they burned "witches," is implying that she does not believe there are any such beings as witches, which is to say, human beings having the supernatural powers and natures the Salemites attributed to the unfortunate women they burned under the description "witch."

If, then, I should read, in DeNora's book, about the "modern conceptions of musical hierarchy and serious musical 'stars' or 'geniuses,'"[1] what am I to make of it? My impulse is to conclude that she is talking about geniuses (so-called); that the political deconstruction of genius leaves it an empty concept. There are no geniuses, as there are no witches; there are only people that political machinery has made us think of in a certain way.

There is, however, another interpretation one might put on DeNora's use of scare quotes around the word "genius." It perhaps signals not the denial of the concept, as in "genius (so-called)," but a drastic change in the analysis of the concept. Thus, DeNora might be construed not as denying that there is such a thing as genius but as denying that genius is of the nature that the commonsense view has, for so long, attributed to it. Natural science is, of course, full of such redefinitions of ordinary concepts. And since what we are dealing with here is the work of a social scientist, such an interpretation of what she is about is not out of place. However, it is a nice question whether, if that is what DeNora is doing, the concept of genius has really been preserved. For if one gives a different *enough* analysis of a concept to what its traditional analysis has been, it is arguable that we now have simply a different concept with the same name. So much of our commonsense "logic" of the concept of genius is lost—even if one accepts what DeNora is doing as a redefinition of genius rather than a denial of its reality—that there is little to choose between saying she is doing the one rather than the other.

It any event, it is all one to me which interpretation is put on what DeNora is doing. Both are deflating in exactly the same way, of the commonsense concept of genius. Furthermore, under either interpretation, I shall argue, the evidence and arguments adduced do not establish the conclusion.

Let us turn now, after these general introductory comments, to the specific case of Beethoven. For it is *Beethoven's* genius that is the subject of DeNora's book, and *its* deconstruction the goal. It is a swing of the pendulum from Mozart to Beethoven yet again, but decidedly *not* a swing back to the Longinian genius.

I begin by providing a commonsense account of Beethoven's genius, its reception, and its ultimate triumph, as I did of the commonsense view of genius in general, against which we can perceive DeNora's contrasting, "constructed" view.

Ludwig van Beethoven was born in Bonn, in Catholic Germany, on (probably) 16 December 1770. His father was a musician and provided the first music lessons for his son, who began to show his musical genius at an early age. He was certainly a prodigy by anyone's standards, although not a match for Mozart in that regard. (Who could be?)

In any event, by the time he left Bonn permanently for Vienna in 1792, Beethoven was a world-class virtuoso on piano and organ, a master at improvisation, and an accomplished composer who had already written some of the finest wind music of the eighteenth century, as well as an impressive Cantata on the Death of Emperor Joseph II (1790), which has moments in it of true magnificence and sublimity that already bear the Beethoven "signature." These clearly are the work of a budding genius.

When Beethoven arrived in Vienna he had very good connections with the aristocracy as well as with established musical figures, including Joseph Haydn—connections which are examined with considerable care by DeNora. He continued his musical studies with, among others, Haydn and Albrechtsberger, and began, fairly early on, to be recognized as both a performer and composer of extraordinary talent—even, some were saying, a *genius.*

In all three periods in which Beethoven's music is still customarily divided, it was never easy for its first listeners to comprehend or appreciate. It was considered by many to be confused, disorganized, dissonant, idiosyncratic, self-indulgent, even bizarre. But during his lifetime Beethoven won over many enthusiasts, not only among professional musicians, but also among the talented amateurs, both aristocratic and middle-class, of which Vienna possessed a large number, as well as the general musical public. In short, very early on, Beethoven's towering genius was beginning to be recognized by many, and he died a revered artist whose funeral was a public event.

According to the commonsense view of Beethoven's genius, then, Beethoven was, from the start, a man apart. He was gifted with a preeminent genius that began to express itself early in life. In Vienna, his genius struggled for recognition: many misunderstood it, but many came to appreciate it as well. And to make the power of his genius all the more remarkable, it triumphed over the worst affliction under which a composer can labor: impairment of hearing and, ultimately, a nearly total loss, which, nevertheless, did not prevent him from writing musical masterpieces that are the wonder of the world. So says common sense about the transcendent genius of Beethoven.

It is now time to move on from the commonsense view of Beethoven's genius to DeNora's alternative—what I have been calling the socio-political view—Beethoven's genius as a "construction."

In the introductory chapter of her book, DeNora provides a kind of preview of the claims she will be making in the ensuing chapters. Perhaps the central claim, so it seems to me, is that

> it is fallacious to argue that the artistic steps Beethoven took were those of a giant, and that if his contemporaries were unable to perceive their inherent value it was because they were too small or lacked vision. To account for Beethoven's talent in any of these ways is to hold a view that flatters the present-day viewer's so-called more advanced perspective; it also imposes our own aesthetic evaluative terms on a group for which they are not necessarily appropriate.[2]

The commonsense view, of course, is that Beethoven *was* a "giant" —that his talent was enormous, genius-talent and this enabled him to write music of supreme greatness, which, because of its departures from familiar models, was difficult for his contemporaries to appreciate. They lacked the vision and perspective that time and familiarity have given to later generations of listeners. But all this, we are being told, is fallacious. In particular, it "flatters" us and "imposes" our aesthetic evaluative terms on a group for which they are not appropriate. "Impress" and "flatters" are terms of a particular kind of abuse: they suggest that friends of the commonsense view are in bad faith; are motivated by their desire for self-aggrandizement and a tendency to force their values on others; they are the bad guys.

Pursuing this thought further, DeNora writes that "Beethoven's recognition, for example, is often explained in ways that over emphasize his 'own' talent at the expense of the social basis of his acceptance and celebration."[3] "Overemphasize" is, of course, something of a weasel word. It suggests that the commonsense view is not mistaken in attributing Beethoven's recognition to his own talent but puts too much weight on it. (What is *too much*?) However, what does DeNora mean to suggest by putting "own" in scare quotes? If "talent" were in scare quotes, of course, we would know that what is meant is talent so-called, which is to say, no talent at all — talent goes the way of witches. To put the quotes around "own," however, is puzzling. It suggests that there is talent, alright, but it is not *Beethoven*'s. What *that* could mean I can scarcely imagine, and so I am inclined to think that the scare quotes around "own" are meant to convey the same meaning as if they were put around "talent." That Beethoven really had talent is (astoundingly) being placed in doubt: Beethoven had "talent" the way Salem burned "witches." That he had no talent of his *own* I take to be equivalent to his having no talent, at least as it is construed by common sense — which is to say, an inborn gift that *he* possesses and that most others do not, albeit an inborn gift that requires all the resources of a certain cultural and institutional structure to nurture and to realize appropriately.

Within the framework of the two claims already adduced, two "inner" themes are pursued with tenacity — themes which are intended, apparently, to both illustrate and support them. The first is a contrast between the careers of Beethoven and one of his more or less forgotten contemporaries — forgotten in the concert repertory (and rightly so) but not by the historians of music, to whom his name is familiar. "By comparing Beethoven's early career with that of Jan Ladislav Dussek, I examine resources that were available to Beethoven but beyond the reach of most of his fellow musicians, and I suggest that it was because of a variety of social and cultural forms of capital that Beethoven was well positioned to become 'the next Mozart.'"[4] Note that, yet again, there is a crucial phrase in scare quotes: "the next Mozart"; in other words, the next Mozart (so-called). There is no *real* next Mozart, no *real* next great genius in the tradition, any more than there are real witches. It is a matter—and note well the term—of your social and cultural "capital." In other words, we are in a marketplace with, one assumes, marketplace motivations. And note, finally, the suggestion of a scientific method, which becomes more apparent when the comparison between Beethoven and Dussek is pursued more fully later on. Had Jones received the drug and Smith the placebo, Jones would not have gotten cancer and Smith would, just as had Dussek been given Vienna, with Beethoven's connections, Beethoven London with Dussek's (lack thereof?)....

The second theme is what DeNora calls "A particular mythic account of Beethoven's relation to Haydn . . . ," in which, she claims, ". . . Beethoven and Haydn were willing to collaborate to produce a fiction that became a resource for the construction of Beethoven's greatness."[5] Note here the bald assertion that Beethoven's musical greatness is a "construction," that it is the result of a "fiction," and that Beethoven and Haydn "collaborated" to produce the fiction, all of which implies that Beethoven really wasn't great, that his greatness (so-called) was the product of a lie, and that Beethoven and Haydn promulgated what they knew was a lie in order to forward Beethoven's (and Haydn's) interests. If this is so, we ought to view Beethoven and Haydn in somewhat the same moral light as the perpetrators of the Dreyfus affair, and Beethoven's musical "greatness" in the same epistemic light as Dreyfus' "guilt." From the commonsense point of view this is pretty heavy, and one is tempted to say that anyone who can believe it—at least, anyone with an ear for music—can believe *anything*.

In exploring how DeNora expands upon these claims and themes, and what she offers in the way of argument and evidence for them, I turn first to the comparison of Beethoven with Dussek. The general idea here seems to be something like this. On the commonsense view, had Beethoven lived from infancy to death in the outback of

Australia, no one in his right mind would think that his genius for musical composition would have flourished. It would have withered on the vine and been lost to the world. But suppose that instead of living and dying in Vienna, as he did, he had spent his mature creative life in London. Suppose, in other words, he and Dussek had changed places. On the commonsense view, Beethoven, because of his transcendent genius, would *still* have composed towering masterpieces, and Dussek still would have been a mediocrity. If, however, genius really is a socio-political construct, then Beethoven would have been the "mediocrity," Dussek the "genius." (Note that we must now add scare quotes, because genius has been deconstructed.)

The question now is: Is it true that if, *per impossibile*, Dussek and Beethoven were to change places, Dussek would have been the genius and Beethoven the mediocrity? DeNora confidently answers in the affirmative. She says: "of course Beethoven was musically competent and musically interesting. The point is rather that there were numerous other musicians who, under different circumstances, could have ended up as celebrities."[6] More specifically, "Had Beethoven been in London at that time, it is unlikely that his particular claims could have been articulated, let alone sustained."[7]

Actually, it seems to me the London thing is a bit of a red herring, aside from the obvious fact that many foreign musicians—Handel, Johann Christian Bach, Haydn—flourished there. Dussek spent only ten years of a fairly long life in London. Most of his musical career played out touring the musical capitals of Europe (as well as some of the tank towns) as a distinguished composer and pianist, with, so far as I can see, more than adequate opportunity and "connections" to stake his claim as a world-class compositional genius, if he had been one. But never mind that. Let us see where DeNora's argument leads us.

It is vital to note not merely what DeNora is claiming here but what qualification she puts on the claim. If genius is a political construction, pure and simple, then it would follow that *anyone,* given the right connections and the requisite publicity, could take Beethoven's place as the transcendental "genius" of his era. But *that* even the most confirmed deconstructivist of genius will have difficulty swallowing. So, of course, constraints must be put on the group of possible candidates for Beethoven's position. Dussek qualifies but, obviously, your average Viennese menial does not. Thus the group of potential "Beethovens" consists of "musically competent and musically interesting" persons, of which we can count Beethoven and Dussek and, possibly, many others as members.

Now the first thing to notice in this regard is that in the process of deconstructing genius, DeNora has helped herself to two other evaluative concepts—musical competence and musical interest—and in a moment I will consider the question of whether she is entitled to them.

But first let us take a look at the claim itself, which these two concepts are meant to qualify. To repeat, it is this: "Had Beethoven been in London at that time, it is *unlikely* that his particular claims could have been articulated, let alone sustained." (The emphasis is mine.) I intend the reader's eye, of course, to fall on the word "unlikely." Under what circumstances do we use that word, and its opposite, "probably"? Clearly, the standard cases are those in which we are basing some conclusion, formally or informally, on an inductive inference. Past experience tells us it is unlikely that there will be a hurricane in March, likely in September. On what grounds do we say it is unlikely that Beethoven would have been the genius he was had he changed places with Dussek? On *inductive* grounds?

Have we experienced *other* cases of composers changing places, and music history rerunning itself like a rewound film? Of course the "experiment" is impossible. The claim is based on no possible experience, hence no possible inductive inference at all. And using the word "unlikely" in making the claim is just idle conjecture masquerading as science. What we have here is merely a "thought experiment."

Well, what's wrong with a thought experiment? Nothing at all, except that if one performs this particular one, it seems that common sense will conclude that were Beethoven and Dussek to change places, Beethoven would *still* be the genius, the important genius, the serious genius, the "big" genius, and Dussek the mediocrity. Common sense got there first, so to speak, so it is common sense that has formed our intuitions about genius. A *Gedankenexperiment* is an intuition pump, and this particular one pumps out, predictably, the commonsense conclusion that, be it London or Vienna or Munich or Prague or even Bonn or Salzburg, Beethoven would be Beethoven, Dussek Dussek. (If Vienna and politics did the trick, what's Salieri doing in mothballs?)

But perhaps, it might be retorted, I am placing far too much weight on the word "unlikely." Sometimes, after all, such words as "likely" and "probably" are merely synonyms for "certain." So perhaps all De-Nora is saying is that *she* is *certain* that were Dussek and Beethoven to change places, Dussek would be the Beethoven-like genius, Beethoven the Dussek-like mediocrity. Then, however, we would want to know what evidence she had for her certainty, and we would be back where we started. Of course, *if* it were true that genius is a sociopolitical construct, *that* would be evidence for the Dussek/Beethoven claim. Then, however, the truth of the Beethoven/Dussek claim would not be evidence for the theory that genius is a political construct, but vice versa. So other evidence, of course, would be required for its support.

DeNora does, indeed, tell us some of the ways in which the London musical scene, musical institutions, and musical forms and predilections differed from the Viennese ones. But, so far as I can see, this provides no evidence at all for the notion that Beethoven's genius (or anyone else's) is a socio-political construct. *If,* of course, we were to establish that it was antecedently, *then* we could point to these institutions, practices, forms, and predilections as possible causal factors, using John Stuart Mill's good old "method of difference." But before we establish the socio-political thesis, there is no prior reason to think that these factors have any crucial efficacy at all, any more than that what makes the difference is that in London they spoke English and had a king and parliament, and in Vienna they spoke German and had an emperor. Or, in other words, to cite the socio-political differences as evidence for the socio-political theory of genius is simply to beg the question from the start, and to try to establish the theory with the Beethoven/Dussek thought experiment (for a thought experiment is all that it can possibly be) produces no result or the opposite one.

Notice that it is impossible to *disprove* the Dussek/Beethoven conjecture, and, of course, I have not attempted to do so. It stands safely above refutation because it is an "experiment" that can never be carried out except in thought. All the more reason, then, to be very suspicious of it: immunity from empirical refutation is not a mark in favor of a scientific theory, even one in the social sciences. But, anyway, there is no need for common sense to refute it. Common sense has the prior claim over the Dussek/Beethoven conjecture. It is for the supporter of genius as construct to disprove common sense, not the other way around. All things being equal, if it's a choice between common sense and the Dussek/Beethoven proposal, common sense wins.

In concluding this discussion of the Beethoven/Dussek business, I want to return briefly to a point mentioned at the outset of the discussion: the point about musical competence and musical interest. If it is assumed, on all hands, as I think it must be, that it is a *reductio ad absurdum* of the constructionist's view of genius if it were to imply that *anyone,* in the proper circumstances, with the requisite connections, could be a Beethoven-like genius, then some constraints must be put on the potential-genius pool. Apparently, the constraints DeNora wants to put on it are those of musical competence and musical interest. Both Beethoven and Dussek were musically "competent," their music "interesting," and so either of these two were potential geniuses, but Beethoven's cook (for example) was not musically competent (although Handel's cook, Waltz, actually was), and Franz Xaver Süssmayr's music (for example) was not interesting.

But note that both "competent" and "interesting," like "genius" itself, are, in part and essentially, value concepts. They demarcate, simply, lower orders of musical value than does the concept of genius. Why shouldn't they too be subject to the same political deconstruction? It's turtles all the way down. The reason Beethoven's cook is not musically competent and the reason Süssmayr is not a musically interesting composer is that *they* did not have the right social environment or the right political connections. So it would seem that DeNora must either arbitrarily designate musical interest and musical competence as immune from deconstruction while, equally arbitrarily, declaring genius eligible, or accept the conclusion which most, I think, would consider a *reductio* of her view: that anyone, *absolutely anyone,* given the right social environment and the right political connections—Beethoven's, for example—could have been the Beethoven genius. Once deconstruction starts, there seems no way to stop it. If musical interest and musical competence are necessary conditions for the construction of genius, never mind. The *reductio* goes through one way or the other.

The next logical step for the constructionist is to somehow defuse the *reductio*. What drives it? At least one vital element here is the concept of artistic or aesthetic *value* (which I shall use here synonymously). Musical genius, musical competence, musical interest are all parasitic on musical *value*. A person is recognized as a musical genius if her compositions have the highest possible musical value; she is recognized as musically competent if her compositions meet a certain minimal standard of musical value; and she is considered musically interesting if her compositions have a certain *kind* of musical value. What makes the notion that just about *anyone* can be a musical genius, or even be musically competent or musically interesting, appear an absurd notion is, I suggest, that *value,* value of any kind, does not grow on trees. As any music teacher knows, musical competence cannot be imparted to all his students, let *alone* musical genius, no matter how much they practice. Some of his students are just "gifted"—*that* is just "common sense."

It appears, then, that a logical strategy for defusing the *reductio* of *anyone* being able to, under the proper socio-political auspices, create musical value, is to defuse value itself. That, in part, I suggest, is behind DeNora's claim that it is "fallacious" for us to pass aesthetic judgments to the effect that Beethoven's music possesses "inherent value" which might perhaps have not been perceivable to his contemporaries. The value question, then, must be our next order of business. The commonsense view of genius endorses the commonsense notion that Beethoven's music *is,* without qualification, music of the highest possible value, and orders of magnitude better, without qualification, than Dussek's or that of any of those other also-rans.

Does DeNora adduce any compelling reasons for giving up that commonsense notion? Her attitude toward the assumption of musical value is apparent in her stated focus of her book:

In this study, I am interested in the responses of Beethoven's contemporaries to his works, as these responses occurred in a social context. I am not interested, however, in evaluating these responses from a musical-analytical standpoint (for example, how initial listeners may have been "mistaken" in their assessments of his work). That kind of enterprise is historically imperialistic, because it makes the responses of previous others subservient to our own, later responses, which are inappropriately projected backward in time.[8]

The first point to notice here is which word appears in scare quotes—for, inevitably, it seems, there will be one or more such instances in every claim DeNora makes. Here the victim is "mistaken," which we must read as: "mistaken so-called." In other words, as there is no such thing as a witch, there is no such thing as being mistaken if you were an "initial listener" to Beethoven in your assessment of his work. *No matter what assessment you made of Beethoven's music, you could not have been mistaken.* (What an extraordinary claim!) Does that mean that everyone was correct in their assessment? If so, then opposite assessments would both be correct, which sounds like a violation of the law of contradiction. To be charitable to DeNora, I presume, therefore, she is saying that there is no such thing as being either mistaken or correct in an initial listener's assessment of Beethoven's music. And this, by the way, would apply both to the judgment that Beethoven's music is or is not interesting and is or is not competent—another reason she is not, by her own lights, entitled to either of these notions in constricting the group of potential geniuses.

But why should we believe this extraordinary claim? As far as I can see, the only reason adduced in the above quotation, if properly a reason at all, is that if we should say that a contemporary of Beethoven's was mistaken in her assessment of his music, we are guilty of being "historically imperialistic," because it makes the responses of previous others subservient to our own later responses, which are inappropriately projected backward in time.

Now, of course, to rebut someone's claim by saying it is imperialistic or fascist, racist or communistic is simply to substitute abuse for argument. It is a kind of political rhetoric that has become all too familiar in public debate when evidence is wanting (as it usually is). Unfortunately, it is becoming all too familiar in the scholarly literature as well, for very much the same reason.

But precisely what "historical imperialism" is, anyhow, is something of a mystery to me. I know what ordinary, garden-variety imperialism is, and why it is morally reprehensible (if it is morality that really is at issue). Imperialism compels people by main force to share the imperialist's beliefs, values, and institutions against their wills and inclinations. It is morally reprehensible because of *that*. Whatever historical imperialism is, it cannot by main force, or by any other means, compel people who are dead to share the historical imperialist's beliefs or values or institutions. I think Rossini was profoundly mistaken in his assessment of Beethoven's Ninth Symphony (except for the Scherzo, which he highly valued). I can hardly, however, be judged immoral—"imperialistic" toward his assessment—since he is forever free of my attempt to compel him to share my view.

In any case, people whom I associate with, and who may claim that some listener of the past is mistaken in her assessment of Beethoven, would not *want* to compel her, by main force or any other means, to share their assessment, even if they could. They would want to *convince* her by argument, and would be open to rational persuasion themselves. Furthermore, even if one were immoral, because a "historical imperialist," in claiming that a contemporary of Beethoven's was mistaken in her assessment of his music, that *still* would be completely irrelevant. Under certain circumstances, it *would* be immoral to tell someone she was mistaken. (You can imagine the circumstances for yourself.) But the immorality of telling that person she was mistaken would hardly be evidence against the truth (or falsity) of what I told her. In sum, then, the charge of "historical imperialism" borders on nonsense and is a cheap shot with no epistemic clout.

Why, then, should anyone think it necessarily fallacious to claim that a contemporary of Beethoven's was mistaken in an assessment of his music? There are some shards of argument scattered here and there (besides the pseudo-argument I have just canvassed) that, on my view, don't amount to much but are at least worth a cursory examination, before I go on to say what I think really is going on here, which, I suggest, is merely the begging of a question, no doubt on the dubious assumption that it is just plain common sense. But it is, I further suggest, only "common sense" to those who have left common sense far behind them.

If we return, for a moment, to the first statement of DeNora's, of what I shall call henceforth her aesthetic value skepticism, we find the following two claims made in support of the view that it is always fallacious to declare mistaken any assessment on the part of Beethoven's contemporaries with regard to his talent or his music. First, "it is to hold a view that flatters the present-day viewer's so-called more advanced perspective," and, second, "it also imposes our own aesthetic evaluative terms on a group for which they are not necessarily appropriate."

Let's look at the second claim first. To begin with, it reveals the same apparent obsession of the author with the notion that disagreeing with someone is a form of oppression, evidenced in the claim, previously examined, that to call a contemporary of Beethoven's "mistaken" in her assessment of the composer's music is "imperialistic." But the notion is plainly false in this place, as it was in the other, and amounts to nothing more than name-calling. To impose "aesthetic evaluative terms" on someone means to *force* her, in one way or another, to adopt them. Aside from the obvious fact that I cannot force a dead person to do anything, to say to someone that she is mistaken is *clearly* not, in itself, a form of imposition, and in my circles it is usually followed by rational persuasion, which is just the opposite of "imposition."

Now, it may be replied that I am being purposely obtuse in understanding DeNora in these cases. After all, are not "imperialistic" and "impose" merely metaphors? Perhaps so, but they are metaphors with a kind of abusive force. They tend to impugn motives without providing anything in the way of argument to show that what they are naming is logically defective in any way. Furthermore, it is plainly false that "our own aesthetic evaluative terms" were not shared by Beethoven's contemporaries, as well as by people in other historical periods. If that were true, we would not even be able to understand what their assessments of Beethoven were. But clearly we do understand them, and DeNora assumes that we understand them. When Leopold II famously said of *Die Entführung,* "Too many notes, my dear Mozart," he was evaluating the work in the very terms we would, and we understand exactly what he meant. Both he and we agree that to say "too many notes" is to pass an adverse judgment on a work for reasons that are too obvious to state. What separates us from Leopold II is that we, like Mozart, think there are just as many notes as are necessary. We agree on terms, we disagree in our value judgments—and history has proved Leopold II mistaken. So far, as well, we have been given no reason to believe it is "fallacious" to say so.

But perhaps we are involved here merely with a *lapsus calami.* Perhaps DeNora meant that we do not share the *values* of Beethoven's contemporaries. This, however, is either a trivially true claim, if it means we do not place the same value on some of Beethoven's works that they did, which no one denies, or that we differ with them about what makes a musical work valuable, which is, by and large, false. For, again, we share with Mozart's and Beethoven's contemporaries the beliefs that too many notes or lack of organization or orchestration that is too heavy in the winds or compositions that are too long—all charges that at one time or another were leveled by Beethoven's contemporaries against his works—are disvalues. What we disagree with them about is whether Beethoven's works possess those disvalues. They say yes; about this we say they are mistaken. And nothing yet brought forward by DeNora shows that we are committing any fallacy by so saying. Least of all does it follow that even if we were imposing our views on dead folks (whatever that could mean), which we patently are not, we would be mistaken or fallacious in our judgment. We would simply not be very nice people. But not very nice people are sometimes right in their judgments, and calling them names cannot count as evidence against their claims.

The first claim, yet again, displays DeNora's tendency to substitute a kind of personal abuse for rational argument, and is a special case of a more general tendency to impugn motives in lieu of rationally examining beliefs. Thus, if I should suggest that a well-known contemporary of Beethoven's was mistaken in thinking the Seventh

Symphony incoherent, I am "flattering" my views at the expense of his. No doubt I am, if I say it immodestly. Although if I am right, and he is mistaken, I presume it is a flattery my views deserve; furthermore, my *motive* is not self-flattery, but even if it were, it would not imply that my view is false any more than if he was motivated by malice, it would show that he was mistaken. The way to show whether or not Beethoven's Seventh Symphony is or is not incoherent is, clearly, to examine the symphony itself, not the motives of its supporters or detractors.

Even more revealing is DeNora's reference to "the present-day viewer's *so-called* more advanced perspective." So it turns out that any estimate of Beethoven's music I or any of my contemporaries have that we deem more advanced than a contemporary of Beethoven's — say, that the Seventh Symphony is not incoherent but a model of tightly organized symphonic structure — is more advanced in exactly the same way in which they burned witches in Salem. It is not possible, contrary to all common sense in the matter, for us to have advanced one whit since the premier of Beethoven's mighty Seventh in our perspective on its value or significance. In spite of the obvious fact that we have a more advanced view on biology, physics, astronomy, ancient Greek culture, medicine, Medieval iconography, and so on, than did Beethoven's contemporaries, we do not, *cannot*, have a more advanced view of the value and significance of Beethoven's music. Why should we believe such an extraordinary thing? There are two reasons, I suspect, lurking in DeNora's book — one, the more important one, never surfacing at all, the other surfacing in a slightly different context. Neither is in the least convincing.

The latter reason can be gleaned from what DeNora says about what she calls "turning points." She writes: "With regard to various 'turning points' or radical departures in Beethoven's work, we need to consider that what we may perceive as a comparatively 'small' distance (between Mozart and Beethoven in the 1790s) may have been perceived by contemporaries as much larger. . . ."[9]

I am not particularly interested here in whether Beethoven's early works are or are not a turning point, a departure from Mozart, or whether, on the contrary, there is only a small gap between late Mozart and early Beethoven. The important point is that DeNora apparently thinks it is wrong to either assert or, in the present instance, deny something's being a turning point in Beethoven's musical style. Why is it wrong to assert that there is a small gap between early Beethoven and late Mozart? Because what *we* perceive as a small musical difference Beethoven's contemporaries perceived as a very large one. *They* perceived a turning point, and we do not.

This reasoning, I suggest, can be extrapolated, and perhaps was meant to be, to estimates of Beethoven's musical worth. Since Beethoven's contemporaries heard incoherence where we hear coherence, or since Beethoven's contemporaries heard strange and mannered music where we hear music of transcendental power and greatness, we must remember that what we may perceive as eminently coherent music of power and greatness may have been perceived by Beethoven's contemporaries as mannered and incoherent. Therefore, because such considerations, DeNora argues, should prevent us from asserting, from our historical perspective, that Beethoven's early works are but a small departure from Mozart's late ones, these same considerations should also prevent us, from our historical perspective, from asserting that Beethoven's music is music of eminent coherence and transcendent power and greatness.

Unfortunately for DeNora, the same argument that prevents us from saying that there is but a small gap separating Beethoven's early from Mozart's late style would prevent us from saying that the greatest scientist in history was born on Christmas Day 1642, because, clearly, none of the folks who were witness to this momentous event saw it as anything but the birth of a perfectly ordinary baby. And it *surely* should have prevented DeNora herself from saying that "A *turning point* in this transition [from pianist-composer to composer] occurred when Beethoven's first instrumental works were published, the Trios op. 1."[10] After all, Beethoven's contemporaries could hardly have seen this as a turning point.

It is hard to know what idea DeNora could have of the practice of historical narrative if she believes, as she apparently does, that it is a fallacy to ascribe to a past event or events some feature that those contemporaneous with the event or events could not possibly perceive them to possess. That is the very point of historical narrative. *Of course* you cannot make a historical judgment about the significance of an event or events until you have seen the consequences played out over time. *Of course* it is only in retrospect that we can know that the birth of the infant Newton was the birth of the greatest natural scientist in history. *Of course* we cannot know that the Battle of Gettysburg was a turning point in the Civil War until long after the event. *Of course* we cannot know that the publication of Beethoven's Op. 1 was a turning point in music history until a good deal of music history has succeeded the event. And *of course* we cannot make a reasonable evaluation of Beethoven's musical works without the perspective that only time and events can give us.

Therefore, an argument to the effect that because those contemporaneous with an event cannot see it the way we do in historical retrospect then our historical assessment of it cannot be valid proves either too much or too little. Either it proves that *all* historical statements are unjustified or inappropriate—including those in DeNora's own book, by the way, which is a *reductio*—or it proves nothing at all about value judgments made with the benefit of historical perspective, which seems just about right to me.

At this point, I think, an inevitable response will be forthcoming to the effect that there is no *reductio* here at all if we simply distinguish between *factual judgments* and *value judgments*. Historical judgments, so this argument will go, are factual judgments about the past. They purport to express truths about what really was the case. And of course one cannot make such judgments without events playing themselves out. Had Newton died at the age of six months, Christmas Day 1642 would not be the birthday of the greatest natural scientist in human history; had the South won the Civil War, the victory of the North at Gettysburg would have been not a turning point in that conflict but merely a temporary setback; and had Beethoven not emerged as the first person known *only* as a composer (actually, I think that happens to be false), then the publication of his Trios, Op. 1, would have been not a turning point in music history but merely an important event in Beethoven's life.

Now one problem with this move is that DeNora herself does not confine her ukase against retrospective historical judgments to judgments about artistic or aesthetic *value*. The judgment that the stylistic gap between early Beethoven and late Mozart is a narrow one is, on her view, *verboten* because Beethoven's contemporaries would have perceived the gap as wide. But this judgment is not, in any obvious sense, a judgment about aesthetic or artistic *value* at all. It is a judgment about style, with no *direct* implication for value either way. So we would have to extend the area of judgments forbidden to the aesthetic and artistic *tout court*, of which aesthetic and artistic value judgments are a subclass. And that begins to look more questionable, even to someone initially sympathetic to skepticism with regard to aesthetic and artistic value judgments. The fact-value gap is familiar to all philosophers, and is thought unbridgeable by some. There is, so far as I know, no strong groundswell for a fact-style gap. And I see no more reason to think that there is anything logically defective in ascribing, in historical hindsight, a narrow stylistic gap between early Beethoven and late Mozart, the judgments of Beethoven's contemporaries to the contrary notwithstanding, than there is to think that it is a logical mistake to say that the greatest natural scientist in human history was born on Christmas Day 1642, or that the Battle of Gettysburg was a turning point in the Civil War, the judgments of the contemporary witnesses to *those* events to the contrary notwithstanding.

Suppose we assume for the sake of argument, though, that DeNora's claim is not that all retrospective historical judgments are logically tainted, but only historical value judgments. What might the grounds be for this claim? Presumably, the grounds would be the familiar ones, that aesthetic and artistic value judgments are not judgments at all, but merely expressions of approval or disapproval. Or, if they are judgments, they are "subjective"—that is to say, not judgments imputing a value property to some object but merely judgments to the effect that the judge is feeling pleasure or displeasure, satisfaction or dissatisfaction in contemplating a work of art (or other aesthetic object). In other words, it would be the old skeptical claim that *De gustibus non disputandum est*. In that case, there is no justification at all for my asserting that Beethoven's contemporaries were "mistaken" in their low estimate of his music's artistic or aesthetic value and, *pari passu,* no justification at all for asserting that my or my contemporaries' high estimate of same is "correct." If aesthetic and artistic assertions of value are merely expressions of approval and disapproval, then they can be neither mistaken nor correct, since it makes no sense to ascribe either to an expression of attitude. And if they are statements about the subjects' feelings, then *all* of them are correct (it being highly unlikely that one can be mistaken about whether, here and now, he is enjoying or not enjoying what he is perceiving aesthetically), in which case it would always be false to say that Beethoven's contemporaries were incorrect in their aesthetic or artistic estimates of value, always otiose to say that mine or my contemporaries' are correct.

If this kind of aesthetic value skepticism is what is driving DeNora's interdict against our making historically retrospective judgments to the effect that Beethoven's contemporaries were mistaken in their low estimation of his music, and if we are correct in our high estimates, then, of course, we require an *argument* to show that aesthetic value skepticism is true. I find no such argument in her book. Perhaps she might reply that her whole book is such an argument; that the deconstruction of genius constitutes a deconstruction of aesthetic value judgments. But that will not do if the deconstruction of genius *assumes* (among other things) aesthetic value skepticism as a premise, which, it appears to me, might very well be the case. In that event we are indeed in need of a justification for it.

Well, I suppose someone of DeNora's stripe might just think that, among enlightened intellectuals, aesthetic value skepticism is simply "common sense." And, indeed, it is, as David Hume famously put it, *a* "species" of common sense. Which is to say that *De gustibus non disputandum est* is abroad in the land. "But," Hume continued,

> though this axiom, by passing into a proverb, seems to have attained the sanction of common sense; there is certainly a species of common sense which opposes it, at least serves to modify or restrain it. Whoever would assert an equality of genius and elegance between Ogilby and Milton, or Bunyan and Addison, would be thought to defend no less an extravagance, than if he

had maintained a mole-hill as high as Teneriffe, or a pond as extensive as the ocean. . . . The principle of the natural equality of tastes is then totally forgot, and while we admit it on some occasions, where the objects seem near an equality, it appears an extravagant paradox, or rather a palpable absurdity, where objects so disproportionate are compared together.[11]

Common sense is divided on the question of whether or not aesthetic and artistic value judgments are "subjective," unarguable, unsupportable, or not, and so cannot be appealed to in favor of one side or the other. Or, to put it more precisely, in Humean terms, common sense perhaps concedes to "subjectivism" where there is a near equality in value, but not where there is a great disparity, as between genius and mediocrity. It may be "common sense" that there is no reasoned way of deciding whether Beethoven's instrumental compositions are greater than Bach's, or the other way around; that, common sense tells us, may be a subjective matter—"a matter of taste." However, that Beethoven's instrumental music is orders of magnitude greater than Dussek's, Bach's than Telemann's—that, common sense tells us, is no matter "merely of taste" but is as "objective" a matter as that an ocean is more extensive than a pond, a mountain not a mole-hill.

Of course, common sense may be mistaken in *either* case. But that it is requires an argument, a philosophical critique. DeNora does not provide one against common sense, which has the prior claim; nor is this the place to provide one in its favor, particularly as the burden of proof is not upon the advocate of common sense. However, in lieu of one—and, as far as I know, there is none on which there is philosophical consensus—I will simply make my stand *on* common sense, indeed, the best common sense that I know: Hume's common sense. And the conclusion to be drawn from all this is that *if* DeNora's (or anyone else's) deconstruction of genius is driven by the engine of naive aesthetic value skepticism, it is driven by a very inadequate engine indeed.

There is, however, one further point to be made concerning aesthetic value skepticism before we can move on. Whether or not De-

Nora embraces the doctrine of *De gustibus non disputandum est* may be debatable. But that she embraces aesthetic value *relativism* is clear. And if aesthetic value relativism is confused with aesthetic value skepticism, if the former is adduced as an argument for the latter; in either case it is an obvious mistake. For aesthetic value relativism neither is aesthetic value skepticism *nor* does it imply the latter. Indeed, it implies its opposite.

The reason I suspect (but cannot be certain) that DeNora is either conflating aesthetic value relativism with aesthetic value skepticism, or assuming that the former implies the latter, is that she writes *as if* she were a value skeptic but never explicitly says that she is, while it appears from what she explicitly says that she *is* a value relativist. Indeed, the last section of her book is titled: "BEETHOVEN, THE CONSTRUCTION OF GENIUS, AND THE RELATIVITY OF VALUE."[12]

That musical value is *relative* it needs no ghost from the grave to tell us. Every sensible person who has thought at all about the question will agree to *that,* to some degree or another. The value of Beethoven's symphonies is measured relative to the standards and criteria of value for Western art music, the symphony in that tradition, and so forth, not the standards and criteria of value for Javanese gamelan, Indian ragas, or Broadway musical comedies. But measured according to those relevant standards and criteria, Beethoven's symphonies are very, very great, those of his lesser contemporaries anywhere from poor to mildly pleasurable to well brought off, and so on. However, it is an "objective fact" that, relative to these standards, Beethoven's symphonies are very, very great, just as it is that Abraham Lincoln was a tall man—tall, of course, relative to the standards for adult males in the mid–nineteenth century, not to those for current players in the NBA.

To get from aesthetic value relativism to aesthetic value skepticism, one must show by argument that one implies the other. And, so far as I can see, the only way to do that is to show that the standards underpinning aesthetic value judgments are themselves unredeemably subjective—in other words, relative merely to individual preferences or to the preferences of small, isolated groups. ("By *your* standards Beethoven's symphonies may be great musical works, but by *mine* they are utter garbage.")

Indeed, DeNora tries at least to show that the standards by which Beethoven's contemporaries judged his works were different from ours. And this is an argument for at least *historical* aesthetic value skepticism. But as I have argued previously, this view is completely false. *Our* evaluations of Beethoven's works may differ from his contemporaries' evaluations. Our *standards,* however, are more or less consistent with theirs. For that matter, when generalized, they are standards for the evaluation of artworks, many of which standards are already in place in Aristotle's *Poetics*. The notion that the standards for evaluating Beethoven's music are variable enough to turn aesthetic value relativism into aesthetic value skepticism with regard to it is philosophically and historically unfounded.

As foundations, then, for the socio-political deconstruction of genius, both aesthetic value relativism and aesthetic value skepticism are foundations built on sand. The former is true, but provides aid and comfort neither to deconstruction nor to skepticism, while skepticism remains unproven and in conflict with, as Hume describes it, one species of common sense.

There is, however, another deconstructive strategy that DeNora brings against the commonsense concept of genius that is independent of whether or not aesthetic value skepticism is true. It might be called "aesthetic *motive* skepticism," or, perhaps, "cynicism." It runs quite obsessively through DeNora's book, and I will conclude this discussion by considering it.

The commonsense notion of genius has it that (in many cases, anyway) the works of a genius like Beethoven are only gradually, and with difficulty, recognized and enjoyed for what they are: works at the very highest end of the musical value scale. Some people, in advance of their time, recognize and enjoy them sooner than do others. But eventually, through "the test of time," there is consensus.

Underlying the commonsense view of genius is the assumption—a reasonable assumption on the commonsense view, indeed, a *commonsensical* assumption—that people are motivated by their recognition of supreme value in a work, and, consequently, genius in its creator, to behave (sincerely) in certain ways. They may bear witness to their discovery by telling others that, for example, Beethoven's music is really wonderful, or write articles and reviews to that effect. They will, doubtless, be motivated to listen to Beethoven's music more and more, since, obviously, with a growing estimate of the music's value and virtues usually comes a growing satisfaction in hearing it. If they are in a position to, they help support the composer, as some of the Viennese aristocracy did. Or, if they are musicians or composers themselves, they may help promote Beethoven's interest among professionals while he is alive or promote his reputation after his death (as did the French and German Romantics). And so on.

However, it is also part of the commonsense view of genius that *some* people who do all of the above are not motivated by the belief that Beethoven's music is supremely great and that Beethoven is a transcendent genius. *These* people are "politically" motivated— "politically" in a rather broad sense of the term. As it becomes more and more fashionable to be known as a believer in the greatness of Beethoven's music and in his genius, it enhances one's reputation as a person of advanced views and superior taste and intellect to be known as one. We all are aware that some people go to opera performances and symphony concerts not because they love operas and symphonies— they are bored silly by the stuff. They attend these cultural events "to be seen," as the saying goes; it is in their "political" (in the wide sense) interest to be known as cultivated and educated men and women of taste—patrons of the arts. Maybe you can even make a business deal or land a job between the acts of *Fidelio*. That's just common sense.

Common sense departs and philosophy, *bad* philosophy, enters when one begins to wonder whether the political motivation might *always* be the operative one. Maybe no one is ever *really* motivated by a genuine belief that Beethoven's music is very, very great and that Beethoven, therefore, is a transcendent genius. With regard to motivations, once again, it's turtles all the way down. Thus, genius is deconstructed not by deconstructing value but by deconstructing *motive*. For if belief in the greatness of music and the genius behind it is never the motivation for "aesthetic behavior," and if political self-interest always is, then such behavior is not, as common sense sees it, a consequence of the sincere recognition of greatness and genius; it is, rather, the construction of greatness (so-called) and genius (so-called). It's all a product of aesthetic "bad faith." Whether or not there is real greatness or real genius, it never figures in the equation (except by accident). The recognition of greatness and genius is a political put-up job, even if, by chance, the process enfranchises true greatness and true genius. It is all the same whether one acquires the good reputation for recognizing true greatness and true genius or whether one acquires the good reputation for recognizing anything else, just so long as *whatever* it is is widely *believed* to be true greatness and true genius. It is the aesthetic version of Machiavelli: it is not aesthetic virtue that counts but the reputation for it.

But why should one be inclined to believe such a general theory of aesthetic motivation? And what evidence is there that, in the case of Beethoven, political motivation lay behind his elevation to the ranks of the immortals rather than sincere recognition of his music's greatness and his genius?

It is not within the purview of this study to undertake an inquiry into the general theory of human motivation. Suffice it to say that anyone familiar with the philosophical literature on this subject will naturally suspect lurking behind aesthetic motive skepticism the doctrine known as *psychological egoism*—the doctrine that the only motivation for human action is *perceived* self-interest. But psychological egoism will not, of itself, yield aesthetic motive skepticism. Rather, aesthetic motive skepticism, at least in the form it appears in DeNora's book, is a special case of psychological egoism in which perceived self-interest is cashed out in terms of perceived *political* self-interest. In other words, in determining what sorts of things human beings perceive to be in their interest, DeNora, like what are called "natural choice theorists," tends to take a pessimistic or cynical view of human nature that is neither argued for nor obviously true.[13]

As to our second question—What reason is there for us to think that Beethoven's contemporaries or their progeny were driven by motives of political self-interest rather than straightforward recognition of Beethoven greatness in elevating him to the pantheon?—it is best to turn to the reasons DeNora adduces, or, at least, the general form of her argument. All will be familiar to anyone acquainted with the way psychological egoism was defended in the days of Hobbes and Mandeville. (We are slow learners.) Here follow three examples of DeNora's strategy.

Haydn, as most music lovers probably know, was Beethoven's teacher for a time. Apparently they did not get on very well, and the relationship was brief. Nonetheless, Haydn openly expressed admiration for Beethoven, and taking him on as a pupil was in itself evidence of his positive attitude toward the young aspirant.

Similarly, Beethoven admired Haydn's music and was obviously influenced by it. He paid his own, musical compliment to the older master by quoting from Haydn's *Creation* in the overture to his ballet, *The Creatures of Prometheus* (also a "creation" story). And when Haydn was honored in old age by the performance of *The Creation*, at which the cream of Viennese aristocracy was present, Beethoven paid homage to the great composer by kneeling down before him and kissing the old man's hands.

What motivated these mutual expressions of admiration between two men who, *personally*, were not exactly *simpatico*? Common sense would suggest that it was genuine recognition, on Haydn's part, of the great talent and promise of the young composer, genuine veneration, on Beethoven's part, of the genius and accomplishments of the old master—an example of the triumph of intellectual and artistic integrity over personal animosity.

DeNora, however, puts a very different spin on these mutual expressions of admiration. You will recall that, early on, in her introductory chapter she referred to Beethoven and Haydn as "willing to collaborate to produce a fiction that became a resource for the construction of Beethoven's greatness." Clearly, the *motives* of both are being called into question, in particular, as we see later on, their motives for expressing mutual admiration.

On Haydn's part, his acceptance of Beethoven as a pupil might have been not a sincere expression of approval but motivated by political self-interest; for, DeNora argues, "given Beethoven's origins in a major electoral kapelle, Haydn could have refused only with difficulty to take Beethoven on as a student."[14] On Beethoven's part, "After Haydn's death in 1809 (and when Haydn was no longer a rival) Beethoven publicly professed admiration for Haydn's genius and publicized his close ties to his former teacher."[15] In other words, when it was in Haydn's political self-interest to be known as Beethoven's teacher he took him on, and when it was in Beethoven's political self-interest (or at least not against it) to publicly pay homage to Haydn, he did so. After all, that's just human nature.

Let us take a look at a second case. It is taken to be a crucially important event in the history of classical Viennese musical style when the Baron Gottfried van Swieten became enamored of contrapuntal music, in particular, the fugues of Handel (in the oratorios) and Bach (in the *Well-Tempered Clavier*). He was perhaps the first to begin the revival of these great Baroque masters, and it was partly through his influence that Haydn, Mozart, and Beethoven enriched and deepened the classical style with increasing exploitation of counterpoint and contrapuntal forms.

Common sense sees van Swieten as a man well in advance of his time in his recognition of the greatness of Bach and Handel, and in his love and admiration for their contrapuntal style. But was it *sincere* love and admiration that motivated the baron? Let's not be too naive about this. There was, after all, social status to be gained from this kind of "learned" taste in music. "*Whether van Swieten recognized it as such*, the issue was simultaneously social and political because of the allignment of music patronage with the pursuit and maintenance of status."[16] Common sense may take van Swieten's love of counterpoint and admiration of Bach and Handel at face value, but the sophisticated are well advised to weigh "the *possible* sincerity of van Swieten's belief in 'those select few great men of our own time' . . ." against the fact "that the cultural practices associated with the baron's musical preferences were socially exclusive." The sophisticated must "consider the extent to which van Swieten's vision of musical seriousness may have been linked to a concern for maintaining a special and dominant position in the Viennese musical world."[17] One doesn't, after all, want to fall for so naive a notion that someone might be motivated to do important things in his life *merely* because he genuinely loves counterpoint and places the highest possible musical value on the musical works of Bach and Handel. There *must* be some ulterior motive also—if not solely at work, *even if not consciously recognized as such by the party in question.*

One further instance of DeNora's motive-critique: Common sense tells us that among what DeNora calls the Viennese "social aristocrats," there was a growing recognition of Beethoven's music as great music, a growing enjoyment of it, and a growing tendency, therefore, to describe Beethoven as a genius. There was, among the aristocrats, much praise heaped upon Beethoven and his music, motivated, as common sense would have it, by this very recognition and enjoyment. But is not common sense here, as elsewhere, too naive, too optimistic, too trusting about human motivation? Surely beneath the surface of this apparently sincere reaction to Beethoven a politically self-interested motive lurks. "Praising Beethoven was, simultaneously, albeit implicitly, praising his aristocratic patrons [i.e. the Viennese nobility]. Through the pursuit of the greatest composers (whose status depended on recognition by aristocratic, powerful patrons), Vienna's social aristocrats could themselves be identified as aristocrats of taste."[18] Scratch a music lover and you will, inevitably, find a status seeker or social climber beneath. Not only that, but there is no need to claim that the people acting on such motivations will reveal it to you or even be aware themselves. "There is no extant explicit testimony from the aristocrats themselves. . . . But why should there be any? . . . To expect the nobility to declare or even to hold such an externalist view of their own situation may be to paint a far too rational portrait of aristocratic consciousness."[19]

What exactly is going on here? In order to answer this question, and evaluate what DeNora is up to, it would be advisable to lay down some ground rules about the concept of "motive."

I am in a restaurant. I decide to order the kidneys in mustard sauce rather than the steak. I will say that the "motive" for ordering the kidneys rather than the steak was my liking kidneys better than steak, if that was really the conscious, operative cause of my choice. Let me just add, as a warning, that this is not meant to be a complete philosophical analysis of what it means to be a motive, which would be a substantial undertaking. All I am doing is laying down a necessary (but not a sufficient) condition.

But suppose I am having dinner with a woman I would like to impress with my very sophisticated taste. I will say that a "possible motive" for ordering kidneys rather than steak is to impress the lady in question, though, in fact, my motive was liking kidneys rather than steak.

It is, to be sure, possible to have "mixed motives" for doing something. I might choose the kidneys *both* because I want to impress my female companion *and* because I like kidneys. I shall say I have "mixed motives" for doing something if I have two or more motives (as defined above) for doing it.

Finally, it would be well to make the catalogue complete by introducing "remotely possible motives" and "impossible motives." I will say that a "remotely possible motive" for my ordering kidneys, judged, that is, by a third party on the available evidence, is that even though I detest kidneys to the point of their making me sick when I eat them, I order them to impress not my companion but a friend of hers whom she will see in one year's time, and whom I hope she will remember to tell that I ordered kidneys. And an impossible motive for my ordering kidneys is my desire to break the current polevaulting record. In other words, a remotely possible motive, judged from the outside by a another party, is one which has at least some tenuous if more or less remote connection with its goal or purpose; an impossible motive, one which has not even a remote connection.

With these distinctions in hand, we can now take a look at the three examples adduced above of DeNora's motive-critique.

What is apparent immediately is that DeNora's main strategy is to present what she takes to be possible motives of political self-interest for behavior that common sense and sometimes the testimony of the principals themselves portray as being motivated by sincere beliefs in the high musical value of Bach's, Handel's, Haydn's, Mozart's, and Beethoven's music, genuine liking for this music, and the sincere recognition, so they see it, that the composers of such music must be geniuses. But what does DeNora wish to show by adducing these putative examples of *possible* politically self-interested motives? We can infer that from looking at some of her statements about what she does *not* want to show in her discussion of the Haydn-Beethoven business. "I am not . . . ," she writes, "suggesting that Beethoven pursued the new line of conduct for purely egotistical reasons—for recognition in and of itself." Or, again, "My intention is not to debunk Beethoven and Haydn by suggesting that their actions were instrumentally careerist."[20] Or, finally,

> This is by no means to suggest that Haydn and/or Beethoven were acting in a calculating and conscious manner—for instance, that Haydn was privately hostile to Beethoven's music, but that he praised it in public for purely instrumental reasons. Rather, it is to call for a more naturalistic imagery of how decisions are made and stances taken towards individuals and works, one which recognizes individuals as often indecisive and ambivalent, and whose ideals and practical circumstances are inextricably and interactively related.[21]

The tenor of DeNora's claim, here, is that she is *not* making an argument for Haydn and Beethoven being motivated *solely* by political self-interest—and these claims, I am assuming, can be extended to van Swieten, the Viennese social aristocracy, and any other individuals or groups for whom similar arguments have been given. In other words, throughout her book, DeNora is *not,* she claims, saying that the *only* motive her cast of characters exhibits is political self-interest.

But for this negative claim to make any sense, she must *also* be making a positive claim, namely, that political self-interest is consistently *one* of the motives of Haydn, Beethoven, van Swieten, the Viennese social aristocracy, and the rest. In other words, she is claiming that all these parties have mixed motives: that they are motivated (always or some of the time?) by their sincere beliefs in the greatness of Beethoven and his music, *and* by the perceived political advantage of being known to have those beliefs. Common sense tells us that, by and large, they are motivated by the former. An *argument* or *evidence,* however, is required to establish the latter motivation. What is the nature of the argument or evidence that DeNora adduces?

So far as I can make out, the *only* evidence or argument that DeNora ever adduces for the claim that one of her principal players is motivated by political self-interest is that it is a *possible* motive. In that case, we can deal with the strategy summarily. That something is a *possible* motive for someone simply does not imply that it *is* a motive (as defined above). To show that it *was* in Beethoven's political self-interest to be known as Haydn's pupil, or in Haydn's political self-interest to be known as Beethoven's teacher, is not to show that political self-interest *was* their motive (or one of them). As Bishop Butler long ago pointed out, in arguing against psychological egoism, that a benevolent action may be in one's interest does not make it any the less a benevolent action.[22] *Pari passu,* being an action that is in one's political self-interest does not make it a politically self-interested action; for the former refers to the action's consequences, the latter to its motive.

As well, many of the instances in which DeNora suggests political self-interest as a possible motive seem to me only to exhibit it as a *remotely possible* one. (It is easy to imagine, for example, courses of action far more potentially fruitful and likely to succeed in the promotion of social status in general, or musical status in particular, given a man of Baron van Swieten's class, than the promotion of counterpoint and fugue!) But that is really beside the point. Even given that all of the cases DeNora adduces are of political interest as a truly possible motive (as defined above), this in no way establishes, in any case, that political self-interest *was* really a motive. DeNora's whole strategy in this regard completely misfires. It died a decent death in the eighteenth century, and deserves to rest in peace.

The second point to notice is that even if by the above strategy, or some other, DeNora succeeded in showing that all the relevant cases were cases of mixed motives—genuine admiration for Beethoven remaining one, prospect of political advantage the other—this would not help to secure DeNora's larger purpose, namely, the political deconstruction of genius. For the commonsense notion of genius grants that sometimes motives are mixed: that some people gave lip service to the admiration of Beethoven for political motives, and others may have been motivated, perhaps, by *both* genuine admiration and political self-interest.

In order for DeNora's strategy to work for her, she would have to go whole hog and show that political self-interest is the sole motivation for the elevation of Beethoven's star to the realms of the immortals. For only that will show that his genius is "constructed." No half measures will do here. If a composer's genius is only partially constructed, then genius is not a constructed "thing," and the more reasonable way to describe the situation is one in which *reputation* is constructed but genius is innate. Only if it is construction all the way down has genius been deconstructed through aesthetic motive critique. If it is not construction all the way down, DeNora's thesis simply is not an interesting one. Acknowledging merely "mixed motives" lets the fox into the henhouse. If it were the case (which it is not) that possible motive proves motive, and the motives of Beethoven's supporters were mixed (which, in some cases anyway, it might have been), then it *might* show that Beethoven's reputation is larger than his genius (which neither I nor most music lovers and musicians believe). It would assuredly *not* show that Beethoven's genius, or anyone else's, is constructed rather than innate.

Finally, a baleful eye must be cast on the rather suspect qualifying phrases DeNora inserts into her statements of what I have been calling the aesthetic motive critique, or aesthetic motive skepticism. Thus, van Swieten's motive for the championing of counterpoint and fugue was "social and political." "Whether [or not] van Swieten recognized it as such. . . . Praising Beethoven was, simultaneously, albeit implicitly, praising his aristocratic patrons. . . ." And even though "There is no extant explicit testimony from the aristocrats themselves . . ." that their motivations were socio-political, "why should there be any?" We should not "expect the nobility to declare or even to hold . . ." that their motives were politically self-interested. To expect it would be "to paint a far too rational portrait of aristocratic consciousness."

Clearly, what DeNora is engaging in here is the preparation of damage control strategy against evidence contrary to her thesis of political motivation. To understand her strategy, it might be well to ask what evidence, aside from the possible motive argument (which, I have claimed, comes to naught), might count *in favor* of the thesis? Not surprisingly, the answer is: *documentation;* which is to say statements by the parties in question, perhaps coming to light in historical research, that in praising Beethoven and promoting his career, they were motivated by political self-interest rather than genuine love and admiration for Beethoven's music; the kind of evidence, for example, that emerges in diaries, letters, private papers, and the like, after the death of a public figure, to show that some crucial decision was made for political reasons rather than the "noble" ones given out to the populace at the time.

But there is no evidence of this kind, so far as I know, for the thesis that the praise and promotion of Beethoven by his contemporaries and following generations was motivated by political self-interest rather than their oft-stated proclamations of love and admiration for his music. Furthermore, lack of such evidence is not merely neutral to the thesis; it is evidence *against* the thesis. That is to say, the absence of any documentary support for the thesis that Beethoven's praise and promotion were political rather than sincere is evidence against the thesis that it was political, and the longer the lack of evidence for the political thesis survives continued historical research, the stronger that lack of evidence becomes *against* the political thesis.

Not to worry, though, the defender of the political thesis responds. First of all, *of course* there is no direct documentary evidence of political motives. In DeNora's words, "Why should there be?" Part of the strategy of politics is to cover up the strategy of politics. Political motives of self-interest are disreputable motives, and no person who says his motives are thus and so, when they really amount to political self-interest, is going to admit it. He is going to cover it up. It is simply a special case of the conspiracy argument. There is a conspiracy; but of course there is no evidence of a conspiracy because part of the conspiracy is the conspiracy to suppress the evidence of the conspiracy. "There is no extant explicit testimony [to their political motives] from the aristocracy themselves...." Of course not. What politician is going to admit he is one?

Second, the response goes, *of course* there is no documentary evidence of political motives. Why should there be? It would be naive to think that people with political motives are *aware* of them. Praising Beethoven, DeNora tells us, may not have been explicitly to praise his aristocratic patrons, but it was "implicitly" to do so. You were doing it whether you were conscious of what you were doing or not. Nor is there need for van Swieten to have been aware of his political motive in promoting the music of Handel and Bach. As DeNora says, "Whether van Swieten recognized it as such . . ." does not matter; it was there as a motive regardless. To insist that people must be aware of their political motivations, to be correctly described as so motivated, is to represent them as "far too rational." We are driven, after all, by motives we know not of, deep down in our inner depths. Political motives may very well be such.

It will not, perhaps, have escaped the reader's notice that, in principle, these two defenses of aesthetic motive skepticism are incompatible. You cannot *both* claim that in some given instance a person is consciously suppressing evidence of his or her political agenda *and* being unconsciously motivated by it. One can, of course, employ the former strategy in a given instance and the other strategy in another. But that strongly suggests an ad hoc policy of playing both sides of the street, the only reason for playing one side being that it didn't work when you played the other. If you can't make out a case for A's suppressing evidence for his motive, then simply claim that it was an unconscious motive (the unconscious being the final refuge for the unproven). That way, the theory is made completely immune from empirical refutation at the familiar cost of forfeiting any claim to be taken seriously as an empirical hypothesis.

There is, however, a serious further charge to be brought against each of these two strategies in the aesthetic motive critique. Against the thesis that there is no evidence political motivations are at work, because part of the politics is to suppress that evidence, the reply is the same one one gives to any conspiracy theory, of which the present case is an obvious instance. It is a circular argument in which the thesis provides its own defense. What is to be *proved* is that political self-interest is the motivation for praising and promoting Beethoven. Counting heavily against this thesis, however, there is a complete lack of explicit evidence that such was the motivation. But that is not really evidence against the thesis, it is replied, because the politically motivated naturally suppress explicit evidence of their political motivations. The argument is circular, clearly, in that the evidence against the thesis is deflected only by assuming the truth of the thesis, which is the very thing that is in doubt. The response involves a basic logical fallacy.

As for the idea that there is no explicit evidence of political self-interest as the motive for the praise and promotion of Beethoven because the praisers and promoters were unaware of their motivation—were, in other words, unconsciously motivated—it is plainly bizarre: a palpable nonstarter. I suggest that unconscious political motivation is close to a contradiction in terms. It is, indeed, a paradigm instance of conscious, *self-conscious,* plotting and scheming. There is no need to appeal, here, to any of the problems surrounding the concept of unconscious motivation, which are legion. That is not the point at all. The point is, if there are unconscious motivations, motivations of political self-interest cannot be of their number. Of motives that might be unconscious, it would be absurd to count political ones. To be political is, characteristically, to be calculating, careful, and acutely aware of what you are doing at every step. To suggest that that can be unconscious is to suggest an absurdity.

Thus, neither of the two strategies DeNora offers for answering the charge that there is no explicit, documentary evidence in favor of political self-interest as the (or a) motive for praising and promoting Beethoven comes to anything. The first is circular, the second either a contradiction in terms or, at least, a plain falsehood. And the lack of evidence for the thesis of political self-interest as a motive stands firm, not merely failing to support it but counting positively against it.

I have argued at some length that DeNora's attempt to reduce Beethoven Genius to a socio-political construction has failed in all particulars examined. It remains to ask: Why Beethoven? Why, in the socio-political deconstruction of genius should the pendulum swing from Mozart to the Unlicked Bear? Why not deconstruct Mozart's genius?

The obvious answer seems to be that, at least on first reflection, the phenomenon of Mozart—the *phenomenal* Mozart—is ill-suited to the exercise. Indeed, the most persuasive *empirical* evidence I can think of giving for the innateness of musical genius would be the extraordinary childhood of Wolfgang Amadeus. To the contemporary observers of this childhood, as to us, the most stupendous musical ability in all its forms in this virtual baby appears to be a prodigy of Nature or a gift from God, but certainly not of human making: "*a miracle in music, and one of those freaks Nature causes to be born . . .*," one contemporary called it.[23] Goethe called it a divine mystery.

Beethoven, on the other hand, although an early starter in music by comparison to the boy next door, was not a Mozart in this regard—nor has anyone else been in the history of Western music. One can see his stature gradually waxing, which seems to invite an alternative to the gradually emerging genius, namely, the gradual construction of one. So, to anyone pursuing the socio-political program of genius reduction, Beethoven must seem, prima facie, fair game, and Mozart a very hard case.

Of course, anyone devoted enough to this line of work is not going to be fazed by appearances. In principle, there is certainly no reason why all the arguments adduced for showing that Beethoven's genius is a socio-political construct cannot be marshalled to show the same for Mozart's—initial difficulties to the contrary notwithstanding. There is politics, one may claim, from cradle to grave. Leopold Mozart, by all accounts, was a pretty sharp cookie, and his promotion of his son's interests was relentless from the start. Had Johann Nepomuk Hummel—another child prodigy—been blessed with an equally energetic advocate from the start, you can anticipate the argument going, and Mozart not so blessed, who is to say that we would not be saying when our toddler accidentally strikes thirds at the piano, "He's another Johann Nepomuk Hummel!," while Mozart would be adduced as just another example of youthful promise not being fulfilled.

One does, indeed, require some kind of fanatical devotion to socio-political deconstruction to really tackle Mozart. But I have no doubt there are such abroad. All I can say about them and their project is that it's uphill all the way. And if they should deploy the strategies of DeNora's that I have examined, they will fail with Mozart's deconstruction as badly as, I have argued, she has failed with Beethoven's.

What drives this project? It is, I suppose, the quite commendable desire to give a rational explanation for a phenomenon that, even before it had a name, was seen as *mysterious*—and not merely *puzzling* but, as the word "mysterious" suggests, bordering on the supernatural. Plato thought it must have divine origins. Longinus and his eighteenth-century followers called it a gift of Nature, but could go no further than that. It was a "divine mystery" to Goethe, and to the Romantics.

But the invocation of mysteries is anathema to the rational inquirer (among whose number I count myself). To call something not merely an unsolved problem but a "mystery" is to hold up a red flag to the philosopher or scientist. The association of genius with mystery is both strong and ancient. "Genius continues to be shrouded in mystery," DeNora writes, in her argument for "genius as a social construction."[24] The social construction, of course, is supposed to dissolve the mystery. We all understand how political reputations are built, and what they are. They and their origins are not mysteries. So if we reduce genius to political reputation we have demystified the ghostly apparition.

I am, myself, no lover of mysteries. But it is a mark, it seems to me, of staggering *hubris* to think that the crude methods employed in *Beethoven and the Construction of Genius* have dissolved the mystery of genius. In fact, as I shall argue in the final chapter of this book, the commonsense notion of genius, mystery and all, is necessary for us— necessary to mark out an irreducible segment of our experience.

Genius *is* a mystery. Not a supernatural mystery, like the Trinity is said to be, but a *natural* mystery: a natural phenomenon that, as yet, we have no explanation for and, indeed, no idea of what form an explanation might take; what an "explanation" would mean. It may, for all we know, be a natural mystery we will *never* understand.

I shall suggest, then, in the final chapter, that we cannot do without the commonsense concept of genius, and that we must accept it as it comes, mystery along with the rest. If there is a "solution" to the mystery, and what it would even look like, we are far from knowing— and that is a well-calculated understatement.

But before I get to these matters, I turn to what might be taken as *another* kind of "attack" on the traditional concept of genius: the so-called feminist critique. It is *not*, in my view, an attack. That, however, requires argument, which is now to come.

XII

Gendering Genius

There is a tendency among contemporary thinkers to cast a baleful eye on the whole genius thing. It is seen as mystery mongering and politically reactionary: enfranchising certain groups to the exclusion of others (a point to which I shall return shortly), as well as perpetuating so-called elitist attitudes toward art at the expense of what are seen as the more "alive" and "relevant" forms of popular and mass culture. Genius has been getting a bad press—DeNora's socio-political deconstruction being but one example.

Who needs the concept of genius, anyway? The answer is that we *all* need it, and *it* seems to stand in need of a defense. *My* defense I have offered, in part, in the previous chapter. The rest of it I offer in the remaining two.

That the concept of genius is to be *defended* in this book may come as a surprise to even the mildly attentive reader. For haven't I, throughout, referred to the concepts of the possessor and the possessed as "genius myths," and insisted on the mythic element in the characterizations of Handel, Mozart, and Beethoven by their contemporaries and by posterity, even though these characterizations may also have some considerable basis in fact? And when one calls things "myths" and "mythic," is one not denying their reality? If genius is a myth, and the characters of the above-mentioned composers mythic, then there is no such thing as genius, or composers who exhibit its putative characteristics.

But we must be careful here to distinguish between the claim that genius has been represented, since antiquity, in mythic—which is to say metaphorical—ways, and the claim that genius is "a myth," in the sense of a falsehood or "fiction." In that sense, genius is *not* a "myth." It exists; it is part of the universe. However, when we want to talk about it, we resort to myth and metaphor, very simply, because we don't know what it is. We know, indeed, some of the ways in which it manifests itself. And we express these ways in myth, in metaphor, for want of more "rational" ways because, in a deep sense, "we don't know what we are talking *about*." Yet we should not argue "mythic therefore false." As Gilbert Ryle put it: "A myth is of course not a fairy story. It is the presentation of facts belonging to one category in the idioms appropriate to another."[1]

To resort to myth is, no doubt, an admission of ignorance. But the myth is a way of presenting facts. And, to continue Ryle's thought: "To explode a myth is accordingly not to deny the facts but to re-allocate them."[2] The problem is (if it *is* a problem) that we cannot "re-allocate" the facts of genius, because we do not know what genius *is*. Until we do, the myths are all we have. Furthermore, to try to "re-allocate" the facts of genius in political constructs is merely silly—I can think of no complimentary word for the enterprise. The political story fails utterly to fit the facts the myths have evolved to express.

Of course some myths may turn out to be "fairy stories," may, in other words, fail, even mythically, to track any facts at all. Further, some myths, as well as some fairy stories, are downright obnoxious or even dangerous. Is that the case with the genius myths? Some have made such claims.

That a theory has obnoxious or even damaging implications, however, does not bear on the question of its truth or falsity, as David Hume long ago warned us. "When any opinion leads to absurdities, it is certainly false; but it is not certain that an opinion is false, because it is of dangerous consequence."[3]

It appears to me that the most vigorously pressed claim that the traditional concept of genius is "of dangerous consequence" emanates from what is known as the "feminist critique." The claim is, simply, that the whole genius thing completely disenfranchises women, for it has been consistently interpreted as implying that women cannot be geniuses so defined. This is, indeed, an obnoxious result, "of dangerous consequence," and should it be used as an "argument" against the traditional concept of genius, it certainly would fall afoul of Hume's warning that undesirable consequences do not impinge upon truth.

There is, however, a far more charitable construction that can be put on the feminist critique of genius, with which I am in deep sympathy. Hume warns us that an undesirable consequence of a theory is no argument against its truth. But he also states the obvious and indubitable precept that if a theory implies an "absurdity," then it is plainly a false theory; that is to say, the theory leads to a *reduction ad absurdum*. And that is precisely how I intend to construe the core of the feminist critique. Put baldly, the argument is:

1. The traditional concept of genius implies that women cannot be geniuses.
2. It is a plain matter of fact that there are, and have been, woman geniuses.
3. Therefore, the traditional concept of genius is false.

I take this to be a valid argument and, if a good argument as well, a *reductio* of the traditional concept of genius. But, I want to urge, it is *not* a good argument because one of its premises is false. I take the second premise to be plainly true on empirical grounds. But the first premise I take to be false, although a good deal of the historical evidence adduced for it does show that the traditional concept of genius has been systematically misinterpreted by its propounders and defenders in ways that appear to validate the implication.

The proof of the second premise, as I have said, seems to me to be overwhelmingly supported by empirical evidence. Genius, as I have suggested common sense and tradition construe it, is the disposition to create artistic masterpieces at the highest level. And it is a plain matter of fact that women have, since antiquity, produced such artistic masterpieces. (It would be otiose to cite the universally known instances.) It therefore follows directly that the second premise of the proposed *reductio* is true.

But what of the first premise, and of the historical evidence adduced in its support? To begin with, I must remind the reader that I have not set out in this book to produce a history of the genius concept.[4] What I have intended to do, rather, is to trace two concepts—or theses, or myths, if you will—of genius that have pervaded music history, from the enshrinement of Handel as genius in the eighteenth century through the successive emergence of Mozart, and then Beethoven, and to show how these two concepts (or theses or myths) constituted a periodic wane and return to the present day. My limited goal, in these, the final chapters of the study, as so conceived, is to argue that these two representations of genius, the possessor and the possessed, and the commonsense notion of genius that they constitute, are necessary for our picture of the art world in which we live and have lived. My immediate purpose now is to show that they—the possessor and the possessed, and the commonsense notion of genius they constitute—in no way support the first premise of the above argument. In other words, in no way do they imply an exclusively masculine domain for the concept of artistic genius (or any other kind, for that matter).

It was very tempting, from the start, to describe the Platonic metaphor for genius as a feminine metaphor, the Longinian as a masculine one. For the Platonic genius is passive, possessed by the god; the Longinian genius active, the possessor of the laws, and frequently portrayed with images of masculine strength and power. I resisted that temptation because such a portrayal would amount to an endorsement of a masculine/feminine stereotype that I emphatically reject. Nevertheless, it is useful to point out that even if one did endorse it, at least *one* of the two traditional ways of portraying genius would not only include the female genius but also, at least sympathetically interpreted, patently endorse her, which is not surprising since the genius possessed is one with the oracle possessed, and the female oracle or prophetess is a familiar figure in ancient Greek culture and its mythology.

But, as I say, I do *not* endorse the male/female stereotype of possessor versus possessed, activity versus passivity, strength versus weakness—nor, I wish to argue, does the dichotomy between the Longinian and Platonic genius metaphors, on any sensible interpretation of them and any sensible understanding of the human animal.

Since it is obvious that the Platonic picture of genius fits to a "t" one very common stereotype of the female of the species, the passive recipient, I will leave it alone for the moment to look at the Longinian picture. The latter, of course, seems to fit equally well the equally common masculine stereotype of action and power; the one who *does*, not the one who is *done to*. It is drawn, metaphorically of course, from the physical stereotype of the male animal, whose flesh is strong, as opposed to the female animal, whose flesh is weak and yielding. (It need hardly be pointed out that stereotypic sexual roles are also implied.)

Now, it should be abundantly clear that even if it makes sense to characterize men and women *physically* in the above manner, that is completely irrelevant to the question of whether the Longinian picture excludes the female, because the Longinian picture is one not of the physical being (except as metaphor), but of the mental one, and it should be obvious that mental strength does not correlate with physical strength. The Longinian genius exhibits "greatness of mind," not greatness of biceps. So anyone with a modicum of common sense can see that the Longinian picture of genius does not exclude the female, since even given the stereotype of the woman as physically weak and yielding, nothing in that implies the woman as mentally weak and mentally yielding. To get the result that the Longinian picture of genius excludes female geniuses, one must extend the claim that women are weak in the flesh to the claim that they are weak in the spirit, or, to put it in Longinian terms, that they cannot possess the requisite "greatness of mind."

Thus a quick, "naive" look at the two pictures of genius we have been considering in this book—the possessor and the possessed, the Longinian and Platonic—with a feminist critique in mind, suggests the following: the Platonic picture fits the common feminine stereotype perfectly, apparently presenting no impediment to the female genius, while the Longinian picture, even though it embodies a metaphor drawn from a common masculine stereotype, does not in any obvious way exclude the feminine, since the metaphor is drawn from a physical stereotype, whereas genius, male or female, is of the mind, and there is no prima facie reason why the female *physique* should imply lack of the mental requirements that are only "like" the male physique metaphorically. To make *either* of these two pictures of genius exclude the woman genius, then, an argument is required to show *why,* appearances to the contrary notwithstanding, they must exclude the female of the species. Furthermore, that argument must, of course, be directed not at the pictures of genius, which are the "givens," but at the mental and emotional character of the female, which have been debated throughout the history of Western thought. The damage done to women by Western philosophy, in this regard, is, as the feminist critique has shown, of the most deplorable kind. Nor should it be surprising to discover that the leading proponent of the Platonic picture in modern times, also the most notorious misogynist in Western philosophy—and of course I mean Schopenhauer—should have put down the notion of the female genius with hardly anything worth calling an argument.

It will be recalled that, on Schopenhauer's view, the genius is one able to become free of the principle of sufficient reason in its four forms. To do this is to achieve "objectivity," in Schopenhauer's peculiar sense of that word. The attaining of this "objectivity," Schopenhauer tersely (and parenthetically) remarks, without argument of any kind, the female of the species can never aspire to: "Women can have remarkable talent, but not genius, for they always remain subjective."[5]

Perhaps, because woman's perpetual "subjectivity" is itself part of the standard stereotype of the woman as basically a feeling, not a reasoning, being, Schopenhauer felt no particular need to argue the point. But without this ill-founded claim in place, there is nothing in Schopenhauer's concept of genius, whatever else one might fault it for, that excludes women as bona fide geniuses in its mold. Furthermore, since, for Schopenhauer, "objectivity" in this context is used not in its ordinary sense but as a term of art, it cannot be assumed that even if women were unable to achieve "objectivity" in the ordinary sense (which I do not believe for an instant), because they are supposed to be feeling, "subjective" beings, it would not follow from that that they could not achieve "objectivity" in Schopenhauer's special, technical sense of freedom from the principle of sufficient reason.

The case of Kant, the leading modern exponent of the Longinian picture of genius, is not nearly so clear as that of Schopenhauer with regard to the possibility of the woman genius. In fact, in the extensive discussion of genius in the *Critique of Judgment,* nothing at all is said on the question. One can turn for possible evidence of Kant's views on this regard, to the precritical *Observations on the Feeling of the Beautiful and Sublime,* however, where there are some detailed comments on the nature of women and their social role, with some direct reference to art and science. But, to begin with, any inferences we make about Kant's views on any subject in the third *Critique* from his views in this earlier work, separated from it by twenty-five years, can be made only under the assumption that Kant did not change his views on that subject between 1764 and 1790. And we know that on a great many subjects in the area of art, beauty, and taste, Kant's views changed radically during that period. Indeed, whether there could be a philosophy—that is, a "critique"—of taste at all was still doubted as late as the second edition of *Critique of Pure Reason,* published in 1787. Thus one takes a chance in extrapolating from the *Observations* to Kant's mature views on genius. But for the sake of argument, let us put such scruples aside and assume that whatever opinions were expressed in the *Observations* relevant to the question at hand remained in place, though unexpressed, in the *Critique of Judgment.* Given that assumption, what can we learn from the precritical work? In particular, does Kant's characterization of women in it, viewed in the light of the third *Critique*'s doctrine of genius, exclude the female of the species?

In the *Observations,* Kant characterizes the distinction between men and women in what we would call aesthetic terms. Thus Kant writes of the woman that "certain specific traits lie especially in the personality of this sex which distinguish it clearly from ours and chiefly result in making her known by the mark of the beautiful," whereas "on the other hand, among the masculine qualities the sublime clearly stands out as the criterion of his kind."[6] This distinction is cashed out, more particularly, in two different kinds of human "understanding." As Kant puts it: "The fair sex has just as much understanding as the male, but it is a *beautiful understanding*, whereas ours should be a *deep understanding*, an expression that signifies identity with the sublime."[7]

The distinction between beautiful and deep understanding in turn implies, for Kant, the not surprising conclusion that science, philosophy, and the pursuit of knowledge in general are closed to women. But what is not so obvious is whether Kant is saying that women are incapable of such pursuits, have no taste for them, or are morally prohibited from engaging in them because that departs from their proper roles in society. That it may well not be the first is suggested by his assertion that "Laborious learning or painful pondering, even if a woman should greatly succeed in it, destroy the merits that are proper to her sex . . . ," the possibility of success obviously implied in the proscription.[8]

But in any event, if Kant *is* saying, which does not seem to be the case, that *all* women are incapable of scientific, philosophical, or scholarly attainments, that would not preclude them from the category of genius, since it is the teaching of the third *Critique* that these are not the province of genius anyway. The province of genius is the fine arts, and, so far, nothing that Kant says has implied that women cannot succeed there.

Now, it might be suggested to some that the apportionment of the beautiful to the feminine and the sublime to the masculine in itself denies genius to women because of the traditional eighteenth-century connection, in the Longinian tradition, of the sublime with genius and the beautiful with taste. But that would not be a proper inference in the case of Kant, even though I have represented him as in the Longinian tradition. For Kant no longer associates genius particularly with the sublime. Indeed, his account of genius is an account of the connection between it and the fine arts—in other words, for him, *schönen Kunst*, the arts of the *beautiful*. The sublime he associates more particularly with Nature, and although he does not deny that the sublime can express itself in works of fine art, the account of genius is explicitly an account of the creation of artistic beauty. Thus, although it might be consistent with Kant's doctrine, that women, because they are associated with the beautiful rather than the sublime, are capable of genius only for the creation of the beautiful, nothing in this implies that they cannot be geniuses in a full-blooded Kantian sense of that concept. In order, then, for it to be shown that the Kantian concept of genius excludes the female of the species, it must be shown that Kant did not believe women capable of creating beautiful artworks. So far that has not been shown by the text.

There is, indeed, only one, maddeningly brief and unelaborated passage in the *Observations* that seems to bear any relevance to the question of whether or not Kant thought women could be creators of art in the appropriate sense. It reads as follows: "Feeling for expressive painting and for music, not so far as it manifests artistry [*Kunst*] but sensitivity [*Empfindung*]—all this refines or elevates the taste of this sex, and always has some connection with moral impulses."[9]

Well, what is this passage saying of relevance to our question? To begin with, it distinguishes, in painting and music, between *Kunst* and *Empfindung* (for the latter term, I prefer "feeling" to the translator's "sensitivity"). In any case, Kant seems to be distinguishing, I would surmise, between the structure of the work, that is, its craftsmanship, and its expressive character. But what is he saying *about* them and, more particularly, about their relation to women?

Kant is clearly recommending to women the appreciation of painting and music as having both a refining effect on female taste, and some kind of positive moral effect as well. And he ascribes both of these effects to appreciating not the craft of painting and music but what we would call their expressive part. He seems, therefore, to be recommending that women attend not to the technical aspects of music and painting but only to their emotive content. (Significantly or not, he says nothing here about the literary arts.) Why should this be so? Kant says nothing about it. But by a series of speculations and assumptions, *which cannot be supported in the text,* we can construct an argument to the effect that what is implied here, in light of the later concept of genius, is an exclusion of women.

Assume, for the sake of argument, that the beautiful understanding cannot grasp the craft or, better, the technique of painting and musical composition but only the expressive part, because the former requires that depth and labor-intensive activity only the masculine, sublime understanding can achieve. Thus, since the female cannot grasp craft or technique, there is no point in her attending to it.

Assume, further, that it is only through grasping the technique and craft of painting and musical composition that one can make the first step toward becoming a painter or composer and, perhaps, awakening one's genius. In that case, women are by nature unable to be painterly or musical geniuses, since they do not possess the requisite understanding that although not a sufficient condition for genius, is a necessary one.

The problem is that, as I said, *there is absolutely no textual support for any of these speculative assumptions.* The dichotomy between the beautiful and sublime as a way of distinguishing between female and male character—here, as in the place previously cited—is perfectly consistent with the possibility of woman genius, as the concept of genius is laid out in the third *Critique*. It therefore seems a false inference to conclude, as Christine Battersby does in her well-known and, in many ways, admirable book *Gender and Genius:* in the *Observations* "it become[s] clear that the sublime—and hence true genius—is properly a male preserve."[10]

Battersby compounds the error, I think, by apparently arguing from Kant's contention in the *Observations* that it is possible for a woman to achieve the male pursuits of philosophy, science, and scholarship at the highest level, to the conclusion that he *therefore* thinks female genius possible, albeit unseemly. But it must always be borne in mind that these male, therefore sublime pursuits discussed in the *Observations* are *not* the pursuits of *genius* as understood in the *Critique of Judgment*. For Kant makes it abundantly clear there that these pursuits, even at the level of an Isaac Newton, are not the province of genius, which, it is also made abundantly clear, has as its sole province the fine arts. If, then, in his *Observations* Kant counts women as capable of male pursuits, which are in that context the pursuits of science, philosophy, and scholarship, and condemns women for pursuing them, on quasi-moral grounds, he is *neither* saying that they are capable of genius *nor* condemning women for being geniuses. And Battersby, I take it, is falsely affirming both when she writes of Kant's

Observations: "For Kant a woman genius is not impossible; but for a woman to aim at the sublime makes her merely ridiculous. . . ."[11] But genius, as understood in the third *Critique,* is simply not a subject even discussed in the *Observations,* nor, so far as I can recall, does the word ever appear in that text.[12] Thus neither the teaching of the *Critique of Judgment* nor any of the related precritical texts with which I am familiar either implies or states the impossibility of the woman genius. The case for Kant as a sexist with regard to genius must, therefore, at worst, be given a Scotch verdict.

Of course, if Kant himself did not exclude women from his Longinian picture of genius, there were plenty of willing hands for that work, as Battersby amply demonstrates in her book. *Gender and Genius* provides, indeed, a well-documented history of the truly deplorable exclusion of the female sex, both in theory and in practice, from the precincts of genius in all its forms. Even where, as in the Platonic genius, the picture obviously favors the female, a sexist spin is put on it. The "feminine" genius is interpreted as "woman-*like.*" But, as a matter of logic, to say X is like Y is to imply that X is *not* Y. So if the Platonic genius is woman-like, that genius cannot be a woman. "The creative genius," in this mold, "resembles woman in that he is guided by something over and above himself. . . ."[13] But *woman* he is not.

Battersby's intriguing study can be described as an exercise in both historical and (briefly, at the close) normative aesthetics. It is first and foremost a thoroughly researched history of the use and abuse, mostly *abuse,* of the concept of genius in the interest of male dominance. It is an angry book — but there is a lot to be angry about. I am in fullest sympathy with the historical part of Battersby's book, although I may disagree with her on some points of textual interpretation, the Kantian texts being a case in point.

It is only in the last, brief chapter that Battersby undertakes what I have described as her book's normative part. A number of themes weave through these densely packed pages. Not all are relevant to present concerns, and those that are not I will naturally leave alone. What does concern me is any suggestion that the feminist critique must have as its conclusion the rejection altogether of the traditional concept of genius, broadly conceived by the Longinians, the Platonists, and common sense. That conclusion I reject because I am an unregenrate believer in that concept. We cannot do without it.

In her last chapter, Battersby distinguishes what she calls "five separate strands in our modern usage of the term genius . . . ," and avers that only one of them can, as she puts it, "be utilised for feminist ends." The five strands are: (1) genius as "a personality-type (an outsider, near-to-madness, degenerate, shamanistic, etc.)"; (2) genius as "a specific mode of consciousness: variously (and conflictingly) described as passion, imagination, instinct, intuition, the unconscious, reason"; (3) genius as "energy (usually sublimated sexual energy)"; (4) genius as "a kind of 'potential for eminence,'" that one can "quantify . . . via tests and statistical surveys"; (5) genius as "the person whose work (a) marks the boundary between the old ways and the new within the tradition, and (b) has lasting value and significance."[14]

Now to begin with, I think it would be useful, for my own purposes, to distinguish between two ways we can construe what Battersby calls "our modern image of the term genius." Battersby's characterizations 1, 2, 3, and 5 all more or less fit in with either the Platonic or Longinian pictures as I presented them, and are part and parcel (again, more or less) of what I have been calling the "commonsense" notion of genius, of which the Platonic and Longinian pictures form a large part. The fourth characterization of genius, however, is another matter. Battersby is quite right in calling it a "modern image" of genius, but it is genius in a very different sense from the other four. In contemporary usage, it is the sense of "genius" as, merely, very great intelligence or aptitude, that is usually associated with the I.Q. test, the Scholastic Aptitude Test, and other such contemporary tools of the testing trade which are claimed to measure it in quantifiable terms. One therefore is sometimes said to have an I.Q. "at the genius level," which, if it means anything more than having achieved a high score on the test that bears that name, means simply that that person is very, very smart. Thus genius has come to mean, in this sense, extraordinarily high intelligence (or "aptitude"). It of course is *not* the sense of "genius" that this book is about, and can be put aside as entirely irrelevant to the question at hand, which is genius as the disposition to produce artistic masterpieces, scientific theories, and whatever else falls under its purview, at the highest possible creative level.

Battersby rejects, as well, the first three "images" of genius that she gives us as irretrievably masculine and (therefore) sexist. "These first three senses of genius are utterly contaminated by past usage, and by the way that the male (still) provides the paradigm for both the normal and supernormal personality-types, consciousness-types and energy types."[15] But this, I suggest, is a serious mistake, both philosophically and, if I may say so, politically.

The basic philosophical mistake, as I have suggested earlier, is to conflate the sexist characterization of women with the (supposed) sexist character of the genius concept. For none of the characteristics of genius in Battersby's first three "images" is exclusively masculine, *if* one has a nonsexist, realistic, respectable view of women. I dare say there are as many women as men who are or can be perceived as outsider, near-to-madness, degenerate, and shamanistic (although perhaps I will not be taken as a friend of the sex to say it). There are as many women as men who exhibit passion, imagination, instinct, intuition, the unconscious, reason, energy (*sans phrase*), and sublimated sexual energy. If these are part of the Longinian, Platonic, commonsense picture of genius (and at least many are), then it is not that picture that has, through history, systematically excluded women but the philosophically and psychologically perverted characterization of the female of the species that has accompanied that picture. It is the characterization of women, not the picture of genius, that must go. The picture must stay.

But as well as being a philosophical error for feminists to reject the commonsense notion of genius, it is a political mistake too. It is a form of political sour grapes. What is essentially being said is: "Okay: so we can't be geniuses. Well, who cares? Who needs your old genius thing anyway? It's just a male boondoggle." Substitute "vote" for "genius" and you have the point I am trying to make. If the feminists throw genius back in the faces of the enemy, they are simply giving up the game. I think, rather, they should fight for genius tooth and nail. They are entitled to it, and *it is important,* as I shall argue in the final chapter.

Battersby, to be sure, does want to appropriate her fifth "contemporary image" of genius for the feminist cause. And as it contains elements of the traditional concept, I certainly support that. Nevertheless, there are some points in this regard that require critical scrutiny.

Of her fifth "sense of genius," Battersby writes: "This fifth sense of genius is a much more pragmatic notion. A person's cultural achievement is evaluated and assessed against an appropriate background of artistic genius and tradition."[16]

With this one can scarcely quarrel, and wonders why it need be stated at all. That artworks are to be evaluated and assessed against an appropriate background of artistic genius and tradition is something that no philosopher of art, art historian, or critic would deny. It must be supposed, therefore, that Battersby fears some inconsistency between that truth—one is tempted to say truism—and the traditional picture of genius. This supposition is reinforced by Battersby's further insistence that feminists are *not* "wrenching the individual artist out of the social context in which her art was produced. The historical dimension is a necessary part of understanding what is involved in creating *as a woman*."[17] But if the feminist critique of genius is emphatically *not* "wrenching" the artist out of history, out of her social context, the implication seems to me to be that the traditional picture of genius is being castigated for being an *ahistorical* concept of genius, where, so the feminist critique claims, it is clearly not. This is a serious charge—but it is due, I think, to a confusion or at least a failure to look closely enough at the concept of historicity itself, as applied to the concept of genius.

There is one perfectly obvious sense in which the concept of genius is a historical concept. In both its Platonic and Longinian forms, it did not become fully formed until the eighteenth century. Neither Plato nor the author of *On the Sublime* had a concept of genius, in the early modern sense, although their texts were sources for it.

But there is *also* a perfectly obvious sense in which the concept of genius is an ahistorical concept. There has been genius at least as long as there has been *homo sapiens*. For genius is the disposition to create works, whether artworks, scientific theories, human institutions, or practical inventions at the highest possible level. Sappho and Sophocles were geniuses long before the concept of genius was fully formed.

So perhaps were the Neolithic cave painters, Solon, some Babylonian astronomers, the discoverer of the Pythagorean theorem, "Homer," and the "inventors" of tools and the wheel. In this case genius can be treated *as if* it were a natural kind. (There was water before there was the concept of H_2O.)

And, finally, genius is a distinctly historical concept in the following "derivative" sense. A genius for composing four-movement symphonies in Classical style could not have manifested itself in ancient Greece or the Middle Ages, nor could the genius of Judy Chicago (if genius she is). I opine that this is the sense Battersby has in mind in her warning about the wrenching of genius from its historical and social context. Again, though, the traditional concept of genius does not contradict this truth or truism. What does is the false doctrine that the works of contemporary feminist artists cannot be works at the level at which we feel compelled to call them "geniuses." But being false, it need not deter us.

Battersby also claims, in reaction to the traditional concept of genius, that "For a feminist, a female 'genius' is not some kind of élite being, different from other (ordinary) women. . . ."[18] But why shouldn't female geniuses be thought of as elite and different from other, ordinary women (and men)?

There are of course "bad" ways of using the concept of eliteness, from which I would be at pains to disassociate myself—the elitism of class or social status or wealth or race or sex. But why in the world should I not recognize the eliteness of genius, wherever and however it manifests itself? It is rare. It is wonderful. It *is* "elite." For feminism to deny the eliteness of its own genius is, once again, to give over to the enemy. (I shall have more to say about the "eliteness" of genius in the final chapter.)

Related to the denial of "eliteness," on the feminists' part is Battersby's insistence that "we are [not] mythologising the act of creation. . . ."[19] But why not? To mythologise is not to falsify. It is, as I have previously argued, to capture a truth with a metaphor because that is the only way we have of capturing it. Metaphors can track the truth or fail to track it, just as literal language can succeed or fail at the task. And the act of scientific or artistic creation remains a mystery, in the sense already well understood by Plato. Genius requires mythology; "we" require genius, whether or not "we" are feminists. (Again, I shall have more to say about the "mythologizing" of genius in the next chapter.)

A further point of Battersby's deserving attention is her discussion of "influence." She writes: "That an artist is influential is a fact that is relevant—though never by itself enough—for allocating 'genius.' And, since women have been excluded from the academies and have found it difficult to have their art-products taken seriously, we should expect (even today) that there will remain fewer female than male 'geniuses.'"[20]

There is nothing in this statement with which I want to take serious issue. But there is more to be said about it relevant to the feminist critique of genius.

To start with, there are two senses of "influence" or, rather, lack thereof, that seem to me to be in danger of being blurred by their being packed together, cheek by jowl, in the last sentence of the passage quoted above. Battersby claims, and rightly so, that woman geniuses have failed to have as much influence as their male counterparts, on the history of art, due to their systematic exclusion from the institutions and practices which nurture and cultivate genius and through which the influence of works of genius is conveyed. The first of these failures is the failure of the works themselves to have influence because, as Battersby puts it, women "have found it difficult to have their art-products taken seriously. . . ." The second failure is not a failure of women's works to have influence, but a failure of women's *genius* to have influence, because they have been prevented from having their genius realized by their exclusion from the nurturing and cultivating institutions, and hence have not produced any works at all, or not produced works at the level they could have achieved, the genius level, had their talents been nurtured and cultivated. I do not call these latter "potential" geniuses, but geniuses properly so called, because I take genius to be a dispositional concept, and a disposition is possessed even in the absence of the conditions necessary for its expression. (In a universe without aqua regia, gold *still* has the disposition to dissolve in it, though that disposition will never be exercised.)

I have nothing to say about the latter, lamentable absence of influence, through absence of works to influence, except to concur with Battersby's explanation of the absence, and to deplore it as much as she. But I think there is more to be said about the former: the apparent lack of influence of works by female artists. Again, I am inclined to agree with Battersby that this is a fact of art history. However, I want to put a slightly different spin on it from hers as regards the traditional concept of genius.

I begin with Battersby's assertion that an artist's influence through her works is relevant to her being a genius, but neither necessary nor sufficient. That it is not necessary or sufficient I think is obviously right. But I wonder even about relevance. Here is my worry, which comes in two parts.

To start with, the trope of the forgotten or misunderstood genius is central to the traditional concept of genius. Thus it is common, under the traditional concept, for the genius *not* to have influence, at least on his or her immediate posterity. Whether or not someone has had influence on art history appears, then, not to be immediately relevant to whether or not he or she is a genius.

Second, it is the stock in trade of art history, literary history, and musicology to pursue the influence of lesser known practitioners on the geniuses. It is a favorite sport to reveal that something thought to be original with some great artist was, in reality, appropriated from a lesser one and made better use of—transmuted, as one might say, by genius, from lead to gold. Again, influence seems irrelevant to genius and, perhaps, it is a fact in the history of the arts that it is just as likely for influence to exert itself *on* the genius as *from* the genius.

It would also be useful to observe that the influence of genius might well be confused with, and should be kept distinct from, what is frequently called the "anticipation" or prescience of genius: that is to say, the apparent anticipation, in works of genius, of future movements that could not possibly have been known at the time but, through the daring originality of geniuses, are prefigured in their creations. Thus, Monet's late paintings are said to "anticipate" abstract expressionism, *Tristram Shandy* the stream of consciousness technique of the twentieth-century novel, and so forth. These anticipations are indeed taken to be signs of genius, although by no means infallible or necessary ones. In any case, they are not examples of influence but, rather, are aspects of genius discovered only after the fact; after, that is, the movements which they are said to anticipate have come to fruition. Indeed, if they *were* influences, then of course they would not be remarkable at all—would then display not the daring prescience of genius but merely the fact that they were the objects of future emulation.

Furthermore, all this suggests that, far from *defending* the lack of influence of the works of female geniuses against the traditional concept of genius, the feminist should perceive that this lack of influence is perfectly consistent with it: just what one might have expected. The forgotten, maligned, disenfranchised female genius is just a special case of that well-known and venerable figure of the traditional genius myth: the genius misunderstood. And what better explanation, after all, for the works of female geniuses being maligned, neglected, as the feminists have insisted (and they are right), than that they have been *women,* and their character and work denigrated by men. If that is established feminist doctrine, it scarcely need make them run scared against genius in its traditional and commonsense form; they are, in fact, running *with it.*

I want to conclude my discussion of Battersby's critique with what essentially is her parting shot and is, in fact, the last sentence of her book: "A female genius is a construct created as we, the feminist consumers and critics, look back at the past, create a new tradition, and project ourselves and our values towards the future."[21]

Readers of the previous chapter will perceive immediately what it is about Battersby's conclusion that is bound to raise my hackles. It is, of course, the notion that a female genius is a "construct." For I am no more in sympathy with the notion that female genius is a construct than with the notion that that is true of genius across the board. Genius, feminine or otherwise, just *is.*

However, I am not at all convinced that Battersby really means literally what she says here or, at least, *needn't* mean what she apparently says, in order to get what she apparently wants. Rather, I think that if charitably interpreted—charitably, at least, from my point of view—she is saying that the realization of female genius is supervenient on other things that *are* constructed in a perfectly benign and uncontroversial sense, as presented in the previous discussion of genius as a historical concept.

The genius for chess, for example, is not "constructed." It exists timelessly in the species as a disposition to excel, at the genius level, at that game. But, clearly, a genius for chess cannot be realized *until* the game of chess has come into being. And the game of chess *is* a construct. It was made, invented, developed by human beings. Neanderthal could not play chess, no matter what his or her aptitude for the game might have been.

Similarly, neither Sappho nor Jane Austen nor George Eliot could have realized her genius for "feminist literature," as presently understood, although that is not to say that the art of all three was not informed by their sex. Their geniuses could realize themselves only in the genres, forms, and social institutions available to them.

Thus it is not that a female genius, in the contemporary sense Battersby is trying to define, is a construct. What *is* a construct—and a construct on which a female genius, so defined, depends—is the collection of genres, forms, practices, and social institutions that will make up the new feminist aesthetic that Battersby and others hope for. Furthermore, I think she says as much when she writes that the feminist project "is to construct a new foundation that enables us to remove the gag (or the veil) that covers the features of the women buried in the past and the present."[22]

The new feminist artwork, then, is a "construct," properly so called. The new feminist genius is the person who will create that kind of artwork at the highest possible level—the genius level. However, the new feminist genius is *not* a construct, although a construct, and a very complex one, is necessary for its expression. I think this captures what Battersby is trying to tell us about the new feminist genius, without committing her to the rejection of the traditional concept of genius in its Platonic and Longinian forms, which has permeated our thinking about art at its highest level since the eighteenth century, personified for musicians and music lovers by the figures of Mozart and Beethoven.

I have argued here that the traditional concept of genius survives the feminist critique, at least as it has been pursued in Battersby's *Gender and Genius,* certainly the most well-known and admired philosophical work in the field. It is not, I have suggested, the traditional concept of genius that has historically excluded the female genius, but rather the insidious (and false) characterizations of women that prevent them from falling under that concept, *under those false and insidious characterizations.*

Most of Battersby's intellectual history in *Gender and Genius,* as I interpret it, is not so much a history of an exclusively male concept of genius as it is of a denigrating male concept of women that makes it seem as if the female of the species cannot fall within the concept. As an account of that deplorable history, Battersby's book cannot be too highly recommended and should, I think, be required reading for the philosopher of art.

But the reader may fairly ask *why* I have been at such pains to defend the traditional concept of genius against its socio-political deconstruction, and its feminist critique. The answer, I have suggested at various points in my story of Handel, Mozart, Beethoven, and their coming to personify, in their respective turns, the genius concept, is that this concept is somehow *necessary* for our understanding of our world. I cannot imagine what my experience of listening to the Mass in B Minor would be, or my reading of *Middlemarch,* or my viewing of the Sistine ceiling, if I believed that genius was a political put-up job or a male power play. I cannot imagine what it would be like not to appreciate these works as having been made by beings apart: by gifted, inspired beings, albeit, like me, *human* beings. We require the Platonic, Longinian, commonsense notion of genius—the whole package, or one like it—to make sense of human achievement at its highest level, and of our experience of that achievement. I spell out and defend this claim in the next, final chapter.

XIII

Reconstructing Genius

According to an anecdote passed down to us as part of the Mozart legend, Mozart and another (lesser) composer were listening to a composition of Joseph Haydn's. At one point, in response to a particularly arresting passage, the other composer said to Mozart in a critical tone of voice: "I wouldn't have done it that way." Mozart is supposed to have replied: "No, nor would I. And do you know why? It is because neither of us would ever have gotten such a good idea."

One fervently hopes the anecdote is true, for it casts such a favorable and touching light on the veneration for the older master that we have some reliable evidence the younger genius had. But apocryphal or not, it expresses the basic truth of the genius concept (already known to Plato under a different description) that getting good ideas cannot be learned, cannot be taught, cannot be explained, cannot be methodized, and is an intensely personal matter. Witness Ion's talent *only* for Homer. It is *as if* these ideas were the word of God or the gift of Nature.

But can I ask the contemporary reader, if not of a deeply religious persuasion, to believe that genius must be supernatural? Clearly I cannot. But nor can I place all the weight of the concept on natural gifts, as we shall see in a moment.

Well, I am certainly not asking you, the reader, to take literally either the myth of the possessed or the myth of the possessor. That is why I have expressed them in terms of "as if," and that is why I have called them *myths*. Plato, indeed, expresses many of his most famous doctrines in mythic form, and has something important to tell us about this mode of expression. In arguing for the thesis that learning is a process of recollecting what we already know but have forgotten in the birth trauma, he presents at the end of the *Phaedo* a mythic account of the transmigration of souls. In the acquisition of knowledge it is *as if* our souls had lived before, learned, and forgot, and are now recollecting what they formerly knew. But, Plato warns us in the *Phaedo,* the narrative content of the myth itself is not important; it is the conceptual content that that narrative content embodies. Another story with the same conceptual content would do as well, and Plato in fact does tell a different story of the transmigration of souls, to the same effect, in *Republic* X. As Socrates tells his friends in *Phaedo:* "No sensible man would insist that these things are as I describe them...." All that is necessary to believe is "that this, or something like this, is true...."[1]

What *is,* then, the conceptual content of the two genius myths and their satellites? It is, in the most general terms, as we have seen before, that geniuses have something we don't have that makes them able to create or discover or invent. But there are *two* myths, and they are not coextensive. In particular, the inspiration myth suggests sudden and singular occurrences, the Longinian myth steady production. Let me suggest why, and why we need them both.

We are all familiar with the phenomenon of the artist who produced one masterpiece that seems to dwarf the rest of his or her work. It is *that* work alone of the artist's that commands the attention of posterity and perpetuates his or her name and reputation. In such instances, we are inclined to say that that artist was "inspired." She somehow went beyond herself, exceeded her own abilities; it is *as if* someone else had possessed her and done the deed, for her track record showed that *she* could not customarily reach that level.

In music, no composer or work has better exemplified the point for the general population of music lovers than Handel and *Messiah*, the *only* of his works that most concertgoers know. Newman Flower puts it in purple prose eminently suitable to the subject.

> It was the achievement of a giant inspired—the work of one who, by some extraordinary mental feat, had drawn himself completely out of the world, so that he dwelt—or believed he dwelt—in the pastures of God. What happened was that Handel passed through a superb dream. He was unconscious of the world during that time, unconscious of its press and call; his whole mind was in a trance. He did not leave the house. His manservant brought him food, and as often as not returned in an hour to the room to find the food untouched, and his master staring into vacancy. When he had completed Part II, with the "Hallelujah Chorus," his servant found him at the table, tears streaming from his eyes. "I did think I did see all Heaven before me, and the great God Himself!" he exclaimed. Of a certainty, Handel was swept by some influence not of the world during that month—an influence not merely visionary. For twenty-four days he knew those uplands reached only by the higher qualities of the soul.[2]

It doesn't matter whether or not Handel *did* go beyond himself with *Messiah*—whether it is his masterpiece, a cut above the rest, a "stroke of genius," as posterity until fairly recently has seen it, or whether, in the wake of the recent revival of his other works, we decide differently. What matters is that there *are* such cases in the arts, and we need a conceptual marker for them. It is *as if* Handel was "a giant inspired," *as if* "Handel was swept by some influence not of the world," *as if* he "had drawn himself completely out of the world." As Plato says, "No sensible man would insist that these things are as I describe them." But "something like this, is true...." That is why we need the myth of the possessed.

But if you think the myth of the possessed marks out singular, extraordinary events in an artist's life, if you don't think that the gods' intervention or "going beyond yourself" is the order of the day—the way things are with us on a regular basis, even if we are geniuses—then you are going to require another myth to capture the way things are. A myth to capture, for instance, the case of Johann Sebastian Bach, writing a cantata once a week, as the preacher wrote sermons, each one a little gem, a small-scale (or sometimes large-scale) masterpiece. That too is genius—the genius, it seems, of hard work. It is the kind of genius exemplified in the "workaholic" theory, which Bach himself alluded to in the anecdote cited earlier.

But we all know in our hearts that no matter how hard one works at anything, one cannot achieve the genius level by that alone. Nor does there seem to be any external measure of who will achieve it, even given, as Graham Greene said, that one is "willing to put in the time."

There is, of course, external evidence that for any large class of people, they will never function at the genius level in a given area. It is perfectly clear, and has been since I was ten years old, that I will never write novels at the genius level or make scientific discoveries of momentous import, no matter how hard I work, no matter how willing I am to put in the time. There were and are abundant external signs for that, in my performance on examinations in school and in my science and literature courses, and so on. That is not at issue.

The relevant cases are those of "gifted" people: children and young adults who are "math wizzes," who have perfect scores on their aptitude tests, who understand quantum theory at the age of twelve, who can compose prize-winning music before they are old enough to vote. They exhibit all the external signs that they *might* be geniuses. Their parents and teachers hold out great hopes for them.

But for every one of these "wiz kids" who does make the cut, there are hundreds and thousands and tens of thousands that "fizzle out." Furthermore, this happens at even the highest level. For a substantial period of time, Hummel showed as many or more of the external signs of possible genius than did Beethoven or Verdi. Yet he lost the genius sweepstakes to them when it comes down to the *only* external sign of genius that counts, the only one there *is:* the production of works at the highest possible level. And when the genius is of the Bach-like kind, who steadily produces masterpieces at the highest possible level, the Longinian myth of natural gifts fits the facts far more believably than the Platonic myth of the genius possessed, for whom a miracle is necessary for every production. Indeed, the latter seems to have all the defects, when supposed to operate on a "regular" basis, of the doctrine of "occasional causes," which requires an act of God for every act of perception or will.

Of course we must constantly be reminded that neither of these myths need be accepted in literal detail. Furthermore, there is a trope that, so to say, "naturalizes" the inspiration myth, essentially making acts of God rather "acts of Nature" or "acts of Life." It has been popular since the advent of the so-called expression theory of art in the nineteenth century, and perhaps even before, to try to connect great works of art with important events in the artists' lives that "inspired" those works. I was told by one of my college German teachers that the Gretchen episode in Part I of *Faust* was "inspired" by an actual case, in Goethe's lifetime, of an unfortunate woman condemned to death for killing her infant born out of wedlock. Beethoven's *Eroica* Symphony is supposed to have been "inspired" by the deeds of Napoleon (*before* he crowned himself emperor). And a recent film depicts *Romeo and Juliet* as having been "inspired" by a love affair of the author's (although I take this claim to be tongue in cheek). An atheist, I suppose, will find this a more believable inspiration story than the possession myth, although anyone else will find it perhaps less plausible, as it assumes a natural coincidence at an unacceptably high level; whereas in a theodicy, I suppose, anything is as probable as anything else. For, as Hume says with regard to the doctrine of occasional causes, "We are got into fairy land...."[3]

If we acknowledge, then, the three phenomena of artistic creation, or any other kind at the genius level, as facts of life, it can be seen that we require both the myth of the possessor and of the possessed to compass them. By all external measures of learning, talent, and skill, two artists are on an equal footing. Yet one of them creates at the highest level, the "genius" level, and the other does not. It is *as if* the former had a "natural gift," an "innate" extra talent that the other does not have. As an ancient proverb has it: *Orator fit, Poeta nascitur.*[4] Or else it is *as if* the former somehow has another source than the latter; it is *as if* some outside force flows through him or her at the moment of creation to lift the chosen one above the other; it is *as if* "they are so beloued of the Gods that whatsoever they write proceeds of a diuine fury."[5]

Furthermore, sometimes a "mere" artist of "talent" overreaches himself and produces a masterpiece: a work at the genius level never approached again by that artist. *Perhaps* that is the case with Bizet's *Carmen,* or Handel's *Messiah,* or Humperdinck's *Hänsel und Gretel.* In such cases, it is *not* as if the composer had a natural gift, or else why did it serve him only once? But it is *as if* the composer were possessed, or else *as if* motivated by some singular event in his life—the death of a loved one, an affair of the heart, a social or political event of great moment. For such cases the myth of a natural gift will not do. It suggests steady output at the highest level, not flashes of brilliance, "strokes of genius."

In contrast, the steady output, at the highest level, of an artist like a Bach or a Beethoven is a phenomenon that demands the notion of some permanent "natural endowment." Inspiration as a steady diet seems to belie the very notion itself of "inspiration."

Thus, to conclude, the myth of the possessor and the myth of the possessed, in their various incarnations from antiquity to the present, have endured precisely because the phenomenon of genius, of creativity at the highest possible level, demands them: "this, or something like this, is true. . . ."

What, then, of the "workaholic" theory, which also has surfaced from time to time—not, to be sure, with the persistence of the possessor and the possessed, but frequently enough to suggest that it too might be tracking a truth. What truth might that be?

Let us take the workaholic myth of genius to be something along the lines of Newton's suggestion, as elaborated by Keynes and Andrade. Let us suppose that the "hard work" that genius is supposed to consist of takes the form of "extraordinary powers of concentration."

Now, extraordinary powers of concentration will not, of course, in themselves *do* anything. The extraordinary power to concentrate on something is a power one might have without ever putting it to use, like the power of my automobile to kill a person, which, of course, it has but, I am happy to say, has never been exercised. In order for one's extraordinary powers of concentration to have any effect, one must *employ* them. Further, they will not be employed if they are not employed for some extended period of time. One may *have* extraordinary powers of concentration and simply not have the desire to concentrate on anything for more than a brief period. In that case, one's powers of concentration—which we *all* normally have to some degree—may well be extraordinary powers of concentration but may never be employed *as such,* and thus may lie dormant forever.

The missing ingredient is the *desire* to concentrate on a problem or project for extended, extraordinarily protracted periods of time. More than a desire, it must be an *obsession.* The workaholic myth of genius, then, has it that genius consists of an obsessive desire to concentrate exclusively and for extended periods of time on a problem or project, and of the extraordinary powers of concentration to do so. Furthermore, when stated in this way, the workaholic myth or theory of genius does seem to strike a resonant chord. There does seem to be something about our intuitions concerning genius that it tracks.

To begin with, recall that one of the character traits regularly associated with genius is "abstraction": obliviousness to one's social surroundings; complete self-absorption to the extent of seeming to be in a trance or a fit—a fit even of madness. The genius dwells in a different world, seems not to be with us. The genius is more often than not "in a brown study." The genius forgets where she is; her mind is on other things.

The anecdotes of Beethoven's "peculiar behavior," forgetting where he is, muttering and singing to himself, careless in his attire to the extent of slovenliness, and so on immediately come to mind, as do the descriptions of Mozart, as a child, so absorbed in his musical activities that he must be dragged from his clavier to his bed. And, of course, the description, quoted earlier, of Handel in the throes of composing *Messiah,* completely oblivious to his surroundings, the demands of his body, and the passage of time. When, of course, these fits of abstraction come in relatively short bursts, they accord well with the Platonic myth of the possessed: it is *as if* all of a sudden one is taken over by the god, for a time, and then released again. The myth and the "madness" were made for one another and, no doubt, fed on one another.

But an inspirational burst like that of Handel's in composing *Messiah* is a bit protracted for the Platonic myth; it is not a stroke of genius, where an idea comes in a blinding flash or even in an hour or two in which, as more than one poet has testified, a sonnet or lyric "dictated itself," as it were, without a glitch. As Newman Flower tells us, "The whole of *Messiah* from beginning to end was set upon paper in twenty four days. Considering the immensity of the work, and the short time involved, it will perhaps remain for ever, the greatest feat in the whole history of musical composition."[6] Twenty-four days—indeed, a remarkably short time in which to compose a work of such dimensions—is, nevertheless, a long time to be possessed by the god. What it does evince, of course, is "extraordinary powers of concentration." Handel "sat down to the work of composition in the little front room of the house in Brook Street" and did not get up out of it until, twenty-four days later, he emerged with the full score of *Messiah*.[7]

During the twenty-four days in which *Messiah* was composed, Handel may indeed have been possessed by a particularly tenacious daemon. But, from the "naturalist" point of view, what this feat best exemplifies is "extraordinary powers of concentration," coupled with the overriding obsession to complete a task—no doubt, given the nature of the text Handel was asked to set (by Charles Jennens), driven by deep and sincere religious conviction.

Moreover, what the workaholic myth in its "Newtonian" version best comports with is the kind of long-term concentration and obsession depicted in the Beethoven character. For whereas Handel may have been oblivious to the world around him for these three memorable weeks, the unlicked bear is portrayed as being more or less oblivious to the world during his entire adult life, the growing deafness, no doubt, contributing to the impression. Beethoven's image, as passed down to us by the "eyewitness" reports quoted from copiously in Chapter 8, was of a man obsessed with the composition of his works above all else, and continually engrossed in that occupation, wherever he was. His "extraordinary powers of concentration" and the obsession to exercise them in company "explain" the distracted, absentminded character who, the legend tells us, walked the streets of Vienna and its environs in a disheveled state, muttering and singing to himself, unaware of his surroundings, unmindful of his companions.

Furthermore, the workaholic myth fits another, not so familiar "character," as we have seen, the distinctly "unromantic" workman, in the persons of Haydn and Bach. There is no evidence that the Cantor of Leipzig was an eccentric, distracted person. Rather, he seems to have led a boringly normal, orderly life, doing his day-to-day job, which just happened to be, among other things, the producing of musical compositions of transcendent greatness on a regular basis, one a week. How does one *do* that? Well, as Bach tells us, one works very hard at it. But when does one do the composing, given that one's life is also filled with the tasks of schoolmaster, conductor, choir director, music teacher, and so on? To a large extent, no doubt, when one is functioning at the level of Johann Sebastian Bach, one does it "in the head" while one is doing all those other, more or less "mindless" things. My own picture of Bach is of a man who, unlike Beethoven, was in two places at once. While the schoolmaster was in the classroom teaching Latin or even preparing the choir, the genius was "somewhere else," composing fugues. I suppose one way of putting it is that Bach could comparmentalize his intellectual activities, as we know Mozart could also do to a remarkable degree—for example, as we know from one of his letters to his sister, copying down from memory a fugue he had just finished composing "in his head" *while* composing the prelude to it. (In light of this, composing while playing billiards seems a trifling matter.) Thus, Bach's extraordinary powers of concentration and his obsession to compose music did not, as in the case of Beethoven, get in the way of his humdrum activities, making, it seems to me, the powers and the obsession all the more extraordinary, which, I suppose, is why Beethoven Genius seems to us so much more like what genius should look like than the genius of Citizen Bach.

Finally, the workaholic theory suggests at least a possible "explanation" for the gap between genius and "talent," where the latter is of a very high order. Could it be that what separates the two is just that power to concentrate and the persistent obsession to do so? As folk wisdom would have it, those who succeed have a "fire in the belly." Could that be the difference?

Of course we all know in our heart of hearts that obsessive powers of concentration are not sufficient condition for genius. A man may spend a lifetime of singleminded concentration building a scale model of London out of matchsticks and tempt no one to call him "genius" for his trouble. And there are obsessive artists in abundance who are as devoted and relentless workers as Bach and Beethoven, with nothing to show for their devotion to their muse than mediocrity. But then there are the Hummels and the Telemanns—men of stupendous talent who, one wants to say, *should have been* Bachs and Beethovens—and, for all of that talent, remained Hummels and Telemanns. Could the difference be that the right "intellectual stuff" is present in both kinds of case but not the right "emotional stuff"—that Bach and Beethoven were possessed of extraordinary powers of concentration, along with a fire in the belly, their desire amounting to obsessive concentration on musical problems and tasks until the last drop of juice is squeezed from them? The Bachs and Beethovens never choose the easy solution, never choose the easy way out.

There is very real content to the claim that Hummel and Telemann, as opposed to Beethoven and Bach, were "lazy" composers. It is true that Telemann composed vast quantities of music—a truly staggering output, really. But a movement by Telemann frequently ends not very long after it begins, with nothing much musically happening to the themes, appealing though they often are. Whereas Bach, not unprolific himself, takes a theme or idea through its paces at length, and in such a way as to make one feel, in the end, that he has exploited that theme or idea exhaustively. And so also with Hummel and Beethoven. In this clear respect, Telemann and Hummel are lazy composers, Bach and Beethoven obsessive workmen who won't let go of an idea until it has completely fulfilled its promise within the musical dimensions set.

It is clear, then, that Bach, Telemann, Beethoven, and Hummel all were tremendously gifted musicians: their musical talents were prodigious. Could it be that what made the difference was "character"— obsession and extraordinary powers of concentration versus less than extraordinary powers of concentration and (or) a complacent streak that led to settling for the easy way out?

I don't know how to answer such questions, although when I am confronted with sheer, overpowering musical beauty, I find it difficult to believe that concentration alone makes the difference between a Beethoven and a Hummel, or a Bach and a Telemann. But answering it, anyway, is not my business. What *is* is to argue that the myths of the possessor, the possessed, and the workaholic together make a conceptual package that is necessary to "save the appearances," to make intelligible our experience of works of genius. It is *as if* Mozart was possessed, Beethoven gifted by Nature, Bach obsessed. "No sensible man would insist that these things are as I describe them. . . ." But "this, or something like this, is true. . . ."

I urge, then, that something like the traditional concept of genius is required to make the phenomenon of art, at the highest level, intelligible. Furthermore, this is so in our individual experiences of works of art as well. What I mean can perhaps be introduced by calling attention to the fact that Kant titles §46 of the *Critique of Judgment* "*Fine art is the art of genius*"; as well, he states there that "fine arts must necessarily be regarded as arts of genius" and, again, "fine art is only possible as a product of genius."[8]

Now is not the time to enter again into a lengthy project of Kant interpretation. So I will simply say straightaway that I am appropriating, for my own purposes, some Kantian insights here, not pretending to accurately represent his doctrine (although if I accidentally do the latter as well, I will not be sorry for it). I appropriate from Kant, to begin with, the idea that there is some necessary connection between the fine arts and genius. In particular, I want to say that there is some necessary connection between the way we, here and now, experience the fine arts *at their highest level* and our conviction that *at this level* the fine arts are arts of genius.

Kant continues his thought, and (here we are going over some ground already covered in a previous chapter):

> Every art presupposes rules which are laid down as the foundation which first enables a product, if it is to be called one of art,

to be represented as possible. The concept of fine art, however, does not permit of the judgement upon the beauty of its product being derived from any rule that has a *concept* for its determining ground, and that depends, consequently, on a concept of the way in which the product is possible.[9]

I spent some considerable time earlier closely reading this and related passages, with the purpose of explicating Kant's doctrine of genius, in the form in which it influenced, so I argued, the representation of Beethoven's creative personality. I now wish to read it in quite a different way: loosely, as an insight into one aspect of our aesthetic experience of artworks, essential to that experience as we know it.

Loosely speaking, then, Kant is saying that we cannot experience works of fine art under "any concept of the way in which the product is possible." In other words, if I am experiencing a "product," an artifact, with knowledge of the method or process or "rules" by which it was brought into being, then I cannot be experiencing a work of the fine arts at all, for works of fine art *cannot* be produced by method or statable process or "rules" but only by the spontaneity of genius. Hence they are *arts* of genius.

Now with one emendation — namely, that we speak here not of the fine arts across the board but only of artworks at the highest level of excellence — I accept Kant's insight, in the following version. When we experience great works of art, we find ourselves unable to conceive how (by what means) such works could have been brought into being, and this engenders in us a sense of wonder, a sense of miracle that is a necessary part of our aesthetic experience. This I take to be the essence, the spirit of Kant's insight — and I think it is dead right.

Imagine, if you will, coming to see how a work of art you are experiencing as a work of genius really did come into being: you "saw through it," as it were. You discovered that it was produced by a method or set of rules that anyone in on the secret could apply — like being shown how shoes are cobbled, or houses framed. (Any reasonably proficient theory student can, for example, with some application, learn to write a credible fugue "according to the rules" that sounds nice.) In such a case, the sense of wonder, the sense of the miraculous that that work conveyed would vanish. Something important and valuable in your experience of that artwork would be lost.

There is no need for you to be *correct* in your surmise, to lose the sense of wonder, only that you become convinced of it. The man who came to believe that Bach possessed a fugue-writing machine must have lost *his* sense of wonder, his sense of the miraculous in Bach's masterpieces.

More relevant to present concerns, if one were to come to believe, as does DeNora, that genius is a political construct, Beethoven a political put-up job, Dussek a political victim, then one perforce cannot experience the music of Beethoven with the sense of wonder and fervor one had when one believed in the traditional concept of genius. To come to such a belief would be, in effect, to come to the belief that there is a "method," a set of "rules" for the creation of works of "genius," although it would be a method or set of rules that went beyond the normal conception of such things as the tools of the musical craft to the tools of the politician—the tools of public relations, backroom deals, bribes, and image-making. In any event, the believer in that, or any other "reduction" of genius to the terms of an expressible method, whether political or otherwise, loses an essential and valuable ingredient in the aesthetic experience of works of art as we now know that experience and have know it since antiquity. He or she loses the sense of wonder, the sense of the miraculous that the greatest works of the fine arts convey.

At this point it seems reasonable for those so inclined to put the charge of "elitism" to the doctrine here advanced, and it is not without some justification. For the Kantian position, unreformed, restricts the concept of genius to the fine arts, and Kant clearly means to include in those only what we would call the "high arts." It is doubtful he would have allowed genius, as a concept, to apply to the "popular" and (now) "mass" arts, certainly not to the "useful" arts such as pottery or quilting. Yet, to not allow that genius can express itself in such arts as moviemaking or popular music or the folk and practical arts but only in the arts enshrined in the Western canon is indeed to leave one open to the charge of elitism in the true, bad sense of that term, with its implications of entrenched privilege, intellectual aristocracy, and snobbery.

However, there is no need for us to confine ourselves to Kant's overly narrow conception of the fine arts, *or* to follow him in his restriction of genius to the fine arts alone, either narrowly or broadly conceived. That the wonder of genius can be evinced in the making of a Hollywood movie or in the throwing of a pot or in a Broadway musical seems evident enough to us, and in no need of a defense—Kant to the contrary notwithstanding (and who can say, anyway, what Kant would have thought of *Oklahoma* or *Bringing up Baby?*). That Kant was "elitist" (if indeed he *was*) in his concept of genius does not require us to be in ours, even while retaining his basic insight.

But now another kind of "elitism" might be detected in the notion that geniuses are people "apart," people above the rest of us in some way—super people, or god-like, as the Romantics were wont to represent Beethoven. And that somehow strikes us as dehumanizing genius, over-Romanticizing the creative artist, making him or her an alien being. Perhaps it was the fear of this kind of thing that led Battersby to insist that "a female 'genius' is not some kind of élite being, different from other (ordinary) women...."[10]

Indeed, one might continue along these lines, what could the works of genius possibly mean to us if geniuses were creatures apart: creatures of a higher order of being, alien to us, to *our* needs, *our* emotions, *our* intelligence? If geniuses are gods or extraterrestrial visitors, they speak not to *us*. But, indeed, they *do*. So we must accommodate two conflicting intuitions: that geniuses are apart from us and that they *are* us: that they eat, sleep, make love, lie, cheat, steal, hate, sacrifice, grieve, are generous, are selfish, are geniuses, in short, are *human,* warts and all.

Perhaps the best way to reassure ourselves that geniuses can *both* be *of* us and *beyond* us is to remind ourselves of a simple fact of logic. Something can become what it is by a process of small increments and yet be *what it is*—something apart from or beyond what it came from. A man once hirsute who gradually becomes bald, perhaps hair by hair, is a *bald* man, not hirsute. And there is a world of difference between the two: witness the amount of time and treasure the one will expend to become again the other.

We know too, as a matter of logic, that with such concepts as bald/hirsute or poor/rich, there is an area, between the absence and presence, of indeterminate character: people who are neither bald nor hirsute, neither poor nor rich, and, as well, an ancient paradox attributed to Eubulides called "the heap," which puts to us the dilemma that since we cannot tell which pebble makes a pile, there are no piles (no hirsute people, no rich ones). I leave this paradox to the logicians. As for the area indeterminate between absence and presence, we all know how to live with it.

It now remains to say that "genius" is a degree concept. What separates the average music lover or amateur musician from Mozart or Beethoven is not the gulf between God and Man, angel and ape. We are all of the same substance as they. And by small increments, you get from me to Mozart. We are separated by degree, not kind. But, of course, in practice no person can become a Mozart; one can only be born one, as a person can, alas, become a bald man and, happily, become a millionaire. If he could, then, of course, the traditional concept of genius would be false. One can, however, in thought, know something of what it must be like to be a Mozart and, as well, how far from us a Mozart really is.

Take piano lessons. Take a course in basic musicianship and music theory. Anyone who can hear a tune can learn to play an instrument at some acceptable level of proficiency, and learn enough harmony and counterpoint to harmonize chorales and compose exercises in "species" counterpoint that are "grammatically" correct. That is the way you learn that performing and composing are *human* tasks that human beings can accomplish. But when you compare your playing to that of Vladimir Horwowitz or your chorales and species counterpoint to Bach's chorales and fugues, you then realize what a gulf, what a galaxy separates you from them, what separates ability, or perhaps even talent, from genius. By this experiment in practice and thought one can get a feeling for both the humanness of genius and what separates it from humanity as we commonly experience it.

Are there, then, degrees of genius? To be sure there are. Was Telemann a genius? I don't think so, though he was a man of prodigious talent and was, perhaps, a borderline case. Were Cherubini and Humperdinck? I *do* think so. But I would describe them as "minor" geniuses. Each produced one or more works that are still in the repertoire—and perhaps more of their works deserve revival. But it seems unlikely they will ever be in the commanding position of Beethoven or Verdi.

Of course the canon of genius, in any art form, is always open to revision. No one who defends the traditional picture of genius need deny that; indeed, it is part of the picture. Be that as it may, there will always be a consensus of some kind about who is a genius, who a minor genius, who a borderline case, who "merely talented," who fallen from grace.

Geniuses are not alien beings. They are *human* beings. We see *our* humanity in them. But we see it at the highest possible level of achievement. Geniuses deserve to be put on pedestals. They do not, as the reductionists would tell us, have feet of clay. They *do* have feet of *flesh,* else they would be naught to us.

But what *is* their flesh? What *is* artistic genius, anyway? To say that it is a "disposition" to make great works of art seems a retreat to the caricature of Aristotelian explanation in which the soporific effect of opium is attributed to its "dormitive virtue."

Nevertheless, that is all we have and, perhaps, all we will ever have. Genius remains for us a mystery marked by myth and metaphor.

Does this mean that genius is some kind of supernatural phenomenon? By no means. The fact that "something" defies our understanding and may, in the nature of the case, do so indefinitely does not put it in the realm of the ectoplasmic, does not make it a subject for psychics or theologians. The "mystery" is not a *divine* mystery.

But were some "reductionist" account of genius to happen along and somehow "dissolve" the "mystery" of genius, what then? Well, as I see it, it could no more leave untouched the wonder we now experience over the mystery of artistic creation and its works, at the highest level, than could the discovery that comets are "merely" dirty ice leave untouched the wonder and awe our ancestors experienced in contemplating these (for them) majestic and ominous portents. In the event, it must drastically change our experience and our very concept of the fine arts—and, in ways already stated, change them for the worse. This is of course no argument against the truth of any reductionist theory of genius, should one emerge; to think it was would be to forget Hume's dictum that the bad consequences of a doctrine are no evidence of its falsity. But nor should those who seriously consider reductionist theories lull themselves into thinking that one can hold such a theory and still, in the aesthetic experience of the fine arts, conduct business as usual.

For my part, I see the myths of the possessor and the possessed outlasting all the reductionists to come. "No sensible man [or woman] would insist that these things are as I describe them. . . ." But "this, or something like this, is true. . . ."

Notes

PREFACE

1. Peter Kivy, "Mainwaring's *Handel:* Its Relation to English Aesthetics," *Journal of the American Musicological Society*, XVII (1964).
2. Peter Kivy, "Child Mozart as an Aesthetic Symbol," *Journal of the History of Ideas*, XVIII (1967).
3. Peter Kivy, *The Fine Art of Repetition: Essays in the Philosophy of Music* (New York: Cambridge University Press, 1993), p. 4.

CHAPTER 1. TIME OUT OF MIND

1. H. C. Robbins Landon, *Haydn: A Documentary Study* (New York: Rizzoli, 1981), p. 193.
2. Quoted in Karl Geiringer, *Haydn: A Creative Life in Music* (London: George Allen and Unwin, 1947), p. 170.
3. *The Iliad,* trans. Richard Lattimore (Chicago: University of Chicago Press, 1952), p. 59. *The Odyssey,* trans. Robert Fitzgerald (Garden City, N.Y.: Anchor Books, 1963), p. 1.
4. Plato, *The Republic,* trans. John Llewelyn Davies and David James Vaughan (London: Macmillan, 1950), p. 90 (397).
5. Plato, *Ion,* trans. W. R. M. Lamb, in Plato, *The Statesman, Philebus and Ion*

(Loeb Classical Library, Cambridge, Mass.: Harvard University Press, 1962), p. 415 (532).

6. Ibid., p. 411 (531).
7. Ibid., pp. 411–413 (531).
8. Ibid., p. 421 (533).
9. Ibid.
10. Ibid., p. 423 (534).
11. Ibid., p. 417 (532).
12. Ibid.
13. Ibid., pp. 417–419 (532–533).
14. *The Dialogues of Plato,* trans. B. Jowett (New York: Random House, 1937), vol. I, p. 287 (532). My italics.
15. Plato, *Two Comic Dialogues,* trans. Paul Woodruff (Indianapolis: Hackett, 1983).
16. *The Dialogues of Plato,* trans. Jowett, vol. I, p. 523 (465).
17. R. G. Collingwood, *The Principles of Art* (Oxford: Clarendon Press, 1955), p. 19.
18. Plato, *Ion,* trans. Lamb, pp. 427–429 (535–536).
19. Ibid., pp. 429–431 (536).
20. I am grateful to my colleague Robert Bolton for checking the crucial passage in Greek for me.

CHAPTER 2. GREATNESS OF MIND

1. Letter from Beethoven to Franz Gerhard Wegeler, in Ludwig van Beethoven, *The Letters of Ludwig van Beethoven,* trans. Emily Anderson (New York: St. Martin's Press, 1962), vol. I, p. 66.
2. Longinus, *Dionysious or Longinus on the Sublime,* trans. W. Hamilton Fyfe, in *Aristotle, The Poetics, "Longinus," On the Sublime, Demetrius, On Style* (Loeb Classical Library, Cambridge, Mass.: Harvard University Press, 1953), p. 125. I am most grateful to my colleague Pierre Pellegrin for going over the Greek text of Longinus for me and straightening me out on this point.
3. Ibid.
4. Ibid., p. 127.
5. Ibid.
6. Ibid., p. 141.
7. Ibid., p. 143.
8. Ibid., pp. 143–145.
9. Ibid., p. 153.
10. Ibid., p. 151.

11. Ibid., p. 153.
12. *Ion,* p. 423 (534).
13. Ibid., pp. 423–425 (534). Nothing is known of this poet but what Plato tells us here, there being, apparently, no other record of him or his poems.
14. Longinus, *On the Sublime,* trans. Fyfe, p. 217.
15. Ibid., p. 219.
16. Ibid.
17. Ibid., p. 225.
18. Ibid., p. 227.
19. Ibid., p. 229.

CHAPTER 3. BREAKING THE RULE

1. *The Spectator,* ed. Alexander Chalmers (New York: D. Appleton, 1879), vol. II, p. 329.
2. Ibid.
3. Ibid., vol. II, pp. 329–330.
4. Ibid., vol. II, p. 332.
5. Ibid., vol. II, p. 333; my italics.
6. Ibid.
7. Ibid., vol. VI, pp. 369–370.
8. For the complete story of the rise of the sublime in eighteenth-century Britain, the reader is recommended to the as yet unsurpassed account by Samuel H. Monk, first published in 1935, and reprinted in 1960. See, *The Sublime: A Study of Critical Theories in Eighteenth-Century England* (Ann Arbor, Mich.: University of Michigan Press, 1960).
9. Again, Monk is to be highly recommended in this regard.
10. Longinus, *Dionysius Longinus On the Sublime,* trans. William Smith (London, 1739), p. xxvii.
11. *The Spectator,* ed. Chalmers, vol. V, p. 33.
12. Ibid., vol. V, p. 34.
13. Edmund Burke, *A Philosophical Enquiry into the Origin of Our Ideas of the Sublime and Beautiful,* ed. Adam Phillips (New York: Oxford University Press, 1990), p. 53.
14. Immanuel Kant, *Observations on the Feeling of the Beautiful and Sublime,* trans. John T. Goldthwait (Berkeley: University of California Press, 1960), p. 47.
15. Marjorie Hope Nicolson, *Mountain Gloom and Mountain Glory: The Development of the Aesthetics of the Infinite* (New York: Norton, 1963).
16. Burke, *Enquiry,* p. 54.
17. Ibid., p. 56.

18. Edward Young, *Conjectures on Original Composition in a Letter to the Author of Sir Charles Grandison* (Manchester: The University Press, 1918), p. 6. The text is that of the second edition, 1759.

19. Ibid., p. 7.

20. Ibid., p. 24. For those who are mystified by the word "fort" in this passage, as am I, all I can tell you is that it clearly means "force" or "strength," but the *Oxford English Dictionary* gives no such meaning for it. It does, however, cite "fort" as an obsolete adjective meaning "strong."

21. Ibid.

22. Ibid., p. 13.

23. Ibid., pp. 13–14.

24. I have omitted in my discussion of the British writers on genius, both in this chapter and in Chapter 7, William Duff's substantial book, *An Essay on Original Genius and Its Various Modes of Exertion in Philosophy and the Fine Arts, Particularly Poetry* (London, 1767). I have done so because I do not believe it contributes materially to the story I am trying to tell in this book. It was published after Gerard, whom I *will* be discussing in Chapter 7, first sketched his own account of genius, in 1759, and before Gerard turned his sketch into a full-length study in 1774. It was Gerard, I shall argue in Chapter 7, who was the major player in the genius game, after Young and before Kant. That, of course, is a judgment call others may well dispute. In a history of the philosophy of genius, Duff would certainly have a place. My book is *not* a history of genius, and I omit Duff with no feelings of guilt.

CHAPTER 4. THE SAXON OR THE DEVIL

1. John Mainwaring, *Memoirs of the Life of the Late George Frederic Handel. To which is added a Catalogue of His Works and Observations upon them* (London, 1760). A portion of the *Observations*, that dealing with the comparison of Handel with "the Italians" (pp. 165–175), was contributed, Mainwaring tells us, by "a Gentleman who is a perfect master of the subject . . ." (p. 164). The "Gentleman" is identified by O. E. Deutch in *Handel: A Documentary Biography* (New York: Norton, 1954), p. 529, as Robert Price.

2. Mainwaring, *Memoirs*, pp. 4–5.

3. Ibid., pp. 5–6.

4. Ibid., p. 8.

5. Ibid., pp. 10–11.

6. Ibid., pp. 13–14.

7. Ibid., pp. 15–16.

8. Ibid., p. 17.

9. Ibid.

10. Ibid., p. 22.
11. Ibid., p. 21. Mainwaring calls him simply Attilio.
12. Ibid., p. 37.
13. Ibid., pp. 43–44.
14. Ibid., pp. 50 and 68.
15. Ibid., pp. 51–52.
16. Ibid., p. 63.
17. Ibid., p. 61.
18. Ibid., p. 159.
19. Ibid., pp. 160–161.
20. David Hume, "Of the Standard of Taste," *Essays: Moral, Political, Literary* (Oxford: Oxford University Press, 1971), pp. 235–236. Cf. Joseph Addison, *The Spectator*, No. 29, Tuesday, April 3, 1711: "music, architecture, and painting, as well as poetry and oratory, are to deduce their laws and rules from the general sense of mankind, and not from the principles of these arts themselves . . ." (*The Spectator*, ed. Chalmers, vol. I, p. 222).
21. Mainwaring, *Memoirs*, pp. 161–162.
22. Ibid., pp. 162–163.
23. Ibid., p. 166.
24. Ibid., p. 168.
25. Ibid., p. 190.
26. Ibid., p. 192.
27. Ibid., p. 193. In a footnote to this passage Mainwaring refers the reader to Section 33 of *On the Sublime*. This is a mistake. The description of Demosthenes occurs in Section 34. The confusion must arise from the fact that Mainwaring uses as an epigraph for his book a quotation from Section 33.
28. Longinus, *Dionysius Longinus On the Sublime*, trans. Smith, pp. 83–84. The notion of the oratorio as peculiarly sublime, among musical forms, filtered down even to that most unmusical of philosophers, Immanuel Kant, who wrote in the third *Critique*: "Even the presentation of the sublime, so far as it belongs to fine art, may be brought into union with beauty in a *tragedy in verse*, a *didactic poem* or an *oratorio* . . ." (*Critique of Judgement*, trans. James Creed Meredith (Oxford: Clarendon Press, 1911), p. 190 (§52).
29. Ibid., pp. 78–79. Lawrence A. Gushee helped me locate this passage in the Greek text.
30. Mainwaring, *Memoirs*, p. 192.
31. Ibid., p. 197.
32. Ibid., p. 201.
33. Charles Avison, *Reply to the Author of Remarks on Mr. Avison's Essay on Musical Expression*, in Deutsch, ed., *Handel: A Documentary Biography*, p. 736. Avison

refers to "his [Handel's] own DRYDEN" because Handel had set two of Dryden's poems to music: *Ode for Saint Caecelia's Day* and *Alexander's Feast.*

34. Ibid.

35. Mainwaring, *Memoirs,* p. 197.

36. Deutsch, *Handel: A Documentary Biography,* p. 849.

37. Charles Burney, *An Account of the Musical Performances in Westminster-Abbey, and the Pantheon, May 26th, 27th, 29th; and June 3d, and 5th, 1784. In Commemoration of Handel* (London, 1785), pp. i–ii.

38. Ibid., p. iii.

39. Paul Oskar Kristeller, "The Modern System of the Arts: A Study in the History of Aesthetics (I)," *Journal of the History of Ideas,* XII (1951), and "The Modern System of the Arts: A Study in the History of Aesthetics (II)," *Journal of the History of Ideas,* XIII (1952), both reprinted in Peter Kivy (ed.), *Essays on the History of Aesthetics* (Rochester: University of Rochester Press, 1992).

40. Kristeller, "The Modern System of the Arts (II)," in Kivy, *Essays on the History of Aesthetics,* p. 35.

41. Burney, *Account of the Musical Performances in Westminster-Abbey,* p. iv.

42. Rob C. Wegman, "From Maker to Composer: Improvisation and Musical Authorship in the Low Countries, 1450–1500," *Journal of the American Musicological Society,* XLIX (1996), p. 411.

43. Ibid., p. 442.

44. Ibid., p. 447.

45. Ibid., p. 465.

46. Ibid., p. 466.

47. Ibid.

48. Ibid., p. 467.

49. Ibid., p. 466.

CHAPTER 5. THE GENIUS AND THE CHILD

1. Kant, *Critique of Aesthetic Judgement,* trans. James Creed Meredith (Oxford: Clarendon Press, 1911), p. 50 (§5).

2. Ibid., pp. 42–43 (§2).

3. The history of this doctrine in the eighteenth century—a doctrine that is primarily a product of British thinkers—is well told by Jerome Stolnitz in "On the Origins of 'Aesthetic Disinterestedness,'" *Journal of Aesthetics and Art Criticism,* XX (1961).

4. Joseph Addison, *The Spectator,* paper no. 411, Saturday, June 21, 1712, *The Spectator,* ed. Alexander Chalmers (New York: D. Appleton, 1879), vol. V, p. 31.

5. Francis Hutcheson, *Inquiry Concerning Beauty, Order, Harmony, Design,* ed. Peter Kivy (The Hague: Martinus Nijhoff, 1973), p. 37 (I.xiv).

6. Kant, *Critique of Aesthetic Judgement,* trans. Meredith, p. 43 ($2).
7. Ibid., p. 44 ($3).
8. Ibid., p. 45 ($3).
9. Ibid., p. 46 ($4).
10. Ibid.
11. Ibid., p. 48 ($5).
12. Ibid., pp. 48–49.
13. Ibid., p. 60 ($9).
14. Ibid., p. 56 ($8).
15. Arthur Schopenhauer, *The World as Will and Representation,* trans. E. F. J. Payne (Indian Hills, Colo.: Falcon's Wing Press, 1958), vol. I, p. 3 (Book I, $1).
16. Ibid., vol. I, p. 184 (Book III, $36).
17. Ibid., vol. II, p. 191 (Chapter XVIII).
18. Ibid., vol. I, p. 175 ($32).
19. Ibid., vol. I, p. 192 ($36).
20. Ibid., p. 184.
21. Ibid.
22. Ibid.
23. Ibid., vol. I, p. 233 ($49).
24. Ibid., vol. I, p. 257 ($52).
25. Ibid., vol. II, p. 372 (Chapter XXX).
26. Ibid., vol. I, p. 196 ($38).
27. Ibid., vol. I, p. 187 ($36).
28. Ibid., vol. I, p. 196 ($38).
29. Ibid., vol. I, p. 185 ($36).
30. Ibid., vol. I, p. 196 ($38).
31. Ibid., vol. I, p. 181 ($34).
32. Ibid., 181n.
33. Ibid., vol. I, p. 190 ($36).
34. Ibid., p. 191.
35. Plato, *Phaedrus,* trans. H. N. Fowler (Loeb Classical Library, Cambridge, Mass.: Harvard University Press), p. 469 (245A).
36. Schopenhauer, *The World as Will and Representation,* trans. Payne, vol. II, p. 389 (Chapter XXXI).
37. Ibid., vol. I, pp. 178–179 ($34).
38. Ibid., vol. II, p. 377 (Chapter XXXI).
39. Ibid., pp. 384–385.
40. Ibid., p. 393.
41. Ibid., p. 394.
42. Ibid., p. 395.

43. Ibid.
44. Ibid., pp. 395–396.

CHAPTER 6. THE LITTLE MAN FROM SALZBURG

1. Franz Niemetschek, *Life of Mozart,* trans. Helen Mautner (London: Leonard Hyman, 1956), p. 13.
2. Ibid., pp. 14–15.
3. Ibid., p. 15.
4. Ibid., pp. 21–22.
5. Otto Erich Deutsch, *Mozart: A Documentary Biography,* trans. Eric Blom, Peter Branscombe, and Jeremy Noble (Stanford: Stanford University Press, 1965), p. 95.
6. Ibid., p. 98.
7. Ibid., pp. 97–98.
8. Ibid., p. 98.
9. Ibid., p. 97.
10. Ibid., p. 100.
11. Mainwaring, *Memoirs of the Life of George Frederic Handel* (London: 1760), p. 5.
12. Friedrich Nietzsche, *Beyond Good and Evil,* trans. Marianne Cowan (Chicago: Henry Regnery, 1955), p. 78 (#94).
13. Niemetschek, *Life of Mozart,* p. 20.
14. Ibid., p. 19.
15. Ibid., pp. 65–66.
16. Ibid., p. 52.
17. Ibid., p. 20.
18. Ibid., pp. 68 and 13.
19. Ibid., p. 69.
20. Ibid., p. 20.
21. Ibid., p. 67n.
22. Deutsch, *Mozart,* p. 225.
23. Otto Jahn, *Life of Mozart,* trans. Pauline D. Townsend (New York: Kalmus, n.d.), vol. I, p. 362.
24. Anonymous, *Berliner Musik-Zeitung Echo,* VI (1856), pp. 198–199. The story is attributed in the journal to "Mozart's son," the one surviving at the time being Karl Thomas (1784–1858). That this anecdote did not surface until 1856 does not speak well for its authenticity.
25. Paul Henry Lang, "Mozart After 200 Years," *Journal of the American Musicological Society,* XIII (1960), p. 197.

26. Johann Wolfgang von Goethe, *Eckermann's Conversations with Goethe*, trans. R. O. Moon (London: Morgan, Laird, n.d.), p. 301.

27. Niemetschek, *Life of Mozart*, p. 52.

28. Goethe, *Eckermann's Conversations with Goethe*, p. 351.

29. Oracular pronouncements are, of course, the paradigmatic instances of inspiration for Plato, to which poetic inspiration is analogized.

30. Johann Wolfgang von Goethe, *Conversations of Goethe with Eckermann*, trans. John Oxenford (New York: E.F. Dutton, 1930), p. 347. My italics. See also Johann Peter Eckermann, *Spräche mit Goethe in dem letzen Jahren seines Lebens 1823–1832* (Leipzig: Der Tempel Verlag, n.d.), vol. II, p. 15.

31. G. W. F. Hegel, *Aesthetics: Lectures on Fine Art*, trans. T. M. Knox (Oxford: Clarendon Press, 1975), vol. II, p. 954.

32. An earlier translator of Hegel's aesthetics suggests both Mozart and Schubert. See G. W. F. Hegel, *The Philosophy of Fine Art*, trans. F. P. B. Osmaston (London: G. Bell & Sons, 1920), vol. I, p. 37n.

33. Goethe, *Eckermann's Conversations with Goethe*, trans. Moon, p. 128.

34. Ibid., p. 287.

35. Ibid., p. 530.

36. Ibid., p. 537.

37. William Stafford, *Mozart's Death: A Corrective Survey of the Legends* (London: Macmillan, 1991), p. 207.

38. *Eckermann's Conversations with Goethe*, trans. Moon, p. 616.

39. Ibid.

40. Ibid., p. 16. The party took place Tuesday, 14 October 1823.

CHAPTER 7. GIVING THE RULE

1. John Locke, *Essay Concerning Human Understanding*, ed. A. C. Fraser (New York: Dover Publications, 1959), vol. I, p. 531.

2. See Peter Kivy, *The Seventh Sense: A Study of Francis Hutcheson's Aesthetics, and Its Influence in Eighteenth-Century Britain* (New York: Burt Franklin, 1976), pp. 80–85.

3. Edmund Burke, *A Philosophical Enquiry into the Origin of Our Ideas of the Sublime and Beautiful*, ed. Adam Phillips (New York: Oxford University Press, 1990).

4. Alexander Gerard, *An Essay on Taste: Together with Observations Concerning the Imitative Nature of Poetry*, 3d edition (Edinburgh, 1780), p. 145n.

5. Ibid., p. 36.

6. Ibid., p. 163.

7. Alexander Gerard, *An Essay on Genius* (London, 1774), p. 239.

8. Gerard, *An Essay on Taste*, p. 165.
9. Ibid., pp. 166–167.
10. Immanuel Kant, *Kant's gesammelte Schriften* (Berlin: Georg Reimer, 1913), vol. XV (*Handschriftlicher Nachlass*), pp. 420–421 (*Reflexion* 949). I am grateful to Paul Guyer and one of his students for locating the references to Gerard and Genius in Kant's manuscripts.
11. Kant, *Critique of Aesthetic Judgement*, p. 168 (§46).
12. Gerard, *Essay on Genius*, p. 8.
13. *Kant's gesammelte Schriften*, vol. XV, p. 303 (*Reflexion* 899).
14. Kant, *Critique of Aesthetic Judgement*, p. 168 (§46).
15. Ibid.
16. Ibid.
17. Ibid., pp. 168–169 (§46).
18. Ibid., p. 181 (§49).
19. Ibid.
20. Ibid., p. 169 (§46).
21. Ibid.
22. Ibid., pp. 169–170 (§46).
23. Ibid., p. 175 (§49).
24. Ibid., pp. 175–176 (§49).
25. Ibid., p. 177 (§49).
26. Ibid., pp. 177–178 (§49).
27. Ibid., p. 176 (§49).
28. Ibid., p. 58 (§9).
29. Ibid., p. 82 (§19).
30. Ibid., p. 179 (§49).
31. On the possible significance of the difference between the "free play" or "harmony" of the cognitive faculties, and their "quickening," see Peter Kivy, *Philosophies of Arts: An Essay in Differences* (New York: Cambridge University Press, 1997), pp. 94–96.
32. See, supra, note 21.
33. I have, quite self-consciously, appropriated for my use the definition that Kant offers in his famous pamphlet, *Was ist Aufklarung?* (What is enlightenment?).

CHAPTER 8. AN UNLICKED BEAR

1. William S. Newman, "The Beethoven Mystique in Romantic Art, Literature, and Music," *Musical Quarterly*, XLIX (1983), pp. 354–355.
2. Quoted in O. G. Sonneck, ed., *Beethoven: Impressions by His Contemporaries* (New York: Dover, 1967), p. 26.
3. Quoted in ibid., p. 70.

4. Quoted in ibid., pp. 145–146. My italics.
5. Quoted in ibid., p. 53.
6. Quoted in ibid., p. 152.
7. Quoted in ibid., pp. 111–112.
8. Quoted in ibid., p. 72.
9. Quoted in ibid., p. 77.
10. Quoted in ibid., p. 59.
11. Quoted in ibid., p. 56.
12. Quoted in Leo Schrade, *Beethoven in France: The Birth of an Idea* (New Haven: Yale University Press, 1942), p. 85.
13. The reader is recommended, in this regard, to Scott Burnham's *Beethoven Hero* (Princeton: Princeton University Press, 1995).
14. Paul Nettl, ed., *The Book of Musical Documents* (New York: Philosophical Library, 1948), p. 164.
15. Ibid., p. 165.
16. Paul Henry Lang, *Music in Western Civilization* (New York: Norton, 1941), p. 763.
17. Quoted in Sonneck, *Beethoven*, p. 140.
18. Quoted in ibid., p. 71.
19. Scott Burnham, *Beethoven Hero* (Princeton: Princeton University Press, 1995).
20. Alexander Wheelock Thayer, *The Life of Ludwig van Beethoven* (Carbondale, Ill.: Southern Illinois University Press, 1960), vol. III, p. 308.
21. Quoted in Sonneck, *Beethoven*, p. 226.
22. Quoted in ibid., p. 69.
23. Karl Geiringer, *Haydn: A Creative Life in Music* (London: George Allen and Unwin, 1947), p. 121.
24. Quoted in Sonneck, *Beethoven*, p. 69.
25. Quoted in ibid., p. 57.
26. Quoted in ibid., p. 87.
27. Quoted in ibid., p. 88.
28. Newman, "The Beethoven Mystique," pp. 157–158.
29. Johan Aloys Schlosser, *Beethoven: The First Biography,* trans. Reinhard G. Pauly, ed. Barry Cooper (Portland, Ore.: Amadeus Press, 1996), pp. 77–78.
30. Quoted in Sonneck, *Beethoven*, p. 147.
31. Quoted in ibid., p. 204.
32. Schlosser, *Beethoven*, p. 136. Actually, Schlosser is referring here particularly to the Piano Trios, Op. 1, which he, as others, saw as Beethoven's first "revolutionary" works.
33. Quoted in Schrade, *Beethoven in France*, p. 23.

34. Quoted in ibid., p. 56.
35. Quoted in ibid., p. 69.
36. Quoted in ibid., p. 94.
37. Sonneck, *Beethoven*, p. 63.
38. Ibid., p. 134.
39. Schlosser, *Beethoven*, p. 148.
40. Quoted in ibid., p. 117.
41. Quoted in Sonneck, *Beethoven*, p. 36.
42. Schrade, *Beethoven in France*, p. 70.
43. Ibid., p. 72.
44. Quoted in ibid., p. 87.
45. Quoted in ibid., p. 83.
46. Quoted in Sonneck, *Beethoven*, p. 23.
47. Quoted in ibid., p. 99.
48. Quoted in Schrade, *Beethoven in France*, p. 32.
49. Quoted in ibid., p. 34.
50. Nicholas Slonimsky, *The Lexicon of Musical Invective: Critical Assaults on Composers Since Beethoven's Time*, 2d edition (Seattle: University of Washington Press, 1969).
51. Schrade, *Beethoven in France*, pp. 34–35.
52. Thayer, *The Life of Ludwig van Beethoven*, vol. II, p. 326.
53. Quoted in Sonneck, *Beethoven*, pp. 49–50.
54. Quoted in Schrade, *Beethoven in France*, pp. 56–57.
55. Quoted in ibid., p. 81.
56. Quoted in ibid., p. 59.
57. Quoted in Sonneck, *Beethoven*, pp. 176, 178, and 179.
58. Quoted in ibid., p. 132.
59. Quoted in ibid., p. 140.
60. Quoted in ibid., p. 62.
61. Newman, "The Beethoven Mystique," p. 381. For Newman's brief sketch of Beethoven's "visual history," see pp. 381–383 of his article and the series of plates, pp. 366–367. For the definitive such study, see Alessandra Comini, *The Changing Image of Beethoven: A Study in Mythmaking* (New York: Rizzoli, 1987).
62. Quoted in Sonneck, *Beethoven*, p. 178.
63. Quoted in ibid., p. 170.
64. Schrade, *Beethoven in France*, p. 41.
65. Quoted in Sonneck, *Beethoven*, p. 83.
66. Kant, *Critique of Aesthetic Judgement*, p. 97 ($25).
67. Ibid., p. 103 ($26).

68. Ibid., p. 109 (§28).
69. Ibid., p. 127 (General Remark Upon the Exposition of Aesthetic Reflective Judgements).

CHAPTER 9. MOZART'S SECOND CHILDHOOD

1. Søren Kierkegaard, *Either/Or*, trans. David F. Swenson and Lilian Marvin Swenson, with revisions and a foreword by Howard A. Johnson (Garden City, N.Y.: Anchor Books, 1959), vol. I, p. 89.
2. Ibid., vol. I, p. 49.
3. Alfred Einstein, *Mozart: His Character, His Work,* trans. Arthur Mendel and Nathan Broder (London: Oxford University Press, 1951).
4. Brigid Brophy, *Mozart the Dramatist: A New View of Mozart, His Operas and His Age* (New York: Harcourt Brace and World, 1964), p. 258.
5. Ibid.
6. Ibid., p. 260.
7. Ibid., p. 257.
8. Ibid.
9. Ibid.
10. Maynard Solomon, *Mozart: A Life* (New York: Harper Collins, 1995). See especially, "Prologue: The Myth of the Eternal Child."
11. Ibid., p. 17.
12. Peter Shaffer, *Amadeus,* ed. Richard Adams (Essex: Longman, 1984), pp. 15–16.
13. Ibid., p. 17.
14. Ibid., p. 8.
15. Ibid., p. 20.
16. Ibid., p. 50.
17. Ibid., p. 20.
18. Ibid., p. 50.
19. Solomon, *Mozart,* p. 117.
20. Shaffer, *Amadeus,* p. 86.
21. Ibid., p. 49.
22. Ibid., p. 41.
23. See Arthur C. Danto, *The Transfiguration of the Commonplace: A Philosophy of Art* (Cambridge, Mass.: Harvard University Press, 1982).

CHAPTER 10. ODD MEN OUT

1. Hans T. David and Arthur Mendel, eds., *The Bach Reader: A Life of Johann Sebastian Bach in Letters and Documents* (New York: Norton, 1945), p. 305.

2. Quoted in ibid., p. 334. I am grateful to James R. Oestreich for reminding me of this Bach anecdote in his very generous account of a lecture on Haydn's genius that I gave at the Bard College Music Festival in summer 1997. See James R. Oestreich, "There's More to Haydn; Much More," *The New York Times,* August 20, 1997, p. B2.

3. Quoted in Vernon Gotwals, ed. and trans., *Joseph Haydn: Eighteenth-Century Gentleman and Genius* (Madison: University of Wisconsin Press, 1963), p. 8.

4. Quoted in ibid., p. 51.

5. Graham Greene, biographical note to *The Quiet American* (New York: The Modern Library, 1992), p. vi.

6. Edward Neville da Costa Andrade, *Sir Isaac Newton* (Garden City, N.Y.: Doubleday Anchor Books, 1958), p. 35.

7. John Maynard Keynes, *Essays and Sketches in Biography* (New York: Meridian Books, 1956), pp. 281–282.

CHAPTER 11. BEETHOVEN AGAIN

1. Tia DeNora, *Beethoven and the Construction of Genius: Musical Politics in Vienna, 1792–1803* (Berkeley: University of California Press, 1995), p. 114.

2. Ibid., p. 5.

3. Ibid., p. 6.

4. Ibid., p. 10.

5. Ibid.

6. Ibid., p. 69.

7. Ibid.

8. Ibid., p. 123.

9. Ibid., p. 125.

10. Ibid., pp. 134–135.

11. David Hume, "Of the Standard of Taste," in *Essays: Moral, Political, and Literary* (Oxford: Oxford University Press, 1971), p. 235.

12. DeNora, *Beethoven and the Construction of Genius,* p. 189.

13. See John Dupré, "Against Reductionist Explanations of Human Behaviour," *Proceedings of the Aristotelian Society: Supplementary Volume,* LXXII (1998), p. 165.

14. DeNora, *Beethoven and the Construction of Genius,* p. 103.

15. Ibid., p. 106.

16. Ibid., p. 57. My italics.

17. Ibid., p. 56.

18. Ibid., p. 48.

19. Ibid., p. 50.

20. Ibid., p. 113.
21. Ibid., p. 112.
22. See, especially, Joseph Butler, Sermons I, II, III, IX, in Fifteen Sermons, *Butler's Works*, ed. W. E. Gladstone (Oxford: Clarendon Press, 1897), vol. II.
23. Quoted in Solomon, *Mozart*, p. 84.
24. DeNora, *Beethoven and the Construction of Genius*, p. 189.

CHAPTER 12. GENDERING GENIUS

1. Gilbert Ryle, *The Concept of Mind* (New York: Barnes and Noble, 1949), p. 8.
2. Ibid.
3. David Hume, *An Enquiry Concerning Human Understanding*, 2d edition, ed. Eric Steinberg (Indianapolis: Hackett, 1993), p. 64.
4. For one attempt in this direction, see, Milton C. Nahm, *Genius and Creativity: An Essay in the History of Ideas* (New York: Harper Torchbooks, 1965).
5. Arthur Schopenhauer, *The World as Will and Representation*, trans. E. F. J. Payne, vol. II, p. 392 (supplements to the Third Book, Chapter XXXI).
6. Immanuel Kant, *Observations on the Feeling of the Beautiful and Sublime*, trans. John T. Goldthwait (Berkeley: University of California Press, 1960), pp. 76–77.
7. Ibid., p. 78.
8. Ibid.
9. Ibid., pp. 80–81. Cf. Immanuel Kant, *Beobachtungen über das Gefühl des Schönen und Erhabnen* (Riga, 1771), p. 55.
10. Christine Battersby, *Gender and Genius: Towards a Feminist Aesthetics* (Bloomington: Indiana University Press, 1989), p. 76. Battersby makes the same inference concerning Kant's *Anthropology from a Pragmatic Point of View;* but it is no more valid there than in the *Observations*, so far as I can see.
11. Battersby, *Gender and Genius*, p. 77.
12. Cf. Immanuel Kant, *Anthropology from a Pragmatic Point of View*, trans. Mary J. Gregory (The Hague: Martinus Nijhoff, 1974). If one looks up any of the references in Gregory's excellent index to her translation under the entries "genius" or "women," there will be no passage found that either states or implies that the female genius is impossible.
13. Battersby, *Gender and Genius*, p. 109.
14. Ibid., pp. 156–157.
15. Ibid., p. 156.
16. Ibid., pp. 156–157.
17. Ibid., p. 157.
18. Ibid.
19. Ibid.

20. Ibid.
21. Ibid., p. 161.
22. Ibid., pp. 160–161.

CHAPTER 13. RECONSTRUCTING GENIUS

1. Plato, *Phaedo,* trans. G. M. A. Grube (Indianapolis: Hackett, 1977), p. 64 (114d).

2. Newman Flower, *George Frideric Handel: His Personality and His Times,* 2d edition. (New York: Charles Scribner's Sons, 1948), pp. 289–290.

3. David Hume, *An Enquiry Concerning Human Understanding,* 2d edition, ed. Eric Steinberg (Indianapolis: Hackett, 1993), p. 48.

4. Sir Philip Sidney, "An Apologie for Poetrie," in G. Gregory Smith, ed., *Elizabethan Critical Essays,* (Oxford: Oxford University Press, 1904), vol. I, p. 195.

5. Ibid., p. 206.

6. Flower, *Handel,* p. 289.

7. Ibid. I hope no musicologist reading these pages will think that I take Newman Flower's romanticized, overwritten, and outdated biography as a reliable research tool for Handel scholarship. As I have repeated often enough before, I am interested here in myths and myth-makers, not state-of-the-art music history.

8. Immanuel Kant, *Critique of Aesthetic Judgement,* trans. James Creed Meredith (Oxford: Clarendon Press, 1911), p. 168 ($46).

9. Ibid. Cf. Chapter VII above.

10. Christine Battersby, *Gender and Genius: Towards a Feminist Aesthetics* (Bloomington: Indiana University Press, 1989), p. 157.

Bibliography

Addison, Joseph and Sir Richard Steele. *The Spectator.* Edited by Alexander Chalmers. 6 vols. New York: D. Appleton, 1879.
Andrade, Edward Neville da Costa. *Sir Isaac Newton.* Garden City, NY: Doubleday Anchor Books, 1958.
Anonymous. Mozart Anecdote. *Berliner Musik-Zeitung Echo* VI (1856).
Battersby, Christine. *Gender and Genius: Towards a Feminist Aesthetics.* Bloomington: Indiana University Press, 1989.
Beethoven, Ludwig van. *The Letters of Ludwig van Beethoven.* Translated by Emily Anderson. 3 vols. New York: St. Martin's Press, 1962.
Brophy, Brigid. *Mozart the Dramatist: A New View of Mozaret, His Operas and His Age.* New York: Harcourt Brace and World, 1964.
Burke, Edmund. *A Philosophical Enquiry into the Origin of Our Ideas of the Sublime and Beautiful.* Edited by Adam Phillips. New York: Oxford University Press, 1990.
Burney, Charles. *An Account of the Musical Performances in Westminster-Abbey, and the Pantheon, May 25th, 27th, 29th; and June 3d, and 5th, 1784. In Commemoration of Handel.* London, 1785.
Burnham, Scott. *Beethoven Hero.* Princeton: Princeton University Press, 1995.
Butler, Joseph. *Butler's Works.* Edited by W. E. Gladstone. 2 vols. Oxford: Clarendon Press, 1897.
Collingwood, R. G. *The Principles of Art.* Oxford: Clarendon Press, 1955.

BIBLIOGRAPHY

Comini, Alessandra. *The Changing Image of Beethoven: A Study in Mythmaking.* New York: Rizzoli, 1987.

Danto, Arthur C. *The Transfiguration of the Commonplace: A Philosophy of Art.* Cambridge, Mass.: Harvard University Press, 1982.

David, Hans T. and Arthur Mendel (eds.). *The Bach Reader: A Life of Johann Sebastian Bach in Letters and Documents.* New York: Norton, 1945.

DeNora, Tia. *Beethoven and the Construction of Genius: Musical Politics in Vienna, 1792–1803.* Berkeley: University of California Press, 1995.

Deutsch, Otto Erich (ed.). *Handel: A Documentary Biography.* New York: Norton, 1954.

———. *Mozart: A Documentary Biography.* Translated by Eric Blom, Peter Branscombe, and Jeremy Noble. Stanford: Stanford University Press, 1965.

Duff, William. *An Essay on Original Genius and Its Various Modes of Exertion in Philosophy and the Fine Arts, Particularly Poetry.* London, 1767.

Dupré, John. "Against Reductionist Explanations of Human Behaviour." *Proceedings of the Aristotelian Society: Supplementary Volume* LXXII (1998).

Einstein, Alfred. *Mozart: His Character, His Work.* Translated by Arthur Mendel and Nathan Broder. London: Oxford University Press, 1951.

Flower, Newman. *George Frideric Handel: His Personality and His Times.* 2d edition. New York: Charles Scribner's Sons, 1948.

Geiringer, Karl. *Haydn: A Creative Life in Music.* London: George Allen and Unwin, 1947.

Gerard, Alexander. *An Essay on Genius.* London, 1774.

———. *An Essay on Taste: Together with Observations Concerning the Imitative Nature of Poetry.* 3d ed. Edinburgh, 1780.

Goethe, Johann Wolfgang von. *Conversations of Goethe with Eckermann.* Translated by John Oxenford. New York: E.F. Dutton, 1930.

———. *Eckermann's Conversations with Goethe.* Translated by R. O. Moon. London: Morgan, Laird, n.d.

———. *Spräche mit Goethe in dem letzen Jahren.* 2 vols. Leipzig: Tempel Verlag, n.d.

Gotwals, Vernon (ed. and trans.). *Joseph Haydn: Eighteenth-Century Gentleman and Genius.* Madison: University of Wisconsin Press, 1963.

Greene, Graham. *The Quiet American.* New York: The Modern Library, 1992.

Hegel, G. W. F. *Aesthetics: Lectures on Fine Art.* Translated by T.M. Knox. 2 vols. Oxford: Clarendon Press, 1975.

———. *The Philosophy of Fine Art.* Translated by F. P. B. Osmaston. 2 vols. London: G. Bell & Sons, 1920.

Homer. *The Iliad.* Translated by Richard Lattimore. Chicago: University of Chicago Press, 1952.

BIBLIOGRAPHY

———. *The Odyssey*. Translated by Robert Fitzgerald. Garden City, NY: Anchor Books, 1963.

Hume, David. *An Enquiry Concerning Human Understanding*, 2d edition. Edited by Eric Steinberg. Indianapolis: Hackett, 1993.

———. *Essays: Moral, Political, Literary*. Oxford: Oxford University Press, 1971.

Hutcheson, Francis. *Inquiry Concerning Beauty, Order, Harmony, Design*. Edited by Peter Kivy. The Hague: Martinus Nijhoff, 1973.

Jahn, Otto. *Life of Mozart*. Translated by Pauline D. Townsend. 3 vols. New York: Kalmus, n.d.

Kant, Immanuel. *Anthropology from a Pragmatic Point of View*. Translated by Mary J. Gregory. The Hague: Martinus Nijhoff, 1974.

———. *Beobachtungen über das Gefühl des Schönen und Erhabnen*. Riga, 1771.

———. *Critique of Aesthetic Judgement*. Translated by James Creed Meredith. Oxford: Clarendon Press, 1911.

———. *Kant's gesammelte Schriften*. 27 vols. Berlin: Georg Reimer, 1913.

———. *Observations on the Feeling of the Beautiful and Sublime*. Translated by John T. Goldthwait. Berkeley: University of California Press, 1960.

Keynes, John Maynard. *Essays and Sketches in Biography*. New York: Meridian Books, 1956.

Kierkegaard, Søren. *Either/Or*. Translated by David F. Swenson and Lilian Marvin Swenson. Revised by Howard A. Johnson. 2 vols. Garden City, NY: Anchor Books, 1959.

Kivy, Peter. "Child Mozart as an Aesthetic Symbol." *Journal of the History of Ideas* XVIII (1967).

———. *The Fine Art of Repetition: Essays in the Philosophy of Music*. New York: Cambridge University Press, 1993.

———. "Mainwaring's *Handel*: Its Relation to English Aesthetics." *Journal of the American Musicological Society* XVII (1964).

———. *Philosophies of Arts: An Essay in Differences*. New York: Cambridge University Press, 1997.

———. *The Seventh Sense: A Study of Francis Hutcheson's Aesthetics, and Its Influence in Eighteenth-Century Britain*. New York: Burt Franklin, 1976.

Kivy, Peter (ed.). *Essays on the History of Aesthetics*. Rochester: University of Rochester Press, 1992.

Kristeller, Paul Oskar. "The Modern System of the Arts (I)." *Journal of the History of Ideas* XII (1951).

———. "The Modern System of the Arts (II)." *Journal of the History of Ideas* XIII (1952).

Landon, H. C. Robbins. *Haydn: A Documentary Study*. New York: Rizzoli, 1981.

BIBLIOGRAPHY

Lang, Paul Henry, "Mozart After 200 Years," *Journal of the American Musicological Society*, XIII (1960), p. 197.

———. *Music in Western Civilization.* New York: Norton, 1941.

Locke, John. *Essay Concerning Human Understanding.* Edited by A. C. Fraser. 2 vols. New York: Dover Publications, 1959.

Longinus. *Dionysius Longinus On the Sublime.* Translated by William Smith. London, 1739.

———. *Dionysius or Longinus On the Sublime.* Translated by W. Hamilton Fyfe. In *Aristotle, The Poetics, "Longinus," On the Sublime, Demetrius, On Style.* Loeb Classical Library. Cambridge, Mass.: Harvard University Press, 1953.

Mainwaring, John. *Memoirs of the Life of the Late George Frederic Handel. To which is added a Catalogue of His Works and Observations upon them.* London, 1760.

Monk, Samuel H. *The Sublime: A Study of Critical Theories in Eighteenth-Century England.* Ann Arbor, Mich.: University of Michigan Press, 1960.

Nahm, Milton C. *Genius and Creativity: An Essay in the History of Ideas.* New York: Harper Torchbooks, 1965.

Nettl, Paul (ed.). *The Book of Musical Documents.* New York: Philosophical Library, 1948.

Newman, William S. "The Beethoven Mystique in Romantic Art, Literature, and Music." *Musical Quarterly*, XLIX (1983).

Nicolson, Marjorie Hope. *Mountain Gloom and Mountain Glory: The Development of the Aesthetics of the Infinite.* New York: Norton, 1963.

Niemetschek, Franz. *Life of Mozart.* Translated by Helen Mautner. London: Leonard Hyman, 1956.

Nietzsche, Friedrich. *Beyond Good and Evil.* Translated by Marianne Cowan. Chicago: Henry Regnery, 1955.

Oestreich, James R. "There's More to Haydn; Much More." *The New York Times.* Wednesday, August 20, 1997.

Plato. *The Dialogues of Plato.* Translated by B. Jowett. 2 vols. New York: Random House, 1937.

———. *Ion.* Translated by W. R. M. Lamb. In Plato, *The Statesman, Philebus and Ion.* Loeb Classical Library. Cambridge, Mass: Harvard University Press, 1962.

———. *Phaedo.* Translated by G. M. A. Grube. Indianapolis: Hackett, 1977.

———. *Phaedrus.* Translated by H. N. Fowler. In Plato, *Euthyphro, Apology, Crito, Phaedo, Phaedrus.* Loeb Classical Library. Cambridge, Mass.: Harvard University Press, 1966.

———. *The Republic.* Translated by John Llewelyn Davies and David James Vaughan. London: Macmillan, 1950.

———. *Two Comic Dialogues.* Translated by Paul Woodruff. Indianapolis: Hackett, 1983.

BIBLIOGRAPHY

Ryle, Gilbert. *The Concept of Mind*. New York: Barnes and Noble, 1949.

Schlosser, Johan Aloys. *Beethoven: The First Biography*. Translated by Reinhard G. Pauly. Edited by Barry Cooper. Portland, Ore.: Amadeus Press, 1996.

Schopenhauer, Arthur. *The World as Will and Representation*. Translated by E. F. J. Payne. 2 vols. Indian Hills, Colo.: Falcon's Wing Press, 1958.

Schrade, Leo. *Beethoven in France: The Birth of an Idea*. New Haven: Yale University Press, 1942.

Shaffer, Peter. *Amadeus*. Edited by Richard Adams. Essex: Longman, 1984.

Slonimsky, Nicholas. *The Lexicon of Musical Invective: Critical Assaults on Composers Since Beethoven's Time*. 2d ed. Seattle: University of Washington Press, 1969.

Smith, G. Gregory (ed.). *Elizabethan Critical Essays*. 2 vols. Oxford: Oxford University Press, 1904.

Solomon, Maynard. *Mozart: A Life*. New York: Harper Collins, 1995.

Sonneck, O. G. (ed.). *Beethoven: Impressions by His Contemporaries*. New York: Dover, 1967.

Stafford, William. *Mozart's Death: A Corrective Survey of the Legends*. London: Macmillan, 1991.

Stolnitz, Jerome. "On the Origins of 'Aesthetic Disinterestedness.'" *Journal of Aesthetics and Art Criticism* XX (1961).

Thayer, Alexander Wheelock. *The Life of Ludwig van Beethoven*. Edited by A. Pryce-Jones. 3 vols. Carbondale: Southern Illinois University Press, 1960.

Wegman, Rob C. "From Maker to Composer: Improvisation and Musical Authorship in the Low Countries." *Journal of the American Musicological Society* XLIX (1996).

Young, Edward. *Conjectures on Original Composition in a Letter to the Author of Sir Charles Grandison*. Manchester: The University Press, 1918.

Index

Abduction from the Seraglio, The (Mozart), 161, 195
absent-mindedness (abstraction), 85, 121–24, 244. *See also* self-forgetfulness
Addison, Joseph, 22–30, 32, 35, 59–60, 78
"aesthetic ideas," 112–13
aesthetics
  aesthetic motive skepticism, 203–15
  aesthetic value relativism, 202–3
  aesthetic value skepticism, 192–203
  beginnings of, 22, 53 (*see also* Addison, Joseph)
  in Gerard's thought, 98, 100–104
  in Hutcheson's thought, 99–100
  in Kant's thought, 57–65, 71, 105, 112–17, 143–44, 224–26
  in Locke's thought, 98–99
  and the Longinian concept of genius, 53, 55 (*see also* Longinian genius)
African American geniuses, 179–80
age, and genius, 16. *See also* child(like) genius
the agreeable 61–63
Agrippina (Handel), 42
Almira (Handel), 41
Amadeus (Shaffer play/movie), *155*, 156–61, 163
Andrade, Edward, 171, 243
anticipation (prescience) of genius, 234–35
Ariosto, Attilio, 41
Arnim, Bettina von, 123, 128–29
art(s)
  expression theory of, 20–21
  fine arts, 107–11, 248–50
  in Longinus' thought, 13–21
  in Plato's thought, 2–10

277

INDEX

art(s) (*continued*)
  popular/useful arts, 250–51
  in Schopenhauer's thought, 68
  women and appreciation of, 226–27
  women as creators of (*see* women as geniuses)
association of ideas, 98–105, 112–13
Avison, Charles, 48

Bach, Carl Philip Emmanuel, 165
Bach, Johann Sebastian, 160, 164–66, *166, 167*, 175–76, 207–8, 240, 246
Barrington, Daines, 81–84
Battersby, Christine, 227–37, 251
beauty, perception of
  in Hutcheson's thought, 99–100, 101
  in Kant's thought, 58–65, 113–16, 224–26
  See also aesthetics
Beethoven, Ludwig van, 119–48
  absent-mindedness, 121–24, 130, 244, 245–46
  on Bach, 175
  birth and early years, 183
  and the commonsense notion of genius, 177–79, 183–85, 188–90, 191, 201
  compared to Mozart, 132–33, 216
  deafness, 123–24, 130–31
  death, 95, 125–26
  DeNora's deconstruction of genius of, 181–217
  Dussek compared to, 185–90
  as ecstatic, 121–23, 130
  familiarity with, 119–20
  feared by acquaintances, 138–40
  and Goethe, 95–96, 128–29
  and Haydn, 127, 169, 183, 186, 206–7, 210–11
  as hero, 124–27, 130, 138–39
  myth of, 120–31, 131–42, 148, 246
  and nature, 129–30, 141–43
  portraits and sculptures, 138–41, *139, 140, 142*
  reverence for, 137–38, 140–43
  as slob, 120–21, 130
  as social rule-breaker, 127–29, 130
  See also Beethoven, Ludwig van (works)
Beethoven, Ludwig van (works)
  The Creatures of Prometheus, 206
  Eroica (Third Symphony), 125, 242
  first period, 183
  initial listeners' reactions to, 183, 192
  inspiration for, 129–30, 143
  Piano Trios, Op. 1, 197–98, 265n32
  recognition/evaluation of, 183–85, 192–213
  rule-breaking in, 134–37, 145–48
  Seventh Symphony, 195–96
  and the sublime, 132–34
  See also Beethoven, Ludwig van
Beethoven and the Construction of Genius: Musical Politics in Vienna, 1792–1803 (DeNora), 181–217
Beethoven: Impressions by His Contemporaries (Sonneck), 120
"Bella mia fiamma" (Mozart; K. 528), 88
Berlioz, Hector, 132, 133, 137
Brophy, Brigid, 152–54
Burke, Edmund, 28–29, 101, 143–44
Burney, Charles, 37, 51–52, 53
Bury, Henri Blaze de, 132

INDEX

Cage, John, 162
Cherubini, Luigi, 127, 253
child(like) genius, 57, 74–76, 84, 150, 153–63, 240. *See also* Mozart, Wolfgang Amadeus
child prodigies, 240. *See also* Handel, George Frideric; Mozart, Wolfgang Amadeus
classical repertory, 164
clavichord, 39
Clemenza di Tito, La (Mozart), 161
Collingwood, R. G., 9
commonsense notion of genius, 177–80, 182, 203–4
and Battersby's five characterizations, 229–30
Beethoven and, 177–79, 183–85, 188–90, 191, 201, 204
and female geniuses, 222
composition
Beethoven and, 122–23, 124, 129–30, 245–46
from craft to fine art, 53–55
of Handel's *Messiah*, 243, 244–45
Mozart and, 80–83, 87–88, 157–60
concentration, 171–72, 243–48. *See also* industry and genius
Conjectures on Original Composition (Young), 27–28, 32–35, 78, 97. *See also* Young, Edward
connections, political, 175–77. *See also* deconstruction of genius
construct, genius as, 235–36. *See also* deconstruction of genius
contemplation, 59–61, 64–65, 71–72
Cowell, Henry, 43
Creation, The (Haydn), 1, 206
Creatures of Prometheus, The (Beethoven), 206
Critique of Judgment (Kant), 105–6,

117, 144, 224–25, 237–38. *See also* Kant, Immanuel
Critique of Pure Reason (Kant), 224. *See also* Kant, Immanuel
Czerny, Carl, 120, 136

Danto, Arthur, 161, 163
Descartes, René, 176
deconstruction of genius, 173–74, 175–217
genius as politics, 175–77
socio-political deconstruction, 177, 180–217
degrees of genius, 251–53
Delacroix, Eugéne, 135
Demosthenes, 46–47
DeNora, Tia, 181–217
devil, Handel compared to, 43
disenfranchised groups, 179–80. *See also* women as geniuses
disinterestedness, 57–65, 69–71, 114
disposition, genius as, 178–80
divine possession. *See* inspiration theory; Platonic genius
Don Giovanni (Mozart), 149–50
d'Ortigue, Joseph, 137
dream metaphor, 176
Dryden, John, 30, 48
Duchamp, Marcel, 161–62
Duschek, Frau, 88
Dussek, Jan Ladislav, 185–90

Eckermann's Conversations with Goethe (Goethe), 89, 91–96. *See also* Goethe, Johann Wolfgang von
ecstatic, genius as, 71–72
Edison, Thomas Alva, 170–71
eliteness of genius, 232, 251
elitism, 250–51

INDEX

Enquiry into the Sublime and Beautiful (Burke), 101. *See also* Burke, Edmund
Entführung aus dem Serail, Die (The Abduction from the Seraglio) (Mozart), 161, 195
Eroica (1949 film), 124
Eroica symphony (Third Symphony; Beethoven), 125, 242
Essay on Genius, An (Gerard), 103–5
Essay on Taste, An (Gerard), 98, 100–104

fact vs. fiction, 38
female genius. *See* women as geniuses
feminist critique of genius, 220–23, 227–37, 251
fine arts, 107–11, 248–50
flaws, 17–20 (*see also* rule-breaking; rules: making)
Flower, Newman, 240, 245, 270n7
Forkel, Johann Nicolaus, 79, 165–66
4′33″ (Cage), 162
Frederick the Great, 165–66

Geist, 112, 115
gender and genius. *See* women as geniuses
Gender and Genius (Battersby), 227–37
General History (Burney), 37
genius
　as accolade, 10
　Battersby's fifth sense of, 229–34
　concept needed, 237, 239–43
　deconstruction of, 173–74, 175–217
　as evaluative concept, 178–79
　as historical vs. ahistorical concept, 229, 231–32
　as mystery, 216–17, 219, 232–33
　reconstruction of, 238–54
　See also specific topics and individuals
Gerard, Alexander, 98, 100–108, 112–13
God
　genius as, 19–21
　inspiration by (*see* inspiration; inspiration theory)
　Romantic concepts of, 141–43
　as rule-maker not -breaker, 43
Goethe, Johann Wolfgang von, 89–96, 128–29, 216, 242
good, the 62–63
Gorgias (Plato), 7
Graun, Karl Heinrich, 160, 175, 176
Greene, Graham, 170, 240
Griesinger, G. A., 166, 169

Halm, Anton, 136, 145–46
Handel, George Frideric, 37–56
　birth, 51
　as child prodigy, 38–42, 83–84
　cook, 190
　death, 35
　in England, 22, 43, 49–52, 78
　Handel festival (*1784*), 51–52
　in Italy, 42–43
　Mozart compared to, 38–39, 41–42, 83–84
　as natural genius, 40, 42, 46–47
　as rule-maker/breaker, 42, 45, 135
　statues of, 49–51, *50*
　See also Handel, George Frideric (works)
Handel, George Frideric (works)
　Agrippina, 42

INDEX

Almira, 41
  chamber duets, 47
  defects in, 47–49, 135
  instrumental works, 47–48
  Mainwaring on, 38, 43, 45–49
  Messiah, 164, 240, 243, 244–45
  Mucius Scaevola, 42
  operas, 41, 42
  oratorios, 45–46, 47, 164
  Rodrigo, 42
  sublimity in, 45–46, 53
  van Swieten and, 207–8
  See also Handel, George Frideric
Haydn, Franz Joseph, 164–65, 166, 169, *170*
  and Beethoven, 127, 169, 183, 186, 206–7, 210–11
  The Creation, 1, 206
  and Mozart, 160–61, 238
  as workaholic genius, 246
Hegel, Georg Wilhelm Friedrich, 92, 93
Heiligenstadt Testament (Beethoven), 124–25
historical judgments, 192–205
Homer, 1, 16, 24, 124, 232
Hugo, Victor, 124, 133, 137
Hume, David, 44, 105, 200–201, 219, 254
Hummel, Johann Nepomuk, 216, 240, 247
Humperdink, Engelbert, 243, 253
Hutcheson, Francis, 60, 99–100, 101
Hüttenbrenner, Anselm, 125–26

imitation
  artistic influence, 109–10, 229, 233–35
  vs. originality, 33–34

imitative genius, 24–26
imperialism, 192–94
improvisation, 82, 122–23
industry and genius, 163–74, 240, 243–48
influence, artistic, 109–10, 229, 233–35
inspiration
  and age, 16
  and the expression theory, 242
  and Kant's concept of genius, 110–11
  and the Mozart myth, 156–60
  strokes of genius, 162–63, 239–40
  See also inspiration theory
inspiration theory, 1–2
  concept needed, 239–40, 243
  in Gerard's thought, 105
  Mozart and, 153, 155–60, 163, 215–16
  in Plato's thought, 2–12, 16–17, 21, 72–74, 91–92, 110, 153 (*see also* Platonic genius)
  and Romantic concepts of genius, 142–43
  and Roubiliac's statue of Handel, 49–51
instrumental vs. intrinsic goodness, 62–63
intelligence, genius as, 229–30
inventive genius, 44, 103, 107
Ion (Plato), 2–10, 73–74
Isaac, Heinrich, 54

Jahn, Otto, 87
Jaquin, Gottfried von, 87
Joseph II, 161, 195
Josquin Des Prez, 54–55
Jowett, Benjamin, 7

INDEX

Kant, Immanuel
aesthetics, 57–65, 71, 105, 112–17, 143–44, 224–25
concept of genius, 68, 97, 106–18, 144–48, 225–27, 248–50 (*see also* Kantian genius)
disinterestedness, 57–65, 69, 71
and female geniuses, 224–28
and Longinian genius, 57, 104–6, 107, 116–18, 144–48 (*see also* Longinian genius)
and Platonic genius, 57, 110–11
and the sublime, 29–30, 116, 143–44
Kantian genius, 68, 97, 106–18, 144–48, 225–27, 248–50. *See also* Longinian genius
Keynes, John Maynard, 171–72, 243
Kierkegaard, Søren, 149–50
Klinger, Max, Beethoven sculpture by, 141, *142*

Lamb, W. R. M., 7
Lang, Paul Henry, 88–89, 94, 125
learned genius. *See* imitative genius
Lexicon of Musical Invective, The (Slonimsky), 135
"Liebes Mandl, wo ist's Bandl" (Mozart; K. 441), 87
literature
ancient vs. modern, 23, 24
and female geniuses, 231, 236
Longinus on, 13–21, 47
poets and poetry, 2–10, 16–17, 19–20, 72–73, 115
sublime in, 14–21, 28–30, 31
Young on, 32–35
Locke, John, 98–99

Longinian genius
in Addison's thought, 23–25, 27 (*see also* Addison, Joseph)
and the commonsense notion of genius, 180
concept needed, 240–43
and female geniuses, 221, 222–23
in Gerard's thought, 102–6
and Kantian genius, 97, 107, 116–18, 144–48 (*see also* Kantian genius)
in Longinus' thought, 13–21, 28, 46–47, 137
Romantic Longinian genius, 57, 129–30, 137, 141–43 (*see also* Beethoven, Ludwig van)
work required for, 159
in Young's thought, 97
See also Beethoven, Ludwig van; Handel, George Frideric; Kant, Immanuel; Longinus
Longinus, 13–21, 28, 46–47, 137. *See also* Longinian genius

madness, genius as, 72–73
Mainwaring, John, 37–48, 55, 78, 83–84
maturity, 150–54
Memoirs of the Life of the Late George Frederic Handel (Mainwaring), 37–48, 83–84. *See also* Mainwaring, John
Messiah (Handel), 164, 240, 243, 244–45
modernist movement, 161–63
Moon, R. O. (Goethe translator), 91
motivation, 208–9. *See also* aesthetics: aesthetic motive skepticism
Mozart, Constanze Weber, 87

INDEX

Mozart, Constanze Weber (fictional character), 156, 160
Mozart, Leopold, 80–81, 150–54, 216
Mozart, Wolfgang Amadeus, 78–95
   Beethoven compared to, 132–33
   "Beethovenization" of, 149–50
   character in *Amadeus*, 154–60, 155, 163
   childhood, 79–86, 89–91, 215–16, 244
   as childlike adult, 84–91, 150–58, 163 (*see also Amadeus*)
   death, 88, 94–95
   deconstruction of genius not attempted, 215–16
   in Goethe's thought, 89–95
   Handel compared to, 38–39, 41–42, 83–84
   and Haydn, 160–61, 238
   Niemetschek's biography of, 79–81, 84–87, 89
   playfulness, 86–88
   portrait, *90*
   psychoanalysis of, 150–54
   recognized as genius, 76
   and Schopenhauer's concept of genius, 68, 69, 75–76, 78–79
   smallness of, 87, 89–91, *90*
   See also Mozart, Constanze Weber; Mozart, Leopold; Mozart, Wolfgang Amadeus (works)
Mozart, Wolfgang Amadeus (works)
   Bastien un Bastienne, 93
   "Bella mia fiamma" (K. 528), 88
   La Clemenza di Tito, 161
   composition style, 246 (*see also Amadeus*)
   and contemporary composers, 160–61 (*see also* Salieri, Antonio (fictional character))
   "daemonic" works, 149–50
   Don Giovanni, 149–50
   Entführung aus dem Serail, Die (The Abduction from the Seraglio) OPERA, 161, 195
   improvisations, 82
   "Liebes Mandl, wo ist's Bandl" (K. 441), 87
   operas, 93, 149–50, 161, 195
   Piano Concerto in G (K. 453), 87
   See also Mozart, Wolfgang Amadeus
Mozart's Death: A Corrective Survey of the Legends (Stafford), 94
Mucius Scaevola (Handel), 42
music
   evaluating, 191–208. *See also* DeNora, Tia
   as fine art, 53–55, 178–79
   in Goethe's thought, 91–93
   in Hegel's thought, 93
   life experience not required for, 92–93
   musical competence, 190
   musical interest, 190
   in Schopenhauer's thought, 68–69
   sublimity in, 30
musicology vs. myth, 38
mystery, genius as, 216–17, 219, 232–33, 253–54
myth, 38, 218–19, 232–33, 239

natural genius
   in Addison's thought, 23–27
   Handel as, 40, 42, 46
   in Kant's thought, 116–17 (*see also* Kantian genius)

INDEX

natural genius (*continued*)
   in Longinus' thought, 14–15, 17, 20 (*see also* Longinian genius)
nature
   Beethoven and, 129–30, 141–43
   and the sublime, 28–30, 133, 144
Neugass, Isidor, Beethoven portrait by, 138, *139*
Newman, William S., 129, 138
Newton, Isaac, 10, 105, 106, 111, 171–72, 198. *See also* industry and genius
Niemetschek, Franz, 79–81, 84–87, 89
Nietzsche, Friedrich, 84
Nissen, George Nikolaus, 87

objective vs. subjective sensation, 61–62, 223–24
Obrecht, Jacob, 54, 55
obscurity and sublimity, 30, 31
Observations on the Feeling of the Beautiful and Sublime (Kant), 29–30, 224–26
obsession, 244
"On the Pleasures of the Imagination" (Addison), 22, 27, 28, 78. *See also* Addison, Joseph
On the Sublime (Longinus), 13–21. *See also* Longinus
originality, 27
   vs. imitation, 33–34
   in Kant's thought, 108–9
Oxenford, John, 91

Pascal, Blaise, 39–40
perception, 68–70. *See also* beauty, perception of; disinterestedness
Phaedo (Plato), 239

Phaedrus (Plato), 72
Philosophical Enquiry into the Origin of Our Ideas of the Sublime and Beautiful (Burke), 28–29
Piano Concerto in G (Mozart; K. 453), 87
Piano Trios, Op. 1 (Beethoven), 197–98, 265n32
Plato
   Gorgias, 7
   and the inspiration theory, 2–12, 16–17, 21, 72–74, 91–92, 110, 153 (*see also* inspiration theory; Platonic genius)
   on learning, 239
   Platonic genius, 72–74
   Republic, 2, 239
   See also Schopenhauer, Arthur
Platonic genius, 72–74, 143
   Beethoven and, 130–31, 142–43
   and the commonsense notion of genius, 180
   concept needed, 239–40, 243
   and female geniuses, 221–23, 228
   and Kant's concept of genius, 107, 110–11
   modern return to, 150, 154–63, 173
   Mozart as, 82–83, 91–95, 155–60, 163 (*see also* Mozart, Wolfgang Amadeus)
   in Schopenhauer's thought, 57, 70, 72–76 (*see also* Schopenhauer, Arthur)
   See also inspiration theory
playfulness, 86–88
poets and poetry, 2–10, 16–17, 19–20, 72–73, 115
Poincaré, Henri, 10

INDEX

politics, genius as, 175–77
popular arts, 250–51
possession
 in *Amadeus*, 156–60
 concept needed, 239–40, 243
 and female geniuses, 221–22
 inspiration/genius as, 4–10, 153
  (*see also* inspiration theory;
  Platonic genius)
possessor, genius as. *See* Longinian
 genius
power, genius as, 15, 17, 33–34, 137.
 See also Longinian genius
Prodhomme, J. G., 120, 125

"quickening," 114

recognition, motivation for, 203–5
recognizing works of genius, 111–12
reconstruction of genius, 238–54
 concept of genius needed, 239–43
 degrees of genius, 251–53
 eliteness of genius, 232, 251
 and elitism, 251
 genius as mystery, 219, 253–54
 genius in the popular/useful arts,
  250–51
 and Kant's concept of fine art,
  248–50
Reflexionen (Kant), 105, 107
Reicha, Anton, 127
Rellstab, Ludwig, 137
representation, 66
Republic (Plato), 2, 239
reputation, 175–76
Ries, Ferdinand, 121–22, 123, 127–28, 136–37, 147
Röckel, August, 138

Rodrigo (Handel), 42
Romantic movement. *See* Beethoven, Ludwig van; Kantian genius;
 Longinian genius; the sublime
Romeo and Juliet (Shakespeare), 242
Rossini, Gioacchino, 193
Roubiliac, Louis-Francois, 49–51
rule-breaking
 Beethoven as rule-breaker, 127–29, 130, 134–37, 145–48
 Handel as rule-breaker, 42, 45, 47, 48–49
 inventive genius and, 44–45, 48–49
 in Kant's thought, 106–10, 116–18, 145–48
 in Longinus' thought, 17–20, 48–49
 in Romantic thought, 32
 Young on, 34–35
rules
 breaking (*see* rule-breaking)
 derived from experience, 44
 following, 24–25 (*see also* imitation; imitative genius)
 making rules, 42–43, 45, 47–49, 106–10, 116–18, 145–48
Ryle, Gilbert, 219

Sabattier, J. B., 135–36
Salieri, Antonio (fictional character), 156–61
Sapho, 231, 236
Saxe-Weisenfels, Duke of, 40
scare quotes, 181–82
Scarlatti, Domenico, 43
Schindler, Anton, 122, 141
Schlichtegroll, Friedrich, 79
Schlosser, Johann Aloys, 129

INDEX

Schlösser, Louis, 120, 125, 129, 132–33, 138
Schopenhauer, Arthur, 57, 65–76, 84, 95, 153, 223–24
Schrade, Leo, 133, 135–36, 137
Schröder-Devrient, Wilhelmine, 137–38
Schulz, Edward, 122
scientific genius, 106, 111
Scudo, Paul, 135
self-forgetfulness, 84–85
senses, 101
Seventh Symphony (Beethoven), 195–96
Seyfried, Ignaz, 133
Shaffer, Peter, 155–56. See also *Amadeus*
Shakespeare, William, 242
Slonimsky, Nicholas, 135
Socrates, 2–10, 16–17, 239
Solomon, Maynard, 154, 157–58
Sonneck, O. G., 120
spark of genius, 112
Spohr, Louis, 134–35
Stafford, William, 94
Stieler, Joseph Carl, Beethoven portrait by, 138, *140*
strokes of genius, 162–63, 239–40
sublime, the
  in Beethoven's music, 132–34
  genius and, 28–32
  in Handel's works, 45–46
  and the infinite, 133–34, 144
  in Kant's thought, 29–30, 116, 143–44, 224–27
  Longinus on, 13–21, 31
  and obscurity, 30, 31
  and terror/danger, 29–30, 32
  sufficient reason, principle of, 66–67, 69–70, 74

taste, 64–65, 98, 100–105, 200–201
techne, 3–6
Telemann, Georg Philipp, 160, 175, 176, 247, 252–53
Thayer, Alexander Weelock, 125–26, 136
thing-in-itself, 66–69
Third Symphony (*Eroica*; Beethoven), 125, 242
thought experiments, 188–90
Tomaschek, Johann Wenzel, 134
Tudor, David, 162
Tynnichus the Chalcidian, 17

unworthy genius, 156–60

value, musical, 191–92, 202. See also music: evaluating
van Swieten, Gottfried, 207–8, 212
Vigny, Alfred de, 132
Virgil, 24

Wagner, Richard, 119
Wawruch, Dr., 126
Weber, Aloisia, 89
Weber, Constanze. See Mozart, Constanze Weber
Wegman, Rob C., 54–55
Westminster Abbey, 49–51
women as geniuses, 179–80, 220–37
  and Battersby's feminist critique, 227–37, 251
  exclusion of, 223, 228, 233–35, 237
  and Kantian genius, 224–28
  and Longinian genius, 221, 222–23
  and Platonic genius, 221–23, 228
  and Schopenhauer's concept of genius, 223–24
Woodruff, Paul, 7

INDEX

workaholic concept of genius, 169–74, 240, 243–48. *See also* industry and genius

World as Will and Representation, The (Schopenhauer), 66–76, 78–79, 84. *See also* Schopenhauer, Arthur

Young, Edward, 27–28, 32–35, 78, 97

Zachow, Friedrich Wilhelm, 40–41